THE NARROW ACT
Borges' Art of Allusion

SITES/Lumen Books
446 West 20 Street
New York, NY 10011
(212) 989-7944

© 1995 Lumen Inc.
ISBN 0-930829-21-2
Printed in the United States of America

SITES Books and Lumen Books are produced by Lumen, Inc., a tax-exempt, non-profit organization. This publication is made possible, in part, with public funds from the New York State Council on the Arts and private contribubtions.

THE NARROW ACT
Borges' Art of Allusion

Ronald Christ

Lumen Books

For my mothers and fathers and teachers
and this time for
Gregory Kolovakos
(1951-1990)

Thoughts hardly to be packed
into a narrow act,
Fancies that broke through language and escaped

"Rabbi Ben Ezra"
Robert Browning

CONTENTS

AUTHOR'S PREFACE

Two unrelated incidents prompted this revision: second, an anonymous book-buyer, ahead of me in line, who wrote a $60 check for a photocopy of the out-of-print book; first, an over-eager publisher who printed the book and its jacket simultaneously with my reading galleys. Between the two came some embarrassments and many kind requests for a reprint. Whatever else, the cover no longer proclaims Borges a novelist, and he is restored to the "narrowness" I intended.

The principal obstacle to this revision was my unwillingness to revise. While I seemed almost alone at the start—I recall that only a tardy *Time* magazine article convinced some professors of English at New York University that my subject merited study—many, more expert than I, have by now devised a vast critical conversation that I do not care to interrupt. (I have read some of it in astonishment yet with little increase in the satisfaction I still take from the sly symmetries that first welded me to Borges' writing or from the discovery of embers of his syntax and diction kindling others' prose. Works by John Sturrock and John Irwin imposingly, impressively stand out, but for me the most notable exception remains: Gene H. Bell-Villada's *Borges and His Fiction* [Chapel Hill, 1981], which speaks to all readers.) So, you have here the delayed correction of typesetter's errors—some of them grave, such as the printing of a quotation from Borges as if it were my prose—and the addition of my interview with Borges that first appeared in the *Paris Review*, whose editors have kindly granted permission for its reprinting.

R.C.
New York, 1995

AUTHOR'S PREFACE TO THE FIRST EDITION

There is no longer any need for introducing Borges to the English-speaking world or for justifying a study of his fiction, perhaps only for questioning why such a study has not already been undertaken. At any rate, no such book-length study was available when I began my work some years ago; at this time no such work is yet available, despite Paul de Man's implicit invitation in 1964: "American and English critics have called him [Borges] one of the greatest writers alive today, but have not yet (so far as I know) made substantial contributions to the interpretation of his works." In full agreement with De Man's evaluation and in response to the deficiency he describes, I present the following pages.

In this work I attempt to provide an introduction to Borges' fiction by focusing on one particular literary device—its esthetic origin, development, and masterful practice. The device is allusion, and the allusions I concentrate on are those to English and American authors. However, it is not my purpose to compile an exhaustive inventory of influences, to search out all verbal echoes, or to document all actual borrowings in Borges' fiction but, instead, to redefine Borges' goals and to reevaluate his achievement in light of certain English-language authors. Documentation of influence may, of course, provide my point of departure, but my fundamental method is that of comparing significant works, not that of detailing the history of Borges' reading and borrowing. I shall try to show not only what Borges borrowed from certain works but also, and more importantly, *why* he borrowed when he did. My aim, then, is not so much scholarly as critical—I omit Walt Whitman and Henry James, for example—and it is always with the *reader* of Borges in mind that I write. That reader, who, like myself when first reading *La historia de la eternidad*, begins casually noting English-language writers as they occur in the text and comes up with an inventory nearly as startling as Borges' own lists: Shelley, Poe, Kipling, Yeats, William Morris, Capt. Burton,

Cardinal Newman, Matthew Arnold, Shakespeare, Hume, Bertrand Russell, Francis Bacon, Gerald Herd, Spenser, Emerson, Chaucer, Wilde, Whitehead, Bradley, Donne, Cyrl Tourner, Swinburne, Tennyson, Swift, Johnson, Shaw, Edward FitzGerald, Swift, Leslie Stephen, De Quincey, Keats, Stevenson, Jeremiah Taylor, Joyce, Middleton Murray, Sir Thomas Browne, Milton, J. S. Mill, and Whitman—not to omit, among many works, Chapman's "Homer" and "los blues."

Generally, I have quoted translations and easily available texts wherever possible, except in the case of Borges himself. What I want to say so often depends from precise usage in his text that I have translated these excerpts myself. For painstaking advice on my translations, I happily acknowledge my friend and colleague Paschal Cantatore of Manhattan College.

Knowing that some readers—myself one of them—turn to the acknowledgment section of a book with the same interest as they turn to the obituary pages of a newspaper, I would like to make this section as long as it really ought to be; but that would violate the reputable convention and spoil the fun, so I shall limit myself to the most important instances. First of all, thanks to Robert Clements, who introduced me to Borges writing, as well as to Humberto Piñera and Ilse Lind, all of New York University, who directed this work in the form of a doctoral dissertation in Comparative Literature; to Manhattan College and the National Endowment for the Humanities for funds that enabled me to travel to Argentina, where I first interviewed Borges; to Eileen McDermott of the Manhattan College Library for helping me to get books I needed; to E. L. Rubinstein of Richmond College, who read the manuscript in its primitive form and imposed some civilization; to Ralph Eepelfeldt, who looked over many of the pages, and, with sadness, to Minnie Eepelfeldt and Oliver J. Hopkins, who carefully overlooked the early pages but did not live to see their publication; to Eduardo Costa, who recommended it to the Literature Program of the Center for Inter-American Relations, whose director, José Guillermo Castillo, ventured to support it with rare good humor and publishing savvy. This section would be neither complete nor accurate if I did not rehearse the true formula: whatever good there is in this book has been elicited by those I have named and whatever faults there are have been preserved by my own stubbornness.

R.C.
New York, 1968

ABBREVIATIONS

In the text, I have abbreviated the titles of Borges' works:

A	El Aleph
EC	Evaristo Carriego
D	Discusión
HE	Historia de la eternidad
F	Ficciones
H	El Hacedor
HI	Historia de la infamia
IA	Idioma de los argentinos
I	Inquisiciones
OP	Obra poética
OI	Otras inquisiciones
P	Poemas
TE	El tamaño de mi esperanza

All page references to the book-length issue of *L'Herne* (Paris, 1964) devoted to Borges are included parenthetically in the text.

FOREWORD

A writer is a user of symbols. This word, in the broadest
sense, may stand for a range of things: tales, metaphors,
plots, word music, and the dramatic moment. Bernard Shaw
once said that the writer does not work from an idea but toward an idea; similarly, Kipling wrote that it is given a writer
to invent a fable but that its morality must be found by the
reader. So, in *Kim*, the native characters are more likable than
the British officialdom Kipling wanted to extol. All these,
of course, are but variations on the old concept of the Holy
Ghost or the Muse. Modern mythology prefers the Sublimi-
nal Self.

Some unsuspected things, many secret links and affinities, have been revealed to me by this book of Ronald
Christ's. I am often asked what my message is; the obvious
answer is that I have no message. I am neither a thinker nor
a moralist, but simply a man of letters who turns his own perplexities and that respected system of perplexities we call
philosophy into the forms of literature. The fact that in one
of my stories the man is both the dreamer and the dream does
not necessarily mean that I am a follower of Berkeley and
of the Buddha. However, the writer must be thankful for
being shown that he has gone beyond what he attempted,
beyond his intentions.

The fact that I am dictating these lines in the very same
room of the Biblioteca Nacional where I first had the pleasure of meeting Ronald Christ makes me feel the reality—
or unreality—of that ungraspable substance, Time.

My gratitude to Ronald Christ.

Jorge Luis Borges
December 17, 1968
Buenos Aires

A manuscript page related to "The Cult of the Phoenix" with sources listed in the margin.

THE ESSENTIALS OF BORGES' ART

Coming upon a story by Borges in an anthology or in a magazine, or merely picking up one of his collections and reading a single story, the reader is likely to be puzzled; perhaps fascinated or irritated, but almost certainly puzzled. The story itself is surprisingly brief; important connections seem to have been omitted; significances are hinted at, but not revealed; emphasis is placed equally upon the seemingly trivial and the obviously important; the direction or import of the story is obscure. The puzzlement may fatigue the reader or it may encourage him to pursue the game. If he does continue, he will quickly find that it is much easier to understand three or four Borges stories than to understand only one. As he reads on, the reader discovers that assumptions and techniques common to almost all the stories gradually emerge and define themselves.

The Esthetic of Negation and Compression

At the beginning of his literary career, long before he had published any fiction, Borges was primarily concerned with the writing of poetry and the formulation of theories of language and literature. Even after he turned to the writing of those short *ficciones* that established his fame outside Argentina, he never forsook either poetry or theorizing; and we must realize that the theories and practices that informed his earliest poems were never abandoned completely, only modified and transformed by passing years and developing interests. Therefore, in order to get at the esthetic notions that govern his fiction, we must go back to his poetic manifestos of the 1920s.

ULTRAISM When, in 1921, Borges returned to Argentina after receiving his *bachot* in Geneva and subsequently spending three years in Spain, he brought with him cosmopolitan literary interests and the fervor of the avant-garde literary movements that had formed in Europe during and after the

World War. Specifically, he introduced Argentina to Ultraism, the movement he had participated in along with his friend Rafael Cansinos Asséns. Later in his life, Borges renounced the goals and techniques of Ultraism with the thoroughness characteristic of a nonbeliever denouncing his early faith; but, Borges' writing, and his fiction in particular, retained the stylistic elements of Ultraism. Ultraism, of course, had much in common with many movements of the time—with Vorticism, for example—but the Argentine, transplanted variety of Ultraism, as Borges subsequently made clear, developed differently from the Spanish stock. The Spanish writers, borrowing their name from the magazine *Ultra*, where many of their works were published, emphasized the notion of *ultra* in the chronological and geographical sense of going beyond the established boundaries, so that Rafael Cansinos Asséns defined the parent movement in the following way:

Ultraism is an exuberant determination that exceeds all scholastic limits. It is an orientation toward continuous and reiterated evolutions, a proposal for perennial literary youth, an a priori *acceptance of every new pattern and of every new idea. It represents the responsibility to go forward with the times.*[1]

Borges, in contrast, defined the Ultraism of Argentina as seeking not the merely modern or new, but the eternal:

The Ultraism of Seville and Madrid was a resolution for renewal; it was the resolve to gird esthetic time in a new cycle; it was a lyric written, as it were, with florid capital letters on the leaves of the calendar, a lyric whose most eminent emblems—the airplane, antennas, and propellers—are spokesmen for a chronological present. The Ultraism of Buenos Aires was the yearning to obtain an absolute art that would not depend on the unfaithful prestige of the authors and that would last in the continuity of the language as a guarantee

*of beauty. Beneath the energetic clarity of lamps, the names
of Huidobro and Apollinaire were frequent in the Spanish
circles. We, meanwhile, weighed lines from Garcilaso, restless and grave beneath the stars of the suburb, demanding
a limpid art that might be as atemporal as the eternal stars.
We abhorred the muddy hues of Rubenism, and metaphor in-
flamed us because of the precision in it, because of its algebraic form of correlating remote things.* (I, 96-97)

The attainment of "a limpid art that might be as atemporal
as the eternal stars" remained a constant ideal in the works
of Borges, and the word *atemporal* is a key to many of his
later works.

A more precise definition of the techniques and principles of Ultraism yields a still more precise clue to the continuing preoccupations of Borges' art. In one of his earliest
articles Borges says:

*Schematicized, the present position of Ultraism can be
summed up in the following principles:*

*1. Reduction of the lyric to its primordial element: the meta-
phor.*
*2. Deletion of intervening sentences, of transitions and use-
less adjectives.*
*3. Abolition of ornamental devices, confessionalism,
circumstantiation, exhortations and studied nebulousness.*
*4. Synthesis of two or more images in one, which will thus
increase the images' power of suggestion.*[2]

These four principles, with only slight modification, are
equally applicable to Borges' fiction. Therefore, they deserve
our careful attention, and perhaps the simplest way to approach them and their relevance to Borges' subsequent career is to examine their resemblance to the Imagist manifesto
issued in 1915 as a preface to the anthology *Some Imagist
Poems*. The six guiding rules of the Imagists are roughly
parallel to the four principles of Ultraism:

These principles are not new; they have fallen into desuetude. They are the essentials of all great poetry, indeed of all great literature, and they are simply these:

1. To use the language of common speech, but to employ always the exact word, not the nearly-exact, nor the merely decorative word.

2. To create new rhythms—as the expression of new moods—and not to copy the old rhythms, which merely echo old moods. We do not insist upon "free-verse" as the only method of writing poetry. We fight for it as for a principle of liberty. We believe that the individuality of a poet may often be better expressed in free verse than in conventional forms. In poetry, a new cadence means a new idea.

3. To allow absolute freedom in the choice of subject. It is not good art to write badly about aeroplanes and automobiles; nor it is necessarily bad art to write well about the past. We believe passionately in the artistic value of modern life, but we wish to point out that there is nothing so uninspiring nor so old fashioned as an aeroplane of the year 1911.

4. To present an image (hence the name: "Imagist"). We are not a school of painters, but we believe that poetry should render particulars exactly and not deal in vague generalities, however magnificent and sonorous. It is for this reason that we oppose the cosmic poet, who seems to us to shirk the real difficulties of his art.

5. To produce poetry that is hard and clear, never blurred or indefinite.

6. Finally, most of us believe that concentration is the very essence of poetry.[3]

The similarities between the two movements are quite evident: both reacted against the prevailing poetry in favor of a timeless verse based on what seemed eternal laws of literature, a verse emphasizing metaphor or image freed from the rules of logical argument or development, liberty in metrical expression, and, finally, precision and concision in expression. At the same time, there is a meaningful difference in the way the two poetic platforms are expressed—a difference all the more interesting because it points to the direction of Borges' own art.

First, Borges' enunciation of his literary principles is much less personal than that of the Imagists: note, for example, the absence in Borges of all personal pronouns. Second, and still more significantly, where the Imagists (like the Spanish Ultraists in this regard) express themselves with "a resolve for renewal," a positive sense of freedom and discovery embodied in the infinitives *to use, to create, to allow, to present, to produce,* Borges empitomizes Argentine Ultraism in three restrictive, even negative words: *reduction, deletion, abolition.* Only in the last principle of each group do both the expression and the goal seem truly parallel—*concentration: synthesis.* One might argue that the problems and opportunities faced by these two groups explain the difference in emphasis, but what is really important for an understanding of Borges' subsequent career is to see that he made his debut as a literary theoretician in 1921 advocating a poetry of concentrated, essential metaphor, stripped of all decoration and logical or descriptive framework. For, once we have seen this, we have focused on the two stylistic concerns— concentration (or brevity) and metaphor—that inform not only the poetry of Borges' Ultraist period but much of his later writing as well.

BREVITY Brevity is the most outstanding quality of all Borges' writing. None of his poems is more than a few pages long, and it is unusual for one of his essays or stories to exceed ten pages. Now, in an era when the greatest "long poem" fills some fifteen pages, this is not strange; but a writer of fiction is still not generally thought to have come into his own, no matter what the quality of his performance, until he has published a substantial novel. Borges, however, never wrote a novel. His brevity is essential to his art; it is wholly intentional and is neither the result of his inability to sustain himself nor of the triviality of his themes nor of the fragmentary nature of his artistic vision. From the beginning of his career he produced only short works and often stated that he would not attempt a long work. Moreover we ought not refer to biography—to Borges' ill health and failing eyesight—in order to explain his wonted brevity; instead we should understand that this brevity is the direct result, first, of an esthetic system elaborated over many years and, second, of the themes he chose to explore. It is, paradoxically, because his themes are so expansive and his views so immense that Borges' stories are so short. The nature of Borges' brevity is perfectly demonstrated in the paragraph that follows his four principles of Ultraism:

Ultraist poems, therefore, consist of a series of metaphors, each of which has its own power of suggestion and condenses a previously unrevealed vision of some fragment of life. The radical difference between current poetry and our own is the following: in the former, the lyric discovery is magnified, made huge, developed; in the latter, it is noted briefly. But do not think that such a procedure lessens the emotional force! "Quintessences accomplish more than farragos," said the author of the Criticón *in a sentence that may be an unsurpassable abbreviation of the Ultraist esthetic.*[4]

Here Borges summarizes the ideal of Ultraism, appropriately, by quoting Baltasar Gracián's epigrammatic statement *"Más obran quintas esencias que fárragos,"* which he calls the *"inmejorable abreviatura"* of the Ultraist esthetic. The brevity that is Borges' subject is mirrored perfectly in the brevity of his expression. What is more, if in the 1920s Borges was able to quote "Quintessences accomplish more than farragos" as the esthetic basis of Ultraism, decades later we can still quote it as the esthetic principle of Borges' art. If he earlier supported a poetry in which "the lyric discovery . . . is noted briefly" instead of "magnified, made huge, developed," he later proposed a fiction that does the same thing:

*A laborious and impoverishing waste—that is what the com-
position of long books is: the expansion to five hundred
pages of an idea whose perfect oral exposition takes a few
minutes. A better procedure is to imagine that these books
already exist and to offer a résumé, a commentary. That is
what Carlyle did in* Sartor Resartus *and Butler in* The Fair
Haven—*works that have the imperfection of being books too,
no less tautological than others. More reasonable, more
inept, more indolent, I have preferred writing notes about
imaginary books.* (F, 11-12)

It would be wrong to take Borges' self-deprecating explanation of his brevity at face value. He is not brief because
he is lazy but because he is always trying to achieve an
"unsurpassable abbreviation" of his subject. His goal is to
write stories that epitomize and suggest rather than stories
that detail and exhaust. The devices he uses to attain this goal
are many, but we may note a few of the outstanding ones that
function on stylistic, organizational, and psychological principles.

An excellent example of the way in which Borges'
style reflects his striving for brevity is his use of adjectives.
The brevity of his stories obviously precludes "useless adjectives," but even so he uses few adjectives and then the
same ones again and again. One reason for the sparing use
of adjectives in his fiction can be found in *The Extent of My
Hope*:

*Any adjective, whether it be pleonastic or equivocal, exer-
cises a power: that of forcing the reader's attention to pause
at the substantive to which it refers—a quality that is suitable for description, not for narration.* (TE, 57-58)

But even in his descriptive passages, Borges' palette is se-
verely limited. His colors are few and elemental. Eliminating most of the transitional or combinational hues, Borges
forgoes the possibility of a colorism such as we find in the
Impressionists; on the other hand, he opens the way to a col-

oristic primitivism, such as we find in Alexander Calder, a colorism that accords perfectly with Borges' emphasis on the essential and primordial in literature. That this search for the basic and essential guides him, at least in part, in his choice of color may be inferred from quotations like the two that follow:

> *the red Adam of Paradise (H, 63)*

> *Not elemental red but grays*
> *Spun her delicate destiny (H, 66)*

Whether Borges is trying to achieve the elemental quality of the primary colors or the simple purity of the unobstructed narrative, he is searching for the basic and universal by means of strenuous selectivity, a search that can be seen not only in the language of his fiction but also in the plots of his stories and the organization of his essays.

One of the organizational devices that Borges uses most frequently in order to achieve a quintessential brevity is the series, marked however, by the suppression of "intervening sentences, of transitions." Just as he suppresses gradations of hue in choosing colors, so in his essays does he often eliminate transitions between examples in series and the thoughts in series those examples provoke. Early in his career Borges showed his own awareness of this quick-cut seriality when, in writing of his essay "The Insignificance of Personality," he said, "But that work, excessively afflicted with literature, is nothing but a series of suggestions and examples strung together without logical continuity" (*I*, 109). He further demonstrated the purposefulness of this technique when he analyzed his methods in the prologue to the first edition of *Universal History of Infamy.* There he explained that his narratives

> *abuse certain procedures: random enumeration, abrupt shifts in continuity, reduction of a man's whole life to two or three scenes. (HI, 7)*

The lack of transitions in his essays briefly emphasizes a series of discrete examples or thoughts; similarly, in his fiction, Borges abbreviates his narrative by distilling it through the narrator's memory, which has let subside the "pathetic bric-a-brac."[5] Borges likes to write stories about events filtered through individual or collective memory, because, in his view, the perspective of memory serves to diminish the extraneous and to emphasize the essential. The narrator of "Examination of the Works of Herbert Quain" is a case in point: "After seven years it is impossible for me to recover the details of the action: this is his plan, just as it is now impoverished (just as it is now purified) by my forgetfulness" (*F*, 78). Historical perspective functions in the same way. The history of the idea of the Eternal Return, as Borges presents it in "Circular Time" for example, consists of what Plato, Nietzsche, and Borges have thought about it: no "intervening sentences"; rather, a series of essential statements with a suppression of "transitions." The selectivity of memory, both personal and historical, is so important to Borges that he has written a story, "Funes the Memorious," on precisely the opposite idea, a story that illustrates the tragic absurdity of absolute memory. The title character's name, Funes, and the dark, melancholy atmosphere are perhaps the best indications of Borges' view of such a memory, and the story may be considered, at least from one point of view, an allegory of the exhaustive, circumstantial approach to literature carried to its logical absurdity.

Borges' essays and stories, then, function on the principle of selective brevity, a principle similar to the one articulated by the Imagist theoretician T. E. Hulme:

Literature, like memory, selects only the vivid patches of life. If literature (realistic) did really resemble life, it would he interminable, dreary, commonplace, eating and dressing, buttoning, with here and there a patch of vividness.[6]

More succinctly and more imagistically, Borges has formulated the psychological realism of this eradicating process in
relation to pleasure: "I cannot walk through the outskirts of
town in the solitude of night without thinking that night-
time, like memory, pleases us because it suppresses idle
details." (*OI*, 243). Brevity achieved by suppression of detail, therefore, is not merely a formal rule with Borges; it corresponds to a principle of memory, and, in his view, such
suppression is one way of guaranteeing a sense of reality in
a story. For example, in "The Man in the Doorway" the narrator invokes Allah to protect him from distorting the true
exoticism of the tale with local color: "My text will be faithful: Allah deliver me from the temptation of adding brief,
circumstantial details or from weighing down the story's
exotic aspect with interpolations from Kipling" (*A*, 143).
Similarly, Borges praises José Hernández for excluding all
the trappings of local color that are usually the earmark of
gaucho literature:

*What was Hernández's aim? Only one, and that very limited:
the story of the destiny of Martín Fierro, related by Fierro
himself. We do not intuit the actions but, rather, the rustic
Martín Fierro telling them. Hence the omission or attenua-
tion of local color that is typical of Hernández. He specifies
neither day, night, nor the color of horses: an affectation that
in our literature of cattlemen corresponds to the British one
of specifying the tackle and rigging, the charts and courses,
the manoeuvres in the literature of the sea, the Englishman's
pampa. He does not silence reality but only refers to it in relation to the hero's character. (Joseph Conrad does the same
with the sailor's environment.) (D, 16)*

But when we have noted the verbal concision of his stories
and the psychological principles that may underpin that concision, we have only begun to perceive the essential brevity
that Borges strives for, not only in expression but also in
form and thought.

The word that most adequately describes what Borges attempts to accomplish in his early work is *abbreviate*; in his later work it is *cifrar:* to abridge, to encompass. He aims to condense the universe in a verbal or narrative abbreviation. The writer's task, as he made clear in "Profession of Literary Faith," is to write at least one page that can stand for his entire destiny:

I have already overcome my poverty; I have recognized, among thousands, the nine or ten words that accord with my heart. I have already written more than one book in order to be able to write, perhaps, a single page. The justifying page, which may be an abbreviation of my destiny. (*TE*, 153)

Therefore we see the special significance when Borges uses the word *abbreviate* to summarize the particular brilliance of Quevedo's adjectives ("In them he abbreviated whole metaphors." [*TE*, 53]) and the concept of abbreviation to support his admiration for Oscar Wilde: "Wilde was not a great poet nor a painstaking writer of prose, but he was a lively Irishman who encapsuled in epigrams an esthetic credo that others subsequently diluted in many pages" (*TE*, 132). The goal of abbreviation justifies Borges' own use of epigrams and his love of encyclopedias, dictionaries, maps, and atlases, all of which figure prominently in his stories as résumés of the universe.

Surely the most intense expression of this stylistic and thematic preoccupation occurs in the story "El Aleph." An Aleph, the narrator discovers "is one of the points of space that contains all the points." (*A*, 160); and an Aleph, Maurice Jean Lefebre has convincingly pointed out, is what each of Borges' works tries to be:

Who does not see that each of Borges' stories, each of his short essays is an Aleph of the dream world? In concentrating an indefinite multiplicity of acts, suggestion and sensation onto a narrow textual surface, in pursuing enumeration with a taste for the eternal, as well as in making each story capable of reflecting itself (in the way facing mirrors do), the author opens our minds to a vertigo, to a problematic and inexhaustible magic, which is what one properly calls literature. (L'Herne, 224)

Emerson, one of Borges' favorite authors, has written that "A work of art is an abstract or epitome of the world. It is the expression of nature in miniature";[7] and the alphabetical character of the Kabbalistic Aleph makes it particularly useful to Borges in his attempt to abbreviate the universe in literature, but the Aleph is also meaningful to the reader as a symbol of all Borges' writing. As the phoenix is an appropriate insignia for D. H. Lawrence's writing, so the Aleph is for Borges' work, a work that has both for its means and its goal an ideal brevity.

METAPHOR Turning to the stories Borges produced about twenty years after his Ultraist period, we may find it hard at first to see the connection between his early poems, which stress metaphor as the essence of literary art, and his later prose style, which persistently avoids metaphorical expression. I say his later prose style because, in fact, Borges' early discursive prose is hardly less metaphorical than his verse. The beginning of *Inquisitions* offers the following examples:

In Torres Villarroel there is a miracle as impenetrable and as clear as any mirror. (I, 12)

Over the days and nights of don Diego de Torres, over each one of the pages he composed, the shadow of his master passed with the loftiness of a flock of birds and the certainty of the wind. (I, 13)

Like swords crossed in intrepid combat, Gómez de la Serna and Rafael Cansinos Asséns are two names united in belligerent brotherhood. (I, 15)

Inquisitions was published in 1925, only four years after Borges' statement of Ultraist principles and bears the imprint of his early metaphorical style; one would have to search Borges' prose of the 1940s, 1950s, and 1960s to adduce any comparable instances of figurative expression. Yet Borges' stylistic development is more consistent than this superficial contrast might suggest: in the words of Herma Briffault, Borges "uses almost no adjectives, no metaphors," but "many of his fictions might be considered as elaborated metaphors."[8] If his concern with brevity led him to strive for a work that in itself is an abbreviation, his interest in metaphor finally led him to forsake individual metaphors in the course of a work so as to create a work that is in itself the expansion of a single metaphor; just as he gradually tightened his rein on the free use of adjectives, so he restrained his figurative imagination. In speaking of adjectives he had said, "Modern poets make of the adjective an enrichment, a variation; the ancients, a pause, a kind of emphasis" (*TE*, 52); and again, "Eliminating adjectives can strengthen a phrase; to search for one can honor the phrase; searching for many is to assure its absurdity" (*TE*, 58). It was, then, specifically toward the practice of the ancients and away from that of the moderns that Borges moved in his decreasing dependence upon descriptive and metaphoric language.

In sum, the evolution of Borges' later style out of his early metaphorical style was precisely that: an evolution, not a sudden mutation, and fully conscious; it is because he constantly pushed himself to logical conclusions, both esthetic and intellectual, continually carried his arguments and propositions to their logical limits, and not as the result of dramatic conversions or reactions, that Borges' art changes and develops. Indeed, to find the precise point in his writings where Borges begins to move away from his exploitation of rhetorical metaphors, we need only turn back to *Inquisitions* itself, specifically to another of Borges' esthetic battle cries, his short essay "After Images."

The title itself indicates that tendency that never permitted Borges to rest content with his achievement but always impelled him to take one more step toward the new. In the essay he briefly summarizes the Ultraist accomplishment in the use of metaphor and then goes on to demand a further advance:

> *To transform a blaze into a tempest, as Milton did, is the work of a wizard. To change the moon into a fish, into a bubble, into a kite—Rossetti did that, making the mistake before Lugones—is less tricky. But there is someone superior to the trickster and the magician. I am speaking of the demi-god, of the angel, whose deeds change the world. To annex provinces to Being, to imagine cities and spaces of contiguous reality, that is a heroic venture. (I, 28)*

Borges' essay is a plea to stop holding the mirror of metaphor up to the world and playing tricks with the reflections; the goal now is to step through the mirror, Alice-fashion, and to populate the reflection-world with the shadowy new creations of art. In a word, the essay looks forward to a literature of *total* metaphor—of fantasy:

> *One must reveal this fantasy transformed into an inescapable reality of the mind: one must show an individual passed through a mirror, one who perseveres in his illusory country (where there are shapes and colors but all controlled by immobile silence), one who feels the shame of being nothing more than a shadow whom the nights obliterate and the glimmering lights allow to exist. (I, 29)*

Even though "After Images" offered the challenge, it was not until his next volume of essays, *The Idiom of the Argentines*, that Borges gave a practical demonstration of what he now demanded in the way of metaphor.

With characteristic awareness that he was working out his own esthetic problems, sketching the history of his own development, Borges returned to the subject in "Metaphor Once Again." In this essay he further rejected the supremacy of rhetorical metaphor in favor of an absolutely metaphorical world of art. After having shown that metaphor is not a characteristic of much popular literature and not even of some impressive passages in poets like Browning and Quevedo, Borges went on to translate the first two lines of Shakespeare's Sonnet CVII as an example of what he was striving for:

Shakespeare begins a sonnet this way: Not mine own fears, nor the prophetic soul/ Of the wide world dreaming on things to come . . . *and so on. The experiment here is crucial. If the locution* prophetic soul of the world *is a metaphor, it is only a verbal indiscretion or merely a personal generalization of the one who wrote it; if it is not a metaphor, if the poet really believed in the personality of a common, universal soul of this world, then the locution is truly poetic.* (*IA*, 60-61)

This passage is especially important because it shows Borges in the very act of transforming a rhetorical metaphor, the staple of his Ultraist period, into a metaphysical proposition, the staple of his mature art. In this record of his reading of two Shakespearean lines is written, in small, the history of his metaphorical art. Here we observe the turning point from his early to his later work along the lines demanded by "After Images." All of Borges' mature fiction—the stories in *El Aleph* and *Ficciones*—is the fully developed response to this demand.

The point of origin for most of Borges' fiction is neither character nor plot, considered in the traditional sense; but, instead, as in science fiction, a proposition, an idea, a metaphor, which, because of its ingenious or fantastic quality, is perhaps best called a conceit. In science fiction, as in Borges' work, the author postulates: "If the world were this way, then . . ." The *if* clause of the proposition, the metaphorical basis of the story is, of course, suppressed, just as the fulcrum, *like* or *as*, is suppressed in a metaphor; but the stories do in fact take place in a world governed by such fanciful introductory assumptions, assumptions contrary to fact or common experience but fascinating to us as the writer works them out logically and precisely. H. G. Wells says that if a man could make himself invisible, then this is what life would be like; Ray Bradbury says that if Mars could nurture human life, then this is what the history of that planet would be like; Borges says that if history is cyclical, then this is how we must understand the assassination of one Fergus Kilpatrick. All three, in accordance with the plan of "After Images," introduce their characters into the mirror world of fantasy where they discover through a confrontation with strange, new worlds that reality is ordered differently from what they had expected. Thus *War of the Worlds* questions the ultimate reality of the universe as it is understood by the pre–space-age man, while "Theme of the Traitor and Hero" questions the discrete identity of man as it is traditionally understood by history and psychology. If we call Wells' and Bradbury's stories "science" fiction, then we might call Borges' stories "metaphysical" fictions.

However, the engendering conceits of most science fiction stories develop from the achievement, real or imagined, of modern technology, and the artist presents them much as boys once displayed the latest construction of their Erector sets: they are the concretion of such fantasies as seem most appropriate to a world dominated by an inventive, creative materialism. Borges' conceits, on the other hand, are speculative, literary, metaphysical. Thus, while he admires the works of Wells and Bradbury, he finds little place in his own work for their scientific paraphernalia. Much comment notwithstanding, Borges' fiction is not scientific: it ignores, first of all, the equipment and typical devices of fictive science—microscopes, rocketships, and the like. To focus on such devices would negate his intention of creating an atemporal art, since nothing is older than yesterday's technology—or, to borrow that phrase directly from the Imagist manifesto of 1915, "Nothing is so uninspiring nor so old fashioned as an aeroplane of the year 1911." Jules Verne, we are constantly asked to remind ourselves, was really very forward-looking, yet the very measure of our appreciation is the distance by which we have superseded his fantasies; Borges, in general avoiding prognostications of a mechanical wonderland or inferno, confining himself to the ageless fancies of metaphysical speculation, does not put himself in danger of evoking our appreciative condescension.[9]

Borges develops his metaphysical conceits in two ways. The first method results in a tale that is hardly narrative at all. In "The Library of Babel," "The Lottery in Babylon," "The Cult of the Phoenix" one discovers no events or characters in the traditional sense; such pieces develop, like Metaphysical poems, by means of descriptive enumeration and elaboration of the basic conceit. While stories that fall exclusively into this category are rare in Borges' oeuvre, many of his stories employ a similar kind of treatment to some degree: the descriptive bibliography that takes up three of the twelve pages in "Pierre Menard, Author of *Don Quixote*," for example, is hardly a narrative, yet Borges obviously intends that bibliography to be taken as a biography of Menard, a metaphor for that writer's life.

Most of Borges' stories, however, are more conventionally narrative in nature. In these stories, the engendering conceit is not described or elaborated but transformed into the inspiring action of the plot. The purpose of the main character in these stories is the realization of the informing conceit. In "Emma Zunz," for instance, Emma's purpose is to create an historical event by an effort of the will—an obvious narrative embodiment of Schopenhauer's thesis abbreviated in the title *Welt als Wille und Vorstellung*; in "The Circular Ruins" the priest-hero's explicit purpose is to dream an individual, to enact the proposition that "la vida es sueño"; while in "The Immortal" the narrator's purpose is to achieve, as if physiologically, the immortality we confer on Homer when we call him immortal.

What should be clear from the foregoing is that Borges turned from lyric metaphor to metaphysical conceit, that he turned from figures of language to figures of thought. The two preoccupations—rhetorical metaphor and metaphysical conceit—had been his, of course, from the early days of his career: *Inquisitions* alone presents us with both "Examination of Metaphors" and "The Insignificance of Personality." But in Borges' mature work, the interest in rhetorical metaphor is evident primarily in his critical treatment of other writers, while the concern with wry and ingenious paradoxes of time, space, and personality informs his own imaginative writing.

The Metaphysic of Negation and Compression

For the source of the metaphysical or philosophical conceits that inspire Borges' fiction, we must turn again to his early writings and to two essays in particular: "The Insignificance of Personality" and "The Crossroads of Berkeley." Despite the order in which they appeared in the 1925 volume *Inquisitions*, we must examine the second first, for an understanding of Borges' basic themes requires first of all a recognition of his relation to Berkeley.

BERKELEY   The essay on Berkeley does not interest us so much for what it has to say about its subject—*that* is neither very new nor particularly informative—but because it serves, with the authority of Borges' own word, to link Berkeley and Borges. As Borges says at the beginning of the essay, "The Crossroads of Berkeley" should situate "the reader along with me at the very source of my thought" (*I*, 109). Like so much of his early prose, Borges' essay is a statement of belief, a kind of metaphysical credo parallel to his "Profession of Literary Faith" in *The Extent of My Hope*, which he actually called "my literary creed" (*TE*, 146), and to the statement on Ultraism that appeared in *Nosotros*. In his essay on Berkeley, Borges reaffirms Berkeley's conclusions in the *Principles of Human Knowledge* and presents some of that book's implications, quoting Berkeley's familiar argument

"*Esse rerum est percipi*" (*I*, 110), explaining it with further quotation, confronting it with some objections drawn chiefly from Spencer's *Principles of Psychology*, defending the theory against these objections, and, finally, redefining it through his own imagery:

And with this I conclude my allegation. As for denying the autonomous existence of visible and palpable objects, it is easy to agree with that by thinking: Reality is like our reflection that arises in every mirror, a simulacrum that exists because of us, that arrives with us, gestures and goes away, but in whose pursuit it is enough to go in order to always encounter it. (*I*, 119)

What Borges found in Berkeley was the stimulus or *acicate* (*I*, 109) to develop a metaphysic based on the same principles and fulfilling the same needs as his rule of style: what the stylistics made possible in the way of expression, the metaphysic provided in the way of thought. Both serve to inform an oeuvre characterized by brevity and quintessence achieved through a denial of all that is either decorative or superficial. Just as Borges' esthetic rejects certain accepted practices in order to arrive at the fundamental element in literature, so too is his metaphysic fundamentally negative in the way it looks at this world. His negations derive from Berkeley's idealism; by manipulating the implications of these negations, Borges arrives at a notion of primordial experience as condensed as his verbal style. Whether Berkeley came before the style or the other way around, I have no way of knowing. Certainly, however, Borges often proceeds from esthetic principle to literary work, as I have argued previously. A metaphysical principle often stands behind an esthetic one, as we can observe in "The Insignificance of Personality," where Borges writes: "Therefore I want to apply to literature the conclusions arising from these premises and to construct on them an esthetic" (*I*, 84). There is no need to quote Berkeley's argument at length, especially since Borges, in characteristic fashion, has recapitulated "the substance of that doctrine":

> *Esse rerum est percipi: perception is the being of things: objects only exist in so far as they are noticed: on this genial platitude rests and rises the illustrious edifice that is Berkeley's system; with that spare formula he exorcises the fictions of dualism and reveals to us that reality is not a re-treating riddle, laboriously decipherable, but rather that it is close by, accessible and open on every side.* (*I*, 110)

Here then is the primary tenet of Borges' metaphysic: a denial of objective, external reality. On the basis of this *hallazgo* or discovery Borges constructs his own system, which is neither borrowed nor new, but an extension in literature of Berkeley's philosophical idealism. Working from his denial of the objective, Borges attacks the metaphysical validity of time and personality just as he attacks the esthetic validity of "intervening sentences, of transitions" and "confessionalism, circumstantiation."[10]

TIME Time is dealt with briefly in "The Crossroads of Berkeley" when Borges rebuts Spencer:

> *Imagine, along with some so-called philosophers, that only a Subject exists and that everything that happens is nothing but a vision unfolding before its spirit. Time would last as long as the vision, which nothing prevents us from thinking of as very short. There would be no time before the start of· the dream nor after its conclusion, since time is an intellectual matter and does not exist objectively. Thus we would have an eternity that would contain all possible time but nevertheless would take up only a few seconds. Similarly, theologians had to translate the eternity of God into a duration without beginning or end, without vicissitude or change, into a pure present.* (*I*, 118-19)

From this quotation we are able to establish the two fundamental points of Borges' denial of time: (1) he accepts time only as a subjective, intellectual fact; and (2) he postulates an eternity existing for perhaps only a few seconds in the subject's mind, that mind itself being a kind of "Aleph," a meeting place for all points of time. To these basic propositions we need add only one more in order to outline Borges' theory of time: the sense of cyclical or circular time probably best and most familiarly exemplified as the Myth of the Eternal Return.

The importance of the Eternal Return in Borges' writing has been widely recognized, chiefly because Borges has taken such care to point out the myth's significance: "I am accustomed to return eternally to the Eternal Return" ["*Yo suelo regresar eternamente al Eterno Regreso*"], he writes at the beginning of "Circular Time" (*HE*, 91), the essay that provides us with the simplest description of Borges' version of the myth.

"Circular Time" is written in the form of its subject. Borges speculates that history is really made up of chronological units repeating themselves with only minor variations throughout eternity and his essay not only describes but also embodies these modified repetitions: just as the first sentence returns forms of both *regresar* (return) and *eterno* (eternal), in a chiasmus, so the entire essay comprises repetitions of the theory itself, each showing how the theory, with only minor changes (like the *regresar, regreso* and *eternamente, eterno* of the first sentence), has repeated itself in the minds of many thinkers widely separated in time and space. Borges emphasizes three principal repetitions and the three representative thinkers who produced them. First there is Plato, who "affirms that the seven planets, their different velocities balanced, will return to the initial point of departure: a revolution that constitutes the perfect year" (*HE*, 91); next, Nietzsche, who sees the necessity for an eternal repetition because, "an *n* number of objects is incapable of an infinite number of variations" (*HE*, 92); and finally Borges himself, who finds "the least frightful and melodramatic concept, but also the only imaginable one, is that of similar but not identical cycles" (*HE*, 94). Thus, by repeating his argument concerning the meaning of repetition—with the weighted suggestion that his own version is "the only imaginable one"—Borges demonstrates the validity of his final quotation, this one from Marcus Aurelius: "I remember that all things revolve, and revolve again through the same orbits, so it is all the same for the spectator to see the orbit in one century or in two or for infinity" (*HE*, 95).

The positive product of Borges' fundamental rejection of time, the Myth of the Eternal Return, sheds much light upon the shape and direction of his entire canon. Indeed, the essay that most satisfactorily brings together these negative and positive propositions—it bears the self-consciously inconsistent title of "New Refutation of Time"—shows Borges in 1944 and again in 1946 (the dates of the two sections of the essay, originally composed as separate versions of the same argument) still working from Berkeley's *Principles of Human Knowledge*, relying, in fact, on many of the same passages cited in his early essay on Berkeley. Here, as nearly always, Borges *returns* to his previous thoughts, adding additional documentation and deepened insights: his oeuvre itself, the unfolding of his own literary mind, then, embodies an eternal return.

Hence, the title "New Refutation of Time" contains two verbal equivocations, not just the *contradictio in adjecto* that Borges himself points out (*OI*, 236), but also the ironic reminder that this is, in fact, an old refutation of time. For even what may seem new for the argument, the peroration of Part One, an account of Borges' intuitive recognition of the timeless present, echoes an anecdote published in 1928, "Feeling in Death" ("*Sentirse en muerte*").

"Feeling in Death" is so nearly central to Borges' thought and esthetic and provides so revealing an account of his theory of time that I want to quote the key portion of it at length:

I stood looking at that simplicity. Confidently and out loud, I thought: "This is the same as thirty years ago. . . ." I guessed at that date: a recent epoch in other countries, but already remote on this fickle side of the world. Perhaps a bird was singing, and I felt a small fondness for it: a fondness about the size of a bird; but what is absolutely certain is that in the already vertiginous silence there was no other sound than the similarly atemporal one of the crickets. The easy thought "I am in the 1800s" ceased to be a few tentative words and deepened into reality. I felt dead, I felt myself an abstract perceiver of the world—vague fear infused with knowledge, which is the best insight of metaphysics. No, I did not think that I had reascended the presumptive waters of time; rather, I suspected that I was the possessor of the reticent or remote meaning of the inconceivable word eternity. *Only later did I succeed in defining that imagination.*

I am writing it now, thus: That pure representation of homogenous facts—serene night, limpid wall, rural odor of honey suckle, fundamental clay—is not merely identical to what was at that corner so many years ago; it is, without similarities or repetitions, the same. Time, if we are able to intuit that identity, is a delusion; the sameness and inseparability of a moment from its apparent yesterday and another moment from its apparent today, is enough to disintegrate Time.

Obviously the number of such human moments is not infinite. The fundamental ones—moments of physical suffering and physical pleasure, of falling asleep, of listening to a single piece of music, moments of great intensity or great ennui—are even more impersonal. In advance I derive this conclusion: life is much too poor not to be immortal too. But we do not even have the certainty of our poverty, since Time, easily refuted by the senses, is not so easily refuted by the intellect, from whose essence the concept of succession seems inseparable. So let the glimpsed idea remain in an emotional anecdote and let stand in the confessed irresolu-

*tion of this page the true moment of ecstasy and the possible
insinuation of eternity which that night did not begrudge me.*

While Borges seems unwilling at the end of this first
part of his essay to go beyond moments of suffering and pleasure, in the second part he does come to ask the question: "*Is
not a single repeated term enough* in order to destroy and
confound the history of the word, to denounce the idea that
there is such a history?" (*OI*, 253). Repetition, then, whether
it be exact or minimally different, denies the succession of
time; whether the repeated term be an identity or a mirror
image, it serves to plunge us into an eternity of the present.
Therefore the discrete moment, the instant of perception, if
apprehended fully as we have it in "Feeling in Death," sheds
its rind of apparent particularity and reveals a core of repetitive reality. While the points of time carefully noted in
Borges' writing have their unmistakably disjunctive function, like the gradations on a clock dial, their placement in
large cycles denies individuality and asserts identity just as
minute gradations, seen in forty-eight-hour cycles, invalidate
distinction and necessitate comparison. An example that runs
throughout Borges' work is the title of a book, *The Arabian
Nights*, which he usually writes as *The 1001 Nights*, the common form of the title in Spanish. The repeated terms of his
version of the title correspond to the repeated nights or stories (the story within the story); the terms are apparently
separated and different (1,000 and 1), but in actuality nothing keeps them apart (0=0) and the repeated terms are identical (1=1). Thus while many of Borges' stories, like "The
Immortal" and "Theme of the Traitor and Hero" assume as
their point of departure a precise date in history (June 1929
in the one and January 3, 1944, in the other), they in fact
demonstrate the meaninglessness of such dates in light of
history's perpetual repetition of itself. The title of each story
makes this point clear. One evokes an immortal, to whom the
passing of time can have no real significance. The other introduces an example of a significant strain of behavior that

has run through man's history: the story as a whole shows how the assassinations of Julius Caesar, Abraham Lincoln, and one Fergus Kilpatrick are not really three separate events but three enactments of the same timeless gesture. Indeed, once one realizes this identity of action, one is logically forced to recognize identity of character: Caesar is Lincoln is Fergus Kilpatrick is, if we are daring enough to accept Borges' train of thought, the immortal who will go on being assassinated throughout eternity. Thus we are led, through Borges' denial of time, to his second basic theme: the insignificance of personality.

PERSONALITY   We have seen that Borges restricts his writing to what he considers the essentials of literature and that he cuts through the seeming intricacies of time to reveal an eternal present. Now we shall see that, as a necessary corollary of this esthetic and metaphysical concision, he eliminates the idiosyncrasies that most writers depend on for revealing personality and focuses instead on an essential or primordial character. Within the chronology of the Eternal Return—really the nonchronology of a single archetypal time—it is necessary that there be archetypal characters. Mythic time demands mythic character.

The decision to suppress personality in his writing, like almost all Borges' esthetic choices, depends on a metaphysical principle enunciated early in his career and founded largely on Berkeley's idealism. To be sure, in "The Insignificance of Personality" we find Borges espousing a nonpersonal literature, seemingly without regard to any philosophical implications:

I want to reduce the unusual preeminence that today is customarily accorded to the "I.". . . I intend to prove that personality is an illusion consented to by conceit and habit, and, moreover, that it is without any metaphysical basis or visceral reality. Therefore I want to apply to literature the conclusions arising from these premises and to construct on them an esthetic hostile to the psychologism bequeathed to us by the last century, an esthetic favorably disposed toward the classics and yet stimulating to the most wayward tendencies of our time. (I, 84)

For the actual metaphysical basis of this principle, we must look to "The Crossroads of Berkeley," an essay that in *Inquisitions* follows "The Insignificance of Personality" but in time actually preceded it by two years.[11]

In an earlier essay entitled "The Insignificance of Personality," I showed in its many derivations the same thought whose explication is the object and end of these lines. But that essay, excessively afflicted by literature, is nothing but a series of suggestions and examples, strung together without rational continuity. In order to correct that fault, I have decided to explain in the following lines the hypothesis that moved me to undertake this writing. . . . Berkeley's idealism was my stimulus. (I, 109)

Borges further clarifies his position in "New Refutation of Time," showing how Berkeley had anticipated the denial of individuality that was later argued by Hume:

Berkeley denied that there was an object in back of sense impressions; David Hume that there was a subject behind the perception of change. The former had denied matter, the latter denied spirit; the former had not wanted us to add to the succession of impressions the metaphysical notion of matter, the latter did not want us to add to the succession of mental states the metaphysical notion of an "I." That amplification of Berkeley's argument is so logical that Berkeley himself, as Alexander Campbell Fraser has noted, foresaw it and even tried to reject it by means of the Cartesian ergo sum. *"If your principles are valid, you yourself are no more than a system of fluctuating ideas, unsupported by any substance, since it is as absurd to speak of spiritual substance as of material substance," reasons Hylas in anticipation of David Hume, in the third and last of the* Dialogues. (*OI*, 251)[12]

Berkeley, then, denied matter; Hume denied matter and spirit; Borges denies matter, spirit, and time. The logic of this cumulative series seems inevitable. But, if we accept Borges' tripartite denial, then we deny the series itself; we deny the separate identities of Berkeley, Hume, and Borges, affirming in their place a single thinker of a single thought. Hence the development from Berkeley's philosophical idealism to Borges' literary idealism demonstrates the central argument of "The Insignificance of Personality."

Since Borges' emphatic denial of time serves to distinguish his participation in the essentially Berkeleyan denial of personality, we can better appreciate Borges' position and, much more importantly, the way that this position affects his writing, if we briefly turn back to his version of the Myth of the Eternal Return. In "Circular Time" Borges formulated two corollaries to the Eternal Return: first, that the myth denied both past and future, telescoping them into an eternal present; and, second, that the myth denied "any newness" (*HE*, 96). If there is only the present and that present allows of nothing new, then what of human, personal experience?

If the destinies of Edgar Allan Poe, the Vikings, Judas Iscariot and of my reader are secretly the same destiny—the only possible destiny—universal history is the history of one man. Strictly speaking, Marcus Aurelius does not impose on us this enigmatic simplification. . . . Marcus Aurelius affirms the analogy, not the identity of the many individual destinies. He affirms that any interval—a century, a year, a single night, perhaps the ungraspable present—contains history completely. In its extreme form, this conjecture is easily refuted: one flavor differs from another flavor, ten minutes of physical pain are not equivalent to ten minutes of algebra.

*Applied to long spans, to the seventy years allotted to each
of us by the Book of Psalms, the conjecture is credible or
tolerable. It comes down to affirming that the number of
perceptions, of emotions, of thoughts, of human vicissitudes
is limited, and that before dying we shall exhaust all of them.*
(*HE*, 96-97)

What Borges says here of history and mankind applies directly to his own fiction. Looking at his stories with this
theory in mind, we see why they emphasize what has happened and not the person to whom it has happened—why,
in a word, his fiction stresses plot at the expense of character. Furthermore, we see why Borges' characters are so
palely, so grayly drawn, and it also becomes evident why
Shakespeare represents the perfect, the most complete man
for Borges: Shakespeare *exhausted* the largest number of
personalities, encompassed so many identities that his own
personality is indefinable or nonexistent: "Nobody was so
many men as that man, who, like the Egyptian Proteus, could
exhaust all the appearances of being" (*H*, 44). The extent of
Shakespeare's protean ability, manifest in the many roles of
his life as well as in the multiplicity of his characters, el-
evates him to a position second only to the divinity:

*History adds that, either before or after dying, he found him-
self before God to whom he said: "I, who in vain have been
so many men, want to be one and myself." The voice of God
answered him from out of a whirlwind: "Neither am I myself. I dreamed the world as you dreamed your work, my
Shakespeare, and you are among the forms of my dream, you,
who like me, are many and no one."* (*H*, 45)

Of course Borges is not so bound by his theory as to represent man without a sense, no matter how transitory, of his
own personality; indeed, he never abandons the tension between the certainty of individuality and the intuition of unity.
Thus Shakespeare experimented with producing and evoking the hallucination of singularity:

Instinctively, he had already trained himself in the habit of feigning that he was someone so that his condition of being no one would not be discovered; in London he hit upon the profession to which he was predestined—that of the actor, who on a stage, plays at being someone else before an audience that plays at taking him for that other person. His acting duties taught him a singular happiness, perhaps the first he knew; but when the last line was applauded and the last dead man taken off the stage, the detested awareness of unreality came over him once more. (H, 43-44)

And the pattern of Shakespeare's life finds analogy in the typical Borges story, in which the starting point is most often the demonstration, through circumstantial detail, of a character's individuality, the conclusion most often the epiphany of his personal insignificance. The progress, in Borges' own terms, is from *everything to nothing*, the alpha and omega terms in the title of his later prose sketch on Shakespeare in *El Hacedor.*

A clue to the kind of nonpersonal experience Borges is interested in can be found in the long passage from "Feeling in Death" that I quoted in the preceding section and more particularly in these sentences:

The easy thought "I am in the 1800s" ceased to be a few tentative words and deepened into reality. I felt dead, I felt myself an abstract perceiver of the world—vague fear infused with knowledge, which is the best insight of metaphysics. (OI, 247)

The two interrelated concepts of time and person that I have emphasized are here evident in a fictional context: the Myth of the Eternal Return in "*I am in the 1800s*" and the insignificance of personality in "I felt dead, I felt myself an abstract perceiver of the world." Furthermore, we see in this passage that the suppression of personality *results* directly from the narrator's intuition of timelessness. The collapse of history brings about the collapse of personality.

By way of instructive comparison to this passage from "Feeling in Death," several analogies offer themselves in addition to the ones Borges explicitly names. First of all, the perception of timelessness in the external world—the intuitive certainty that the world confronted in the present is identical to the world others encountered in the past—this perception is familiar to us all from Keats' "Ode to a Nightingale":

> *Thou was not born for death, immortal Bird!*
> *No hungry generations tread thee down;*
> *The voice I hear this passing night was heard*
> *In ancient days by emperor and clown:*
> *Perhaps the self-same song that found a path*
> *Through the sad heart of Ruth, when sick for home,*
> *She stood in tears amid the alien corn:*
> *The same that oft-times hath*
> *Charmed magic casements, opening on the foam*
> *Of perilous seas, in faery lands forlorn.*[13]

Perhaps it is this very "self-same song" Borges had in mind when he wrote "On Beginning the Study of Anglo-Saxon Grammar":

> *After fifty generations*
> *(Time affords such abysses for us all).*
> *I return to the far edge of a great river*
> *That the dragons of the Vikings never reached,*
> *To the rough and difficult words*
> *That, with a mouth turned to dust,*
> *I used in the days of Northumbria and Mercia*
> *Before being Haslam or Borges.*
> *Saturday I read that Julius Caesar*
> *Was the first who came from Romeburg to discover*
> *England;*

Before the grapes ripen again, I shall have heard
The voice of the nightingale of the enigma
And the elegy of the twelve warriors
Who surround the tomb of their king. (H, 93)

It is Keats' notion of immortality expressed in the "self-same song" and Ecclesiastes that Borges refers to when he has the imprisoned priest in "The Writing of God" say: "The mountain and the star are individual entities, and individuals decay. I sought something more tenacious, more invulnerable. I pondered the generations of grain, of grasses, of birds, of men" (*A*, 117). And again in *"El Sur"* when Borges tells us that while Dahlman petted a cat he thought: "That contact was illusory, and they were as if separated by a mirror, because man lives in time, in succession, and the magic animal in actuality, in the eternity of the present" (*F*, 190). If Keats provides an illuminating parallel to the intuition of eternity in the passage under discussion, we can also find enlightening parallels to the notion of identity or personality expressed there.

The situation described in "Feeling in Death" is roughly equivalent to Marcel's threefold discovery at the end of *À la recherche du temps perdu*, and Borges, like Proust, re-creates the experience in terms of ecstacy (*OI*, 248). However, if we look closely at the state Borges describes, we see that fear is the only feeling precisely named in connection with the act of intuition and even that is defined as "vague." In fact, the dominant impression is of a lack of emotion. The culminating phrase is, in effect, *"Me sentí muerto"* or "I felt dead": to feel dead is to feel nothing, or, more exactly, not to feel at all, and the moment of ecstasy consists in the subject's absorption in a transcendent vision, a state described by Celia in T. S. Eliot's *The Cocktail Party:*

> *I have often thought at moments that the ecstasy is*
> *   real*
> *Although those who experience it may have no*
> *   reality.*[14]

And it is a state Borges returns to, using the words of "Feeling in Death," in "The Garden of the Forking Paths": "I felt myself, for an indeterminate time, an abstract perceiver of the world" (*F*, 102). In this respect Borges is closer to Emerson than to Proust, which is not odd since Borges has remarked that, in naming writers who have mattered to him, he "should have spoken more of Emerson."[15] In fact there is a striking parallel between this passage in "New Refutation of Time" and that famous passage in "Nature":

In the woods is perpetual youth. Within these plantations of God, a decorum and sanctity reign, a perennial festival is dressed, and the guest sees not how he should tire of them in a thousand years. In the woods, we return to reason and faith. There I feel that nothing can befall me in life—no disgrace, no calamity (leaving me my eyes), which nature cannot repair. Standing on the bare ground—my head bathed by the blithe air and uplifted into infinite space—all mean egotism vanishes. I become a transparent eyeball; I am nothing; I see all; the currents of the Universal Being circulate through me; I am part or parcel of God.[16]

Though the grotesque image of the transparent eyeball is patently more memorable than Borges' "abstract perceiver," the two phrases are profoundly similar, not only in their intrinsic sense but also in the way they recall Berkeley's God, who, Borges says, "is not a maker of things; rather, a contemplator of life or an immortal and ubiquitous spectator of living" (*I*, 114). Similarly, "I felt dead" and "I am nothing" are equivalent, and in both passages the moment of visionary clarity entails the loss of self. Both writers, stressing the transcendental elevation at the expense of the ego, insist that to be is not to be. Embodying these metaphysical principles in his fiction—the cyclical nature of history and the resultant negation of individuality—Borges creates a world of echoing events and telescoped chronology and peoples this world with characters that are barely distinguishable from one another or that are chiefly recognizable as analogies to other characters. In other words, each of Borges' stories tends to present an action that reveals the repetitiveness of history and characters that are the manifestations of a single being. In creating character, Borges largely relinquishes or reveals the meaninglessness of the circumstantial and the idiosyncratic—the world of conventional fiction—in order to reach the primordial world of myth. Like the epic poet whom Ortega describes as writing of the same world, Borges also "knows that his song is not his alone."[17] Borges' writing is therefore consciously primitivistic, but different from the verbal primitivism of Gertrude Stein, Sherwood Anderson, or Ernest Hemingway; his work rests on tenets of primitive ontology. In fact, we must turn to the lore of anthropology to find a writer whose interests in the primitive reflect Borges' own; and in this respect Mircea Eliade's book, *Cosmos and History*, is among the most useful.

When in *Cosmos and History*, originally published as *Le mythe de l'éternel retour: archétypes et répétition* (Paris, 1949), Eliade speaks of primitive or archaic man, his descriptions exactly fit the aspects of Borges' fiction I have been discussing; the reality or "world" of primitive man as described by Eliade is precisely the reality of Borges' stories. Compare this passage with Borges' denial of individual personality:

An object or an act becomes real only insofar it imitates or repeats an archetype. Thus reality is acquired solely through repetition or participation; everything which lacks an exemplary model is "meaningless," i.e., it lacks reality. Men would thus have a tendency to become archetypal and paradigmatic. This tendency may well appear paradoxical, in the sense that the man of a traditional culture sees himself as real only to the extent that he ceases to be himself (for a modern observer) and is satisfied with imitating and repeating the gestures of another. In other words, he sees himself as real, i.e., as "truly himself," only, and precisely, insofar as he ceases to be so.[18]

Although based on Platonic rather than Berkeleyan idealism, the points of correspondence between this passage and Borges' fiction are basic. Moreover, the following corollary of Eliade's major point further illuminates Borges' mythic quality:

Insofar as an act (or an object) acquires a certain reality through the repetition of certain paradigmatic gestures, and acquires it through them alone, there is an implicit abolition of profane time, of duration, of "history"; and he who re-produces the exemplary gesture thus finds himself trans-ported into the mythical epoch in which its revelation took place. . . . Just as profane space is abolished by the symbol-ism of the Center, which projects any temple, palace, or building into the central point of mythical space, so any meaningful act performed by archaic man, any real act, i.e., any repetition of an archetypal gesture, suspends duration, abolishes profane time, and participates in mythical time.[19]

Myth is therefore a paradigmatic narrative that takes place *in illo tempore* and whose characters and actions are arche-typal; it is the essential story on which all others are based; and in precisely this sense, Borges strives to be mythic, to retell the eternally recurring actions of the mythical hero and thereby reveal the secret of his eternal reality. Sometimes Borges limits his focus to one particular aspect of myth—the question of mythic time, for example, in "The Secret Miracle"—but even here, in the isolation of one mythic ele-ment, Borges' fiction still draws its force from the whole content and method of the myth. In mythological fiction, cutting through the boundaries of time and personality, he finds the essential narrative that is the proper subject for his essential style.

From metaphor, the primordial element of lyric ex-pression, to mythology, a metaphorical narrative with a pri-mordial subject, the quest of Borges' art has been for the quintessential. As we have seen, he achieves his goal with a remarkable parity of form and subject. Now it remains to point out a single literary device, perhaps the most obvious characteristic of his writing, that implements both his esthetic criteria and his metaphysical scheme. The device, of course, is allusion.

The Function of Allusion

Borges' writing is so thoroughly controlled by his esthetic/metaphysical scheme that when we examine any detail of his style we must not only ask ourselves whether it is a significant characteristic of his writing but also whether it helps Borges to achieve his goal of quintessential brevity. For example, Borges frequently uses words in their older or etymological sense, not merely for "poetic" effect but because such words are in themselves abbreviated symbols of the collapse of time. As James Irby points out, words like *universo* and *unánime* communicate, in addition to their usual denotation, Borges' notion of the underlying unity of all things, of the world as a uni-verse. Moreover, at the same time that these words swiftly take us back to the Latinity of their roots, they neatly carry that archaic Latinity into contemporary Spanish, thereby negating the lapse of time between the ancient and the modern language. Such words are transparent vessels that bear within themselves antiquity and modernity in a perfect, impersonal, or super-personal solution and are therefore invaluable to Borges in his search for "a limpid art that might be as atemporal as the eternal stars." The explicit justification for this etymological emphasis can be found in an early essay on one of the English authors who matters most to Borges, Sir Thomas Browne:

It is my conjecture that the frequent Latinity of his time was neither mere sonorous cooing nor an artifice to expand the writing, but an ardor for universality and clarity. (I, 37)

Until we understand that *all* elements in his style, like this etymological element, are expressive as well as idiosyncratic, we cannot begin to come to terms with the complexity of Borges' art.

Literary allusion is an inescapable characteristic of Borges' writing. Borges himself calls our attention to the pervasiveness of allusion in his work with footnotes, explanatory prefaces, and pages of notes at the end of stories and books. For Borges, allusion first of all expresses the collapse of time and the disintegration of personality. In an allusion, as in a metaphor, two distant things are brought together so that the reader is forced to become aware of their relationship or resemblance. Borges is such a master of these allusive equations that Marcial Tamayo and Adolfo Ruiz-Díaz have written: "This perfect adjustment induces one to believe that the quotation and the text obey a single creative process; that is, that the quotation does not proceed from a former exercise of choice but rather that in his esthetic elaboration Borges moves in a world of quotations."[20] The perfect balance between allusion and text, making both appear the product of a single author, is precisely the goal Borges works toward. If we recall that a single repeated term is sufficient to deny succession and that a repeated idea denies the separate identities of the thinkers, then we can see that an allusion, the embodiment of both these modes of repetition, denies both time and individuality. Allusion unites text and reference in a point of time and space that eliminates both the separateness of the passages and of their authors. This union may be approximate, as in a footnote that indicates a parallelism of thought; it may be near perfect, as in a textual allusion that blurs the boundaries of the actual text and the cited work. In either case, Borges' technique destroys chronology and treats identical ideas as emanations of the same mind: to think the same is to be the same. To make allusions is to demonstrate the timeless universality of the human mind. Moreover, as Borges tries to show how all time and individuality may be compressed in the brief thought of a single mind, he attempts, too, to create a sense of the very diversity he compresses. The Aleph, we recall, is a single point containing all others; therefore, the literary work that aspires to the condition of the Aleph must itself be brief and unified but must also announce ontological variety. Frequent and crucial allusions remind us of the diversity of autonomous minds that have moved toward precisely the same imaginative experience and verbal expression. Allusion further serves Borges' intention by introducing an element of the fantastic into his writing. In a new and often unexpected contexts, literary and philosophical writings create the disturbing quality of novelty and unreality that Borges understands as the source of the fantastic. But allusions used in this way and for this purpose lead us to a comforting symmetry: if Borges' text sometimes resembles a nest of Chinese boxes, his allusions point out that while each box is of a different size, all are always the same in essence. Thus allusion evokes in Borges' work the systole and diastole of metaphysical, unified reality and fantastic, diversified appearance.

Borges' dependence on allusion cannot be overvalued, nor can the extent of allusion in his writing be overestimated. In part, allusion is his substitute for rhetorical metaphor—reference replaces figure of speech, citation supplants comparison. If we find the meaning of other writers concentrated in their metaphors, we often find Borges' meaning distilled in his allusions. His stories are allusions to other stories, his characters are allusions to other characters, and their lives are allusions to other lives. In this single literary device, at once familiar and simple, we find a key to his work.

Characteristics of Allusion in Borges

Before proceeding to categorize Borges' allusions it might be good to list three of their general characteristics. They tend, first of all, to be brief and incisive. Borges' constant concern with extracting the essence is as evident here as in any other aspect of his work: Berkeley, for example, though the source of so much in Borges' thought, is referred to in the shortest of passages, and the extracts from Berkeley that actually make their way into Borges' work are also brief.

Second, Borges' allusions tend to be recurrent: Borges returns again and again—eternally—not only to the same authors but often to the same passages. Again, Berkeley provides a good example, as I have already demonstrated in my discussion of Borges' notions of impersonality. Finally, Borges' allusions tend to be drawn from English and American writers—but this point is so nearly central to my thesis that I will develop it in the next chapter.

MODES OF ALLUSION IN BORGES If we bear in mind the purpose of allusion in Borges' work, its function in demonstrating the temporal identity of thoughts and minds, we should not be surprised that we must define the word more broadly than usual when applying it to his work. When speaking of Borges' literary allusions, then, I refer not only to any passage in his writing where the words or ideas of another writer are explicitly or tacitly referred to but also to any passage that is patterned on other works. Hence the following categories:

Referential allusion. Cleon Capsas has suggested that "Borges has developed the idea of the artistic use of the footnote in his prose. He is probably the first author in Spanish to do so, but admits that the idea came from Carlyle's *Sartor Resartus*."[21] Turning to an introduction Borges wrote to a translation of *Sartor Resartus*, we find not only a justification of this practice but an excellent example of referential allusion:

Literature is a game with tacit conventions; to violate them partially or totally is one of the many joys (one of the many obligations) of the game, whose limits are unknown. For example: each book is an ideal orb, but we are usually pleased that its author, in the space of a few lines, confounds it with reality, with the universe. We are delighted that the protagonists of the second part of Don Quixote *have read the first part, just as we have. It delights us that Aeneas, wandering through the streets of Carthage, looks at sculptures of the*

Trojan War on the facade of a temple and also sees, among so many mournful images, his own effigy. It delights us that on the six hundred and second night of the 1001 Nights, *the queen Scheherazade refers to the story that serves as the preface to all the others, with the risk of arriving once again at the night on which she relates it, and so on into infinity. It would delight us if* Pantagruel *itself appeared in the ridiculous catalogue of the library visited by Pantagruel. It delights us that the protagonists of* Hamlet *attend, as we do, a tragedy whose subject is the poisoning of a king. It delights us that the author of* Sartor Resartus *pretends that this book already exists and that the volume published by him is a small facsimile of the original.*[22]

Carlyle's footnotes, as the quotation explains, blur the boundaries of the world that contains the book and the book that contains the world, and Borges' own footnotes, documentary citations, and explanations of derivation not only perform precisely the same function but in addition erase the literary boundaries separating the essay from the story.

Borges here tells us more about his own methods than about those of Carlyle. This "Preliminary Note" is characteristic of Borges' writing on any point of artistic innovation, or for that matter, on almost any intellectual or historical topic. Although the ostensible subject of his paragraph is Carlyle's device, Borges presents that device last in a long series of examples that in effect denies Carlyle's originality. By the end of the passage we see *Sartor Resartus* as a variation on an ancient theme. Of course, to situate the work he studies in literary tradition is always a legitimate part of the critic's function, but Borges' repeated use of this pattern in opening paragraphs and even in whole essays should indicate its special importance for him. The paragraph is in fact a résumé of his metaphysic: the reference to *The Arabian Nights* introduces the theme of the Eternal Return, while the references to Virgil, Cervantes, Shakespeare, and Carlyle illustrate the theory of "the insignificance of personality." If our view is long enough or broad enough, Borges seems to be saying, we shall see that there is no such thing as an original artist, that there is only the archetypal artist working at the archetypal art object. In other words, Borges' references in this paragraph function as literary allusions, establishing the single identity of all the writers mentioned. A parallel example of this device in the form of a more or less traditional footnote occurs in "Examination of the Works of Herbert Quain":

Alas for the erudition of Herbert Quain! Alas for page 215 of an 1897 book! An interlocutor of the Politician *had already described a similar regression: that of the Sons of Earth or Autochthons who, subjected to the influence of a reversed rotation of the cosmos, would pass from old age to maturity, from maturity to childhood, from childhood to disappearance and nothingness. In his* Phillipic *Teopompo also speaks of certain northern fruits that originate in those who eat them—the same reverse process. . . . It is more interesting to imagine an inversion of Time: a state in which we would remember the future and would be ignorant of or barely foreknow the past. Cf. the tenth canto of the* Inferno, *line 97-102, where prophetic vision and farsightedness are compared.* (F, 79-80)

Borges' references, then, whether they occur in the text or as adjuncts to it, serve their scholarly, referential, or informative purposes as well as their artistic purpose, not the least of which is the expression of the underlying metaphysic of his work.

Paradigmatic allusion. Passing from explicit to tacit allusion, we move from the simple to the more complex, from allusions that often seem subordinate or ancillary to allusive words that prove to be as nearly crucial as any others in the text. Tacit or covert allusion is thus less mechanical: tacit allusion is comparable to metaphor, in which the identity of two things is asserted, and explicit allusion to simile, in which the mechanism of comparison, the telltale *like* or *as*, tends to emphasize the resemblance yet at the same time subtly affirms the essential difference of the things compared.

One kind of tacit allusion that Borges uses with notable effect is the paradigmatic. Here there need be no specific verbal reference; instead, parts or even the whole of a story are modeled on another work. By means of this kind of allusion, which we are probably most familiar with in the epic tradition, one work informs another, and thus, for Borges' purposes, negates the time separating the two works as well as the individuality of the two authors. Since it is necessary that the reader be aware of such nonverbal allusions, or at least of their possibility, Borges frequently appends notes to his work to indicate the correspondences: the epilogue to *El Aleph* (*A*, 171-72) comprises references that remind us in form if not in intention of Eliot's controversial notes to *The Waste Land* or of the hints and explanations Joyce gave to Stuart Gilbert with the understanding that they be published. (If the modern writer sometimes thinks of himself as Dedalus, builder of labyrinths, apparently he is also compelled to think of himself as Ariadne, giver of clues; the reader, in turn, is obliged to think of himself as Theseus, threader of labyrinths and slayer of monsters.) However, Borges does not always cite all his paradigms—he never reveals, for example, that his story "The Cult of the Phoenix" develops from a passage in De Quincey's "Secret Societies."[23] But whether the paradigm is revealed to the reader through notes or hidden from him (as it is usually hidden from the characters themselves), it is the purpose of paradigmatic allusion to embody the secret but recurrent patterns that inform human life: Borges models his works on other writings, builds these parallels into his work in relentless, recurring demonstrations of his belief in the unity of mind and the meaninglessness of passing time.

Evocative versus substantive allusion. Before we can approach the category I shall call substantive allusion, we must briefly consider one type of allusion, common to many writers in the twentieth century, that Borges does not use— evocative allusion. Eliot in *The Waste Land*, for example, incorporated many passages from other writers for what they would say in his context as well as for what they would carry with them from their previous context. When Eliot wrote:

> *Unreal City*
> *Under the brown fog of a winter dawn,*
> *A crowd flowed over London Bridge, so many,*
> *I had not thought death had undone so many*[24]

he did not merely compare the citizens of Unreal London to dead souls; he incremented this comparison with all the particular emotional and dramatic significance that the line bears in Dante's poem. Eliot invoked an image, a scene, a feeling, even a judgment. His allusion is clearly evocative, and evocative allusions are not simply informative or descriptive: they function like evocative images, not only making comparisons but also regulating and directing the reader's response to the comparison. Borges, for all his dependence upon allusions, avoids those that use the words of another writer in such a way as to evoke that writer's style and his personality: Borges alludes to the theme and topic, extracts the essential, and, in so far as possible, eliminates the personal, the specific words of the writer, condensing as he translates, even going so far as to alter the phrasing of book titles with a freedom that only appears to be the result of erudite carelessness.

Yet Borges' allusions do bear an important resemblance to Eliot's in another respect. In Borges' writing, as in Eliot's or Joyce's, allusions are used in such a way that their very frequency implies a significance distinct from that of any of them taken singly: for the act of alluding is, in itself, a meaningful gesture, and the main expressive value of the allusions is implicit in their prevalence. Allusion, in other words, becomes a substantive act, an expression of a profound and ubiquitous cultural impulse. This kind of substantive allusion represents one solution to a problem faced by every writer who tries to deal with experience that transcends the personal. F. O. Matthiessen isolates the problem in *The Achievement of T. S. Eliot*, and the modern solution Matthiessen describes applies to Borges' writing no less aptly than Eliot's:

The modern educated man possesses a knowledge of the past to a degree hardly glimpsed a century ago, not only of one segment of the past, but, increasingly, of all pasts. If he is sensitive to what he knows, he can feel, in Eliot's words, "that the whole of literature of Europe from Homer . . . has a simultaneous existence." But also, owing to the self-consciousness which results from so much knowledge (scientific and psychological as well as historical and literary), he will have a sense in any given moment, as Eliot has remarked of Joyce, "of everything happening at once."

Such a realization can lead either to chaos or to a sense of the potential unity of life. . . . The problem for the artist is to discover some unified pattern in this variety; and yet, if he believes as Eliot does that poetry should embody a man's reaction to his whole experience, also to present the full sense of its complexity. He can accomplish this double task of accurately recording what he has felt and perceived, and at the same time interpreting it, only if he grasps the similarity that often lies beneath contrasting appearances, and can thus emphasize the essential equivalence of seemingly different experiences. Such understanding and resultant emphasis constitute Eliot's chief reason for introducing so many reminiscences of other poets into the texture of his own verse. In this way he can at once suggest the extensive consciousness of the past that is inevitably possessed by any cultivated reader to-day, and, more importantly, can greatly increase the implications of his lines by this tacit revelation of the sameness (as well as the contrast) between the life of the present and that of other ages.[25]

By labeling Eliot's allusions "reminiscences," Matthiessen suggests something of their essentially personal, evocative, non-Borgesian quality, yet at the same time reminds us that they are not so much quotations from other authors as symmetries of thought that illuminate one manifestation of the metapersonal mind—namely, the mind of the contemporary man of letters that is most clearly defined by a commonly accessible treasury of literary experience.

Hence we return to the central, inescapable point: Borges' allusions are an abbreviated demonstration of the Eternal Return, of the mind timelessly turning upon its own universal experience, of "everything happening at once"; they embody the metaphysical principles from which his work develops. In few writers of Borges' stature can we discern such a fixed and limited set of intellectual propositions, so much variety at the service of such unyielding consistency.

Notes

1. Quoted by Borges in "Ultraísm," *Nosotros* XV (December 1921): 468.
2. *Nosotros*, 468.
3. *Some Imagist Poems* (Boston and New York: 1915), vi-vii.
4. *Nosotros*, 468.
5. Review of *An Anthology of Contemporary Latin American Poetry*, *Sur* 102 (March 1943): 64.
6. Notes on Language and Style," ed. Herbert Read, *The Criterion* III, 12 (July 1925): 497.
7. "Nature," *Complete Essays and Other Writings* (New York: 1950), 13.
8. "Homenaje a Jorge Luis Borges," *La voz* (Noviembre 1962): 15.
9. Borges' attitude toward what we might call the local color of science fiction emerges in his 1936 review of *Things to Come*, the film based on a story by H. G. Wells; and he extends that basic attitude into a characteristic though infrequent denunciation:

   Tyrants offend Wells but laboratories please him, hence his forecast of scientists joining together in order to unite a world wrecked by tyrants. Reality has yet to resemble his prophecy: in 1936, the power of almost all tyrants derives from their control of technol-

ogy. Wells reveres chauffeurs and aviators; the tyrannical occupation of Abyssinia was the work of aviators and chauffeurs—and the fear, perhaps slightly mythological, of Hitler's laboratories.

"Wells the Visionary," in Edgardo Cozarinsky's *Borges in/and/on Film*, tr. Gloria Waldman and Ronald Christ (New York: 1988), 36.

10. For a more detailed analysis of Borges' use of Berkeley, see Ana María Barrenechea, *Borges the Labyrinth Maker*, tr. Robert Lima (New York: 1957), 121-24.

11. *Inquisitions* appeared in 1925 while "The Crossroads of Berkely" was published in *Nosotros* (January 1923 XII, núm. 164, tomo 43): 359-65.

12. The original passage reads:

> *Notwithstanding all you have said, to me it seems that, according to your own way of thinking, and in consequence of your own principles, it should follow that you are only a system of floating ideas, without any substance to support them. Words are not to be used without a meaning. And, as there is no more meaning in spiritual Substance than in material Substance, the one is to be exploded as well as the other.*

As presented in the *Harvard Classics* (1909) XXXVII, 270, the lengthy section from which the passage has been extracted carries Fraser's note, to which Borges alludes:

> *This important passage, printed within brackets, is not found in the first and second editions of the* Dialogues. *It is, by anticipation, Berkeley's answer to Hume's application of the objections to the reality of abstract or unperceived Matter, to the reality of the Ego or Self, of which we are aware through memory, as identical amid the changes of successive states.* (XXXVII, 269)

13. *The Poetical Works of John Keats*, ed. H. W. Garrod (London: 1956), 208-209.

14. T. S. Eliot, *The Complete Poems and Plays* (New York: 1952), 363.

15. The statement occurs in one of the few substantive passages deleted from my interview with Borges that appeared in the *Paris Review* (Winter-Spring 1967), 116-64, and that appears at the end of this volume:

> *No, what I think I have said is that writers I have read and reread most are such writers as Shaw, Chesterton, Schopenhauer . . . Sir Thomas Browne, Samuel Butler, and also, but I think I should have spoken more of him—Emerson. I'm very fond of Emerson; he is a very great writer. I remember that Nietzsche said that he couldn't praise Emerson, because he found that they were so close that it was like praising himself. But I think Emerson a finer writer and*

*a finer thinker than Nietzsche, though most people wouldn't say
that today.*

16. *Complete Essays*, 6.
17. José Ortega y Gasset, *Meditaciones del Quijote, Obras Completas* (Madrid: 1957) I, 374.
18. Mircea Eliade, *Cosmos and History*, tr. Willard R. Trask (New York and Evanston: 1959), 34.
19. *Cosmos and History*, 35-36.
20. Marcial Tamayo and Adolfo Ruiz-Díaz, *Borges, enigma y clave* (Buenos Aires: 1955), 19.
21. Cleon Capsas, "The Poetry of Jorge Luis Borges, 1923-1963," unpublished dissertation (University of New Mexico: 1964), 6.
22. Jorge Luis Borges, *Preliminary Note to* Sartor Resartus (Buenos Aires: 1945), 9.
23. Thomas De Quincey, "Secret Societies," *The Collected Writings*, ed. David Masson (Edinburgh: 1890) VII, 181-205.
24. Eliot, *Complete Poems*, 39.
25. F. O. Matthiessen, *The Achievement of T. S. Eliot* (New York: 1959), 34-36.

ACCESS TO THE COSMOPOLITAN

Development of Borges' International Literary Interests
Borges' relation to English literature is idiosyncratic: while we observe in his writing a wide range of references to English authors, we also observe that his interest tends to fall either upon odd, distinctly minor figures or upon curious sidelights of our major authors. It is true that his stated admiration for Shakespeare and Milton is appropriately great; but authors who really influence his work, the reflection of whose writing can be seen in his fiction, are Chesterton, Wells, and Kipling. Even in a course of lectures on English literature he gave at the University of Buenos Aires, the same odd preferences showed up. In fact, one of his students suggested in an interview that Borges' subjective approach to authors was not always advantageous to the student—as, for example, when Borges emphasized William Morris in an introductory course in English literature. One sympathizes with the student, but at the same time, one sees a greater importance in her summary complaint: "The problem is that Borges sometimes chooses what is most important for Borges and not what is most important in that literature" (*L'Herne*, 49). What the student says is equally and more significantly true of Borges' writing, both the essays and the stories: his connection with English is personal, subjective and not, in the usual sense of the word, academic. If we are to understand this relationship adequately, if we are to ascertain its influence on his work, we must recognize both its origin and development. In other words, we must examine this relation both from the point of view of biography and from that of esthetics.

The key to Borges' curious intimacy with English literature, as well as his growing concern with other foreign literatures, lies in his childhood and is alluded to both in his own writing and in some of the biographical pieces about him. Drawing from these sources, we can see how the combined powers of heredity, environment, and education—here evident in his grandmother's influence, his father's library, and his tutor's instruction—worked together to awaken a lasting, personal relationship with English literature. First of all, his mother tells us about Borges' early education:

Georgie was born in the same house I was, in the center of Buenos Aires on Tucumán Street. But he did not stay there very long: a few years after his birth we moved to a large house with a garden in the section called Palermo. . . . He lived in that house until he was thirteen, and it was there that he first learned to read English, at the beginning with a governess; and it was from there that he went to school.

And Borges complements his mother's statement:

I believed for many years that I had been raised in a suburb of Buenos Aires, a suburb of adventurous streets and visible sunsets. What is certain is that I was raised in a garden, behind a wrought-iron gate, and in a library of unlimited English books. (*EC*, 9)

Finally, Victoria Ocampo tells us:

The fact of having had an English grandmother has had a great influence on the life and work of Georgie, because he passed his childhood, as a little boy who loved to read, with Dickens, Stevenson, Kipling, Bulwer-Lytton, Mark Twain, Edgar Allan Poe. He read and re-read Huckleberry Finn. H. G. Wells's The First Men on the Moon *made a very strong impression on him.* (*L'Herne*, 21)

The first two quotations emphasize the long-standing familiarity with English literature that underlies much of Borges' work, while the last is useful for understanding how that familiarity influenced his writing.

Borges' relationship to English literature is just that, a relationship, neither a critical investigation nor an academic study; a relationship, furthermore, growing out of childhood reading in an atmosphere whose comfortable familiarity with English is epitomized in the affectionate diminutive "Georgie." Finally, it is a relationship that, while supported by ancestry, by familial encouragement, and by private instruction, was based above all on a child's tastes and pleasures. Having begun with English literature on this basis, Borges seldom shifted to any other. "I am a hedonistic reader," he explains (*D*, 93). This statement illuminates his unusual, seemingly noncritical attitude toward many authors, an attitude pinpointed by his assistant at the University of Buenos Aires: "Borges, I think, is never objective and never could be objective. Moreover his view is never that of a critic but really that of a reader" (*L'Herne*, 49). The inevitable result of such an approach is exemplified in Borges' comment on his acquaintance with Chesterton: "I read and re-read him, and I find that he is like a personal friend" (*L'Herne*, 383).

Borges' fondness for Chesterton and for his other favorite authors is rather like Virginia Woolf's affinity for many English authors, and she too may be said to have grown up in her father's library. But whereas Woolf's critical essays and her literary skylarking in *Orlando* cover the entire range of English literature, Borges' writing reveals his tracing several thoughts or metaphors through all the books he read. "Perhaps universal history is the history of a few metaphors," he has written (*OI*, 13), and we can see that the metaphors that inform his work are all traceable, in their germinal form, to his childhood reading and that the books he enjoyed then have proved worthy of his continuing, adult attention. While Borges' childhood reading established his enduring preferences, his mature writing justifies that reading and those preferences by drawing from them the stuff of his art. Hence the curious way in which Borges often seems to ignore the most obvious and sometimes the most important aspects of a writer's work in order to focus on some peculiar, even idiosyncratic aspect.

Beyond all question is the thoroughness of Borges' early acquaintance with English literature, a thoroughness that qualifies the seeming extravagance and pettiness of his interests. We only begin to appreciate the full extent of young Borges' close relationship with English authors when we learn that at the age of nine he published his first work: a translation of Oscar Wilde's fairy tale *The Happy Prince*. No mere student's exercise, this translation was adopted as a text in an English class by a local teacher who mistook it for the work of Borges' father (*L'Herne*, 21). A tribute both to Borges' linguistic gifts and his diligent study, this ironic misunderstanding moreover tempts us to cite the incident possibly as a cause, certainly as a circumstantial foreshadowing, of Borges' subsequent theories of the meaninglessness of individual personality. A more prophetic, an even more ironic debut for his future career would be hard to imagine.

At any rate, Borges' knowledge of foreign literature and his interest in it, publicly announced by his translation of Oscar Wilde, continued to develop and expand in the subsequent years. In addition to English, Borges learned French at an early age, and between the reading of English and French books he had little time for Spanish works. Victoria Ocampo tells us:

He had, on the other hand, very little to do with Spanish authors, just like all the young readers of that period who, having the privilege, not always enviable, of a French governess at home, were devoted to French. Don Quixote, *however, was his bedside book, and he also read* Facundo *and* Fausto. *All this between the ages of ten and eleven.* (*L'Herne*, 21)

And this trend toward cultivating an international literary sensibility at the apparent expense of an intimate knowledge of his native literature was further confirmed when, in 1914, he went to Switzerland to study French. While preparing for his degree, which he took in 1918, Borges taught himself German, and it was through German, his mother tells us, that he first discovered Chinese literature, just as he had earlier developed an interest in German literature from reading William Morris' translation of the *Volsunga Saga* (*L'Herne*, 21). From Oscar Wilde to Chinese literature—by this stage the track of Borges' development seems to have twisted further and further away from its starting point in his boyhood reading; yet there was still one great literature Borges had to approach in the conscious way he had come to French, German, and English before he could begin his career as the writer of supranational literature. Ironically, the last important step in his international development took him to Spain and aroused within him a vital, personal concern with the literature of his native language.

Of course Borges had been reading Spanish authors during his youth, but at the end of the World War, when he became intimately involved in the Ultraist movement, he addressed himself to the problems of contemporary verse in Spanish. However, from 1919 to 1921, while he was in Spain, Borges expressed himself chiefly in conversation and discussion; it was not until he returned to Argentina that he embarked seriously upon a writer's career. The impact of his return is apparent in these early writings: even when discussing Ultraism, Borges explained its Argentine variety, carefully distinguishing it from the Spanish parent. And when he published a volume of poems in 1923, the title, *Fervor of Buenos Aires*, made clear the extent of his absorption in the task of singing his native city in his native language and of the distance between his new preoccupations and his earlier interest in foreign literatures. So fervid was Borges' discovery of his Buenos Aires (it can hardly be called a rediscovery) that he virtually shut out his international, multilingual education, almost as though attempting to compensate for lost time and experience. In this first period of his writing career, his subject was the city of his childhood, not his reading, and the early poems make little use of literary allusions. Obviously this is the period, or at least part of that period, Borges referred to when he said: "I believed for many years that I had been raised in a suburb of Buenos Aires, a suburb of adventurous streets and visible sunsets." (*EC*, 9); and the major influence seems to have been not that of any book but of an individual—Macedonio Fernández, whose name appears frequently in Borges' early writings in connection with the mythification of Buenos Aires and the development of Borges' esthetic and metaphysical thought. In *Inquisitions* Borges explains that "The Insignificance of Personality" and "The Crossroads of Berkeley" were conceived in discussions with Fernández, who in Borges' own words was a "passionate spectator of Buenos Aires." Consequently this period was the least international in Borges' career.[1]

The first poem of *Fervor of Buenos Aires,* "The Streets," embodies the interests and the goals of this period:

> *The streets of Buenos Aires*
> *are the entrails of my soul.*
> *Not the active streets*
> *disturbed by hustling and bustling people*
> *but the pleasant streets at the edge of town*
> *softened by trees and sunsets,*
> *and those other streets still farther out,*
> *barren of compassionate trees,*
> *where austere little shacks hardly dare*
> *to thrust themselves into the distant view*
> *of vast plain and vaster sky,*
> *so hostile are the immortal spaces.*
> *For one who covets souls*
> *all streets are a promise of adventure,*
> *because in their shelter so many lives join,*
> *belying the isolation of houses;*
> *and along them with a heroic will for self-deception*
> *walks our hope.*
> *Toward the four points of the compass*
> *the streets have spread out like banners.*
> *May those banners wave*
> *in my upright verses.* (*P,* 13-14)

True, we can single out certain foreign writers as important to Borges in these early years when he was writing the texts and defending the principles of Argentine Ultraism—and we would certainly want to name Whitman here, whose influence is apparent no less in the matter than in the method of "The Streets"—but there can be little doubt that this phase was his most Spanish, or more properly his most Argentine. Even the audience he chose for himself excluded the literary expatriates, those who had, presumably, been educated, as he had been, and whose intellectual and artistic nostalgia for Europe prevented their discovery of Argentina: "I want to speak to the natives: to the men who experience life and death in this land, not to those who believe that the sun and the moon are in Europe" (*TE*, 5). This opening sentence of *The Extent of My Hope*, so Whitmanesque in its sentiment and rhetoric, is further strengthened by "My argument today is the fatherland." (*TE*, 5). And the title of the collection of essays that followed *The Extent of My Hope* in 1928 indicates the continuing nationalistic focus of Borges' attention: *The Idiom of the Argentines*. Though in these books Borges did sometimes deal with foreign figures, his chief concern was Spanish literature and, more specifically, Argentine literature in its most recent manifestations.

This intense involvement with the literature of his own country was the last step in Borges' development before he entered upon the major phase of his career. The effects of this early period on his subsequent writing cannot be overestimated, for it was then that he began to create for himself the peculiar literary personality that would eventually incorporate the huge range of international literature that he had assimilated before becoming, in literature at least, a full-fledged Argentine. Now "Argentine" in no way implies a literary nationalist in the usual sense of that word, for we should keep in mind the peculiarly cosmopolitan character of much Argentine literature as described by Ana María Barrenechea:

*Of all South American countries, Argentina is the most open
to foreign influences; it is a country where one of the national
characteristics is the possibility of not withdrawing into the
merely native, but, instead, of being interested in the manifestations of other countries and then of elaborating them in
a personal way.*[2]

What we must understand, and what often has not been understood, is that Borges' Argentine phase was neither a stopping point nor an aberration nor a false start but, instead, the
culminating moment in the first phase of his career.
Borges'incarnation in a literary nationalism necessarily preceded his transfiguration in a universal mythology: Argentina, and all it represented in the way of language, literature,
culture, and personality, provided one inevitable step toward
the cosmic.

The Beginnings of Borges' Universalism
That it was, indeed, toward a literature of macrocosmic significance that Borges developed is evident even in his early
works that so persistently focus on the microcosm of Argentina. We can detect signs in his strongly nationalistic years—
principally the decade beginning with his return to Argentina in 1921—signs of his predisposition to universalize,
signs that point, first to the writing of *Universal History of
Infamy* in 1935 and ultimately to the stories of *Ficciones* and
El Aleph. Observing Borges' tendency to mythologize his
subjects and his continuing attention to English writers, we
can discover the steadily growing nucleus of Borges' later
work within the constricted periphery of his Argentine period.

MYTHOLOGIZING OF SUBJECT   By the tendency to
mythologize, I refer to the predilection in Borges' early poetry to view Buenos Aires under the aspect of depersonalized
eternity. Having already noted the strongly Whitmanesque
character of his verse, which is one kind of mythification,

we must also recognize basic similarities to the infinite elegiac afternoons of architectural perspective we find in the paintings of De Chirico:

> *At that hour of fine, sandy light*
> *my steps chanced upon an unknown street,*
> *opening into the noble breadth of a terrace,*
> *showing in the cornices and walls*
> *soft colors like the sky itself*
> *that stirred the background. . . .*
>
> *Perhaps that unique hour*
> *increased the prestige of the street,*
> *giving it privileges of tenderness,*
> *making it as real as legend or verse. (P, 17-18)*

In these poems, Borges searches out the fundamental, unchanging Buenos Aires, not trying to paint the picturesque but, instead, to find the moment that reveals the city in immortal light:

> *In search of the afternoon*
> *I combed the streets in vain. (P, 21)*

The city of these poems is one whose timelessness is manifested in site and object, a city for the most part devoid of individuals; and the scenes Borges presents are scenes, really, of time, not place; or, more accurately, of infinite duration revealed in an apotheosis of present place. Like Eduardo Mallea in *Historia de una pasión argentina* (Buenos Aires: 1940), Borges also focuses on "the movement of eternal things" as he parallels Mallea's distinction between "visible Argentina" and "the invisible country."[3]

Poems like *"Último resplandor," "Atardeceres,"* and *"Campos atardecidos"* all show Borges transcending the actual and focusing on eternity embodied in a point of space: each scene, each object is like a rock in the stream of time, interrupting the flow and causing a deep pool to well up there. Necessarily, such a vision avoids the human individual and the limitations of his chronological and spatial existence as in the significantly titled poem, "Empty Room":

> *The mahogany furniture perpetuates,*
> *amidst the indecision of brocade,*
> *its everlasting coterie. (P, 29)*

Similarly, in "The Card Game" and "The Guitar" we do not see the players clearly but concentrate, rather, on the game and the instrument respectively, on gestures and sounds that erase all identities and boundaries. Even when Borges does focus on people, they are usually the dead heroes and villains of Argentina's past. In this way Borges substitutes history for a kind of legendary or epic past and thus transcends the present moment at the same time that he preserves the uniquely Argentine flavor of his subject. Here, his procedure, perhaps by force of circumstance, somewhat resembles Hawthorne's retreat to the Puritan past in order to discover an essential, near-legendary American subject. Both writers are constrained by the comparative youth of their respective countries; both writers abjure the actual to achieve the permanent significance of *illo tempore*. In "Sepulchral Inscription," whose very title evokes most of Borges' earliest verse, he writes typically of his own great-grandfather, whom we see as a hero of epic proportions and mythological significance:

> *His valor spread over the Andes.*
> *He fought mountains and troops.*
> *Boldness was the habit of his sword.*
> *At Junín he put a successful end to the fight*
> *and to Peruvian lances gave Spanish blood.*
> *He wrote his list of deeds*
> *in prose as rigid as battle-crying trumpets.*
> *He died locked in implacable exile.*
> *Today oblivion is the threshold*
> *of so much glory. (P, 25)*

Following the words of his poem named for the famed cemetery in Buenos Aires, La Recoleta, we may say that people appear in these poems chiefly in the light of death and eternity:

> *The serenity of the tombs is lovely:*
> *the union of marble with flower,*
> *and the small squares with the coolness of patios,*
> *and the eternal isolation and eternal individuation;*
> *each one was a contemplator of his death,*
> *unique and personal like a memory.* (*P,* 15)

In sum, the first volume of Borges' poems is a monument to the past and the distant as alive in the present of Buenos Aires, so that taken together the poems comprise an epic of the city. It is this epic quality that Borges will exploit in his later career, but for the present we should be content to see how, paradoxically, the plunge into national, civic literature immersed Borges in vast seas of myth.

ATTENTION TO ENGLISH AUTHORS   In his writing about foreign authors, particularly English authors, we find the second indication that Borges was not completely cut off from wider possibilities during his nationalistic phase. His essays on Edward FitzGerald, Sir Thomas Browne, Oscar Wilde, and Milton, for example, found their way into the collections that appeared in 1925, 1926, and 1928, and provided an indicative counterpoint to the predominating essays on Argentine and Spanish subjects, a counterpoint, incidentally, that increases appreciably as the years go by and is never wholly absent from his writing. Perhaps even more symptomatic of how Borges was keeping up with the world of English literature is his early reading of Joyce's *Ulysses,* his translation of the novel's first page, and his writing of a short essay, "Joyce's *Ulysses,*" in which he was able to say: "I am the first Spanish adventurer to dock at Joyce's book" (*I,* 20).[4] In the same period, Borges was also ambitiously undertaking a translation of Whitman that was announced in a local journal:

NEW VERSION OF WALT WHITMAN—Jorge Luis Borges is currently occupied in completing a translation of Leaves of Grass. *To put Whitman's compact poetic work into our language is an important undertaking, and its particular interest consists in doing it in the form conceived by Borges: to bind himself as strictly as possible to the model and the original concept of the author in order to put the reader in contact with what is truly Whitman—with his familiar style, and even with his vocabulary drawn from the argot or low English of North America. Only one version of this work is known in Spanish, the one by A. Vasseur, which does not fulfill these conditions.*[5]

There can be little doubt, then, that even while his poetry gives little indication of it, Borges was continuing his relationship with English literature in important ways: storing his mind and imagination, refreshing his memory with those English books whose influence flowered in *Universal History of Infamy*, a work that emerged from both the mythologizing of the previous decade and Borges' reading.

The First Universal Book

Universal History of Infamy is a Janus-like book; its physiognomy, though unmistakably its own, primarily interests us for the opposing directions in which it looks. The book's mien is one of uncertainty, and Borges himself always asserted the tentative quality of his stories of infamy, calling them in the first prologue "exercises in narrative prose" (*HI*, 7) and explaining in the second prologue that they are the irresponsible game of a timid man who was not courageous enough to write stories and diverted himself by falsifying and distorting (sometimes without esthetic justification) stories by others. (*HI*, 10). At the same time, *Universal History* is the first of Borges' imaginative works to show him deliber-

ately looking beyond personal and parochial subjects arising from his relation to the city, his country, and their history: it looks forward to the Borges we know best. For one
thing, the book is almost entirely devoted to fiction. For
another, the first section, which gives the book its title, is
typical of the worldwide scope that Borges had previously
allowed himself only in his essays. Thus he gives prime importance to stories about international scoundrels ranging
from American gangsters to a female Chinese pirate. The
very title of the book, with its key word *universal*, indicates
Borges' widened perspective. Even though Borges himself
later referred to this title as "excessive" (*HI*, 9), and even
though the book's most perceptive reviewer, Amado Alonso,
was provoked by the title to apply the adjective *desaforado*
(outrageous, outsized), the title is wholly appropriate, emphasizing Borges' attempt to reveal a mythic pattern of
behavior and announcing, like the earlier "History of the An-
gels" and the subsequent *History of Eternity*, Borges' pen-
chant, strongly developed in later years, for treating subjects
as a series of rhyming incidents, characters, and thoughts
occurring at irregular intervals in expanses of time and space.

Most important for my purpose, however, is that
both the expanded perspective and the timid narrative experiment of *Universal History of Infamy* are closely associated
with English books and may in fact be seen as the immediate product of Borges' reading of certain English authors, so
that the fruition of Borges' reading and mythologizing are
found side by side, both being important qualities of this
volume. The tendency to myth-making is evidenced in "Man
from the Pink Corner," the only story concerned with specifically Argentine material, as well as a tale distinct from
the group of narrations about infamy, that, by itself, comprises one of the volume's three sections. About this story,
certainly the best of Borges' early fiction, Amado Alonso
wrote:

*There is nothing here that recalls stylistic procedures from
either the cultivated or popular epic; . . . And nevertheless,*

59

the epic tone is more powerful than ever, depending here neither on devices or mechanics but on the nature of the emotion and on the glowing halo of mythification that surrounds the characters and permeates the scene.[6]

On the other hand, the impress of English on *Universal History of Infamy* is evident on the very surface of the book from beginning to end. On the first page of the prologue to the first edition we find Borges explaining:

The exercises in narrative prose that comprise this book were executed between 1933 and 1934. They derive, I think, from my re-readings of Stevenson and of Chesterton and even from the first films of von Sternberg and perhaps from a certain biography of Evaristo Carriego. (HI, 7)

Next we encounter the book's dedication, which provides an example of Borges' own literary English:

I inscribe this book to S. D.: English, innumerable and an Angel. Also: I offer her that kernel of myself that I have saved, somehow—the central heart that deals not in words, traffics not with dreams, and is untouched by time, by joy, by adversities. (HI, 13)

In the seven stories of infamy we meet, among others, the American land pirate John A. Murrell, the New York gangster Monk Eastman, the English impostor Arthur Orton, the English pirates Mary Read and Anne Bonney. At the same time, we find a sprinkling of English words and phrases like "Run away to sea" (*HI*, 31) and "Go West!" (*HI*, 67). Finally in the index of sources, we discover that almost all of Borges' sources are English books or works translated into English, a fact Alonso had noted in his review.[7] Clearly, then, *Universal History of Infamy* not only marks a beginning of a new phase in Borges' career but also reaffirms his relationship with English literature.

Perhaps the most striking characteristic of Borges' newfound subject matter is its bookish quality, a characteristic that signals a reaction against the subjects of his Argentine period in favor of his earlier international interests. If Borges' view seems to have suddenly opened up, it is not to the external world around him nor even to his own subjective world. Instead, he seems purposely to have abjured both those realms and to have elected as his own special province the wide world encapsulated in a library, an institution that is itself an Aleph. That this election was a fully conscious one, at least in recollection, one gathers from Borges' prologue to his biography of Evaristo Carriego. I have already quoted the first sentence of this prologue in connection with his early career, but the subsequent sentences are pertinent to the development marked by *Universal History of Infamy*; in fact, the division of the two phases is indicated precisely by the hiatus between the first two sentences:

I believed for many years that I had been raised in a suburb of Buenos Aires, a suburb of adventurous streets and visible sunsets. What is certain is that I was raised in a garden, behind a wrought-iron gate, and in a library of unlimited English books. (EC, 9)

Looking rearward with Borges, we see that the shift from Buenos Aires and its streets to a garden and a library betokens the renunciation of the particular circumstances of environment in favor of the pandemic patterns of romance and fantasy, a shift emphasized by the following sentences:

Palermo with knives and guitars (they assure me) gathered at the corners, but those who populated my mornings and gave agreeable horror to my nights were the blind buccaneer of Stevenson, agonizing under the horses' hooves, and the traitor who abandoned his friend in the moon, and the time traveller who brought a withered flower from the future, and the genie imprisoned for centuries in a Solomonic jar

*and the veiled prophet of Jorasan, who hid his leprosy be-
hind stones and silk. (EC, 9)*

Borges creates his own biography here, choosing which
events and circumstances he will allow, in his writing, to be
responsible for his authorial personality, and, in doing so, he
rejects the seemingly real world of national or urban identity and elects the imaginary, the literary, the universal world
of romance. Borges may indeed be fictionalizing his life in
this account, but there can be no mistaking his intention: to
create for himself a universal character by confronting his
Argentine nationality and his international intellect, the one
reified in his native language and environment, the other
developed, in part, by his European education and most
strongly founded on his early reading.

    Universal History of Infamy is the first of Borges'
books laying claim to that territory of universal myth and
character that he was to mine with such success in later years,
and his preface to *Evaristo Carriego* serves to call our attention to that readjustment of goals and techniques that is embodied in the tales of infamy. What Yeats accomplished by
confronting his early romantic tendencies with antagonistic
esthetic and emotional demands, what Eliot and James
achieved, partly, by establishing themselves as American-
Englishmen, Borges, in his own way, effected by turning
from *calles* (streets), *ocasos* (sunsets), and *guitarras* (guitars)
to the universal themes and the fabulous adventures he had
first encountered in his childhood reading. The deliberate-
ness of Borges' choice should probably not be questioned:
his notes and references are there to instruct the reader; the
advantage of the choice cannot be doubted because it was,
in the deepest sense, a return to himself: the Eternal Return
is shown in small by the rebirth of the boy who read about
blackguards and treasures in the man who wrote about pirates and impostors.

The English Sources for Borges' Universalism

The world with which Borges chose to replace "Palermo with knives and guitars" is the world specifically named in the quotation from his prologue to *Evaristo Carriego*—the world of *Treasure Island, The First Men in the Moon,* and *The Arabian Nights*, and it was with memories of these books and their like that Borges turned to the writing of the *Universal History of Infamy.* In the preface to that book he cites his rereading of Stevenson and Chesterton as sources from which his book derives—surely the Stevenson of *Treasure Island* or *Kidnapped* and the Chesterton of the Father Brown stories, rather than either of these men in their roles as essayists or critics. However, in the index of sources he names books upon which his tales are factually based. Therefore, in recognizing the derived quality of Borges' stories, we must distinguish between the quality and nature of the sources cited in prologue and index—between the primary or influential and the secondary or factual, the first providing the informing spirit and the second the data. The secondary sources are principally drawn from the world of fact or pseudofact, that is, from history, chronicle, and legend, while the primary influences come from the realm of art, from story, novel, and film. Both, however, correspond closely to Borges' childhood absorption in adventures of fascinating scoundrels. Borges' stories in *Universal History of Infamy* not only synthesize a thematic pattern in human behavior but also indicate an underlying interest in his own reading and writing.

PRIMARY SOURCES   While Borges' references to Stevenson, Chesterton, and von Sternberg in the preface to the *Universal History* at first seem merely a courteous acknowledgment of a literary debt, their mannered scrupulosity indicates a subtle intention. Borges is not simply naming his sources of inspiration so as to facilitate the work of future scholars, nor is he only deprecating his creative powers according to the conventions of authorial humility, although neither of these motives would be uncharacteristic of the personality he consciously assumes in writing; rather, and more importantly, Borges is showing in his preface, as much as in his stories, that his writing develops out of an established tradition and is, in fact, the epitome of both a basic human pattern of behavior and a narrative mode—more the latter than the former. From the very start, then, his fiction establishes itself, legitimizes itself as it were, in reference to other books, realizing itself in the extent to which it embodies and reflects basic motifs of life and literature.

Describing the source of Borges' stories in this way, I do not at all deny the personal significance of these references. The pleasure Borges discovered as a child in reading Stevenson and Wells is one he pursued throughout his career, both as reader and storyteller: namely, the oxymoronic sensation of "agreeable horror." As a reader he first experienced it in *Treasure Island,* when Blind Pew is trampled to death by his comrades and, in *The First Men in the Moon* when Bedford abandons Cavor to the Moonmen. Apparently he experienced it again in the early films of von Sternberg that deal with the same kind of exciting and infamous behavior in the world of the American gangster. And Chesterton, too, aroused this reaction with stories of crime and murder that are mysteriously religious in intention. Turning from his reading (and moviegoing) to his writing, we find Borges dealing with characters and situations yielding this "agreeable horror," not only in *Universal History* but also in his mature fiction, where he describes a shy, nondescript girl who commits a brilliantly contrived murder in "Emma Zunz"; an impostor who crushes his sleeping victim's head under a stone in "Abenjacán el Bojarí, Dead in his Labyrinth"; a spy who shoots an innocent scholar in order to communicate a traitorous message in "The Garden of the Forking Paths." Borges treats each of these deeds metaphysically, true, but it is no less true that the metaphysical presentation proceeds directly from the infamous act. We must never forget that this writer who did so much to inform fiction with philosophic and scientific conjecture also wrote, along with Adolfo Bioy Casares, books like *Six Problems for Don Isidro Parodi* and served as the co-editor (as well as a translator into Spanish) for two series of *Best Detective Stories* published in Buenos Aires (1943, 1951). The pirates of his youth may have become the criminals of his maturity, but the esthetic satisfaction he derives from stories of infamy is undiminished.

Borges' continuing interest in stories about criminal or infamous behavior always had the same focus: the atrocious deed, not the mind of the agent. In the first prologue to *Universal History* he said, most emphatically, that his stories "are not, do not try to be, psychological" (*HI*, 7). Hence, his preference for adventurous tales that stress action over individual psychology—for Stevenson, who emphasizes plot over character analysis. In aligning his stories at the very beginning of his fiction-writing career with those of Stevenson, Borges elected the adventure story as his special province and explicitly rejected the psychological bias of much nineteenth- and twentieth-century fiction; nor was this election unprecedented—even in 1935—resulting, as it did, from a critical reaction he had expressed a full ten years earlier:

In its esthetic productions, the past century was radically subjective. Its authors were inclined to demonstrate their personality rather than to create a work: a judgment that also applies today to those who, comprising a huge and much praised crowd, take advantage of the comfortable embers of their predecessors' fires. (*I*, 90-91)

From this statement we can see more clearly why Borges might choose to associate his writings with English authors less representative of what was accomplished in the nineteenth century; his preference for minor figures may have led him to a minor tradition in our literature, but in his eyes it permitted him an escape from the besetting illusion of individual personality.

Borges'escape from individuality was also an escape to metaphysics, for if he fled by means of the adventure story, perhaps an exaggerated refinement of Stevenson's elegantly economical narratives, he fled to the kind of narrow adventure story that is ventilated by piercing drafts of the fantastic and supernatural, rather in the manner of Chesterton's stories, which hybridize "the detective story mechanism" and a "mystical undercurrent" (*F*, 35). If this "undercurrent" in Borges' fiction is only that, an undercurrent, it is surely there both in Borges' narrative invention and in his rhetoric.

When Hugh Kenner said of Chesterton that "his especial gift was his metaphysical intuition of being; his especial triumph was his exploitation of paradox to embody that intuition,"[8] he could as well have been talking about Borges, whose first stories, eclipsing the individual, give swift hints of a nightmarish reality that underlies all earthly appearances. By its title alone, *Universal History of Infamy* indicates its search for a pattern of behavior larger than the individual, and, in scenes like the one where the samurai attack their enemy's fortress, such phrases as "that very lucid nightmare" suddenly redefine the ultimate significance of the particular narrative:

History knows the diverse moments of that very lucid nightmare: the risky, pendulous descent down rope ladders, the drum sounding the attack, the haste of the defenders, the archers posted on the roof, the direct destiny of the arrows toward man's vital organs, porcelain defamed by blood, the burning death that then turns icy, the shames and disorders of death. (*HI*, 78)

A few lines later, when the villain escapes through "a narrow window disguised as a bronze mirror" (*HI*, 79), we are on the threshold of Borges' own metaphysical world: a mirror-window serving as a door invites us to the wonderland of Borges' best stories. Similarly, Chesterton's paradoxes find their counterpart in Borges' tales. *Paradox* is one of

Borges' favorite words, and he relies heavily upon the word and the figure it labels as early as *Evaristo Carriego*; but in *Universal History* paradox becomes the dominant perceptual mode, epitomizing Borges' stylistic emphasis, which Amado Alonso correctly described:

Without denying its close relationship to the previous ones, this book by Borges presents a very special stylistic appearance. From the title of the first story, the new style is fully embodied. It consists of a bifocal vision of things, of a double emotional reaction on different planes, which the grammatical course of the sentence wittily presents as a single plane.[9]

Obviously the equivalent of Chestertonian paradox, this bifocal vision is no less the stylistic embodiment of Borges' reaction of "agreeable horror," so it is not surprising to find that *Universal History* abounds in oxymora of the simple verbal kind like "the terrifying benefactors" (*HI*, 24), as well as in such larger oxymoronic descriptions as that of the "porcelain defamed by blood, the burning death that then turns icy" (*HI*, 78). Seeing these oxymora and paradoxes as an indication that Borges takes "his subjects as mere themes,"[10] Alonso is surely close to the truth; but, when we look back at these tales from the vantage point of Borges' later fiction, we are compelled to view this rhetorical play as the perfect reflection of Borges' childhood reaction to literature, as the fruits of a personally satisfactory rhetoric, as well as the initial opening up of Borges' prose to the metaphysical possibilities inherent in his subjects. Hence, in naming both Stevenson and Chesterton at the start of his book, Borges has led us directly to the twofold source of his fiction: the narrative of action and a mystic or metaphysical perception of reality.

The equivalent weight Borges puts on Chesterton and Stevenson is evident in the syntax of his preface, as is the subsidiary emphasis he places on von Sternberg and the biography of Evaristo Carriego. To make my point clear, I emphasize the significant words:

*The exercises in narrative prose that comprise this book were
executed between 1933 and 1934. They derive, I think, from
my re-readings of Stevenson and of Chesterton and even
from the first films of von Sternberg and perhaps from a
certain biography of Evaristo Carriego. (HI, 7)*

Why Borges underplays von Sternberg here, lightly questioning the director's importance, perhaps downgrading movies
themselves, is not altogether clear, unless that importance is
overshadowed by the long-standing significance of a writer
like Stevenson. In both substance and technique Borges' stories owe much to von Sternberg's films, which present the
adventures of infamous characters—the accent is once again
on the event, not the psychology—at the same time that they
display the paradoxical glamor and excitement of the bad:
if Jim Hawkins lives most intensely when he is with Long
John Silver, if Father Brown is interesting chiefly because
he thinks like a crook, von Sternberg's heroes demonstrate
that power, if it is not separated from passion, corrupts mag-
nificently. Since von Sternberg views his material from the
point of view of the infamous, the same procedure Borges
follows, and since in his early films—*Underworld* (1927),
The Drag Net (1928), *The Docks of New York* (1928), and
Thunderbolt (1929)—he dealt in scenes of "agreeable horror" taken from the world of the American gangster, we can
justifiably posit von Sternberg as an influence at least on
"The Purveyor of Iniquities Monk Eastman."
　　But von Sternberg, and Chesterton too, influenced
these stories in still another way: that is, with respect to particular literary techniques. This influence is made clear in the
second half of the passage I quoted from the preface to *Universal History:*

*[The exercises in narrative prose] abuse certain procedures:
random enumeration, abrupt shifts in continuity, the reduction of a man's whole life to two or three scenes. (HI, 7)*

Admittedly, the last of these procedures—a "visual scheme" Borges calls it in the next sentence, differentiating it from a rhetorical one—depends less on outside sources than on Borges' own metaphysic; the "certain biography" from which it derives is doubtless Borges' own biography of Carriego, published in 1930, the salient narrative method of which has been described by Tamayo and Ruiz-Díaz in such a way as to suggest its development out of Borges' metaphysical system:

Borges distinguishes, then, an unattainable and leisurely sense of actions which would correspond to the successive profusion of existence, from an atemporal narration—true knowledge—in which the divergent historical manifestation becomes intelligible.[11]

The other two narrative procedures Borges mentions, however, can be traced to outside influences and more particularly to von Sternberg and Chesterton.

The "abrupt shifts in continuity" are, in fact, simply the literary equivalent of a technique in movie montage, and Borges may have borrowed the device (as perhaps Eliot did too) directly from movies. While the suppression of "intervening sentences" and "transitions" characterizes Ultraism, *Universal History* offers *narrative*, not lyric; if the sources of Borges' brusk cutting are not exclusively in von Sternberg, the filmmaker's methods of editing demonstrated the narrative applicability of an esthetic principle Borges had reached in another way. Besides, the connection between von Sternberg's editing techniques and Borges' "history" of infamy is almost explicitly established by Borges himself in "The Disinterested Murderer Bill Harrigan": "History (which, like a certain director of movies, proceeds by discontinuous images) . . ." (*HI*, 68).[12] In this respect, von Sternberg's effect on Borges may be termed profound and lasting: the rapid cutting from scene to scene, and even from sentence to sentence, remains a constant feature of Borges' prose fiction.

Similarly, for "random enumeration" Borges found significant precedents in Chesterton—though the influence of Chesterton here cannot be discerned without reference to that of Whitman, despite the fact that the American poet is not named in the preface to the *Universal History*. Whitman's catalogues are notorious, and Ana María Barrenechea has noted their importance for Borges whenever he, like Whitman, wants to express "the planet's vastness." The model for this procedure can be found in St. John's visions in the *Apocalypse*, which has had many imitators, among them Whitman, whom Borges admired and followed since his earliest poems."[13] But as Borges noted, Chesterton was comparably impressed by the richness of life: "Like Whitman, Chesterton thought that the mere fact of being is so great that no misfortune should exempt us from a kind of cosmic gratitude" (*OI*, 120); in Chesterton, too, we find lengthy catalogues imitating the abundance of the earth. Hugh Kenner calls our attention to this little–noted trait of Chesterton's style, at the same time noting its appearance in other authors:

It is the same instinct for being, less rationalized and more akin to simple wonder, that led the Elizabethan poets into catalogues, inviting their reader to share the simple pleasure of naming over created things. . . . It was the instinct for being, manifesting itself in a similar pattern, that led James Joyce, reviving in our own day the patristic tradition, to pack into the vast celebration of the One a multitude of names of particulars; that led him to weave into the river chapter of Finnegans Wake *the names of five hundred rivers.*[14]

The Chestertonian device of the catalogue along with the appropriate "astonishment" (*asombro*), appears frequently in Borges' early stories, and we have only to look at the disparate catalogue in "El Aleph" to assess the centrality of the technique to Borges' meaning. Thus, at an early age he was able to say: "I am a man astonished by the world's abundance; I testify to the unity of all things" (*I*, 97).

In a word, the effect of English authors is manifest not only in the general universalizing impulse of Borges' work but in several recurrent and definitive rhetorical gestures.

SECONDARY SOURCES The matter of Borges' earliest fiction is, like its narrative modes, the product of his childhood reading, but that matter reflects Borges' systematic pursuit of a topic at least as much as it mirrors his personal response to a narrative subject, for Borges brings to bear on his theme the weight of an eccentric erudition. We may be reading tales of adventure in Borges' *Universal History*, but we are always aware of their bookishness, of the fact that we are dealing with written chronicles, neither sailing with Jim Hawkins on deep waters nor ascending with Cavor and Bedford in thin air but, instead, following Borges through many volumes. Mediating between the child's reaction to the literature of adventure and the young man's creation of a history of infamy, we find not only the cleverness of a controlled, ironic style and the shaping force of a metaphysical system but also all the gleanings of a theme deciphered from the Sybil's leaves of a card catalogue.

Nowhere is the lineage of books connecting Borges' boyhood reading to his early fiction more simply evident than in the first story of *Universal History*, "The Terrible Redeemer Lazarus Morell," which derives from works by one of Borges' favorite childhood authors and from a book about that author. The "terrifying redeemer" is the famous American land pirate John A. Murrell, whom Borges apparently first encountered in Mark Twain's writing. Although the index of sources lists only Twain's *Life on the Mississippi* and Bernard De Voto's *Mark Twain's America*, we know from Victoria Ocampo that as a boy Borges read and reread *Huckleberry Finn*, so it is not too much to suppose that he may also have read *Tom Sawyer*, in which, as De Voto points out, "an old saying was recalled that Murrell's gang used to be around here one summer.'"[15] Moreover, while we do not know when Borges first read *Life on the Mississippi*, De Voto emphasizes the connection between that book and *Huckleberry Finn*, a connection that Borges, the devotee of *Huckleberry Finn*, can hardly have ignored:

Life on the Mississippi, *written over the period when Huck was gestated, has many incidents on their way to fruition. The Darnell-Watson feud is the Grangerford-Shepherdson trouble in chrysalis, a desultory tale told by a passenger as the* Gold Dust *passes through the chute of Island Number 8. On the upstream voyage as yet anonymous strollers forecast David Garrick the younger and Edmund Keen the elder. John A. Murrell's inheritors hint at revenge in the staterooms of a wrecked steamboat and other creatures of the midnight presage the turmoil of search and escape through underbrush.*[16]

Here, then, is an unbroken chain of books, a chain that links Borges' first reading of Twain in the early 1900s to his reading of De Voto's book and the writing of the *Universal History* in the early 1930s, a chain that isolates in both of Borges' avowed sources a minor incident or interpolation appealing to and extending his childhood love of pirate stories, and that demonstrates once again that what fascinates Borges takes precedence over what is outstanding in his reading. To see the chain in this way is to understand at once how in his reading of a factual or nonfictional book like *Mark Twain's America*, Borges remained faithful to his earliest responses to literature, at the same time exploring and enriching these responses rather than allowing them to stagnate in nostalgia; to understand this is to understand the allusive method of *Universal History of Infamy*.

Most of the matter in Borges' seven stories comes from contemporary sources, that is, from early twentieth-century anthologies, biographies, and histories, each of which is somehow connected with the theme of adventure, often explicitly with piracy. In this latter sense the books are out of the way and reflect Borges' personal reading tastes, but in another sense they announce a lifelong preoccupation in his writing: the discovery of the esthetic in historical, philosophical, scientific writing. That Borges himself, as always, is aware of this tendency is made clear in his epilogue to *Other Inquisitions,* where he remarks that in correcting the book's proofs he noticed his own inclination "to appraise religious or philosophical ideas for their esthetic value and even for what they contain of the unique and marvelous" (*OI*, 259). From the start, then, we must be prepared to find Borges' secondary sources treated minutely rather than extensively; bent to his esthetic principles rather than explored; playfully modified in self-conscious justification and explanation of his themes and procedures as well as in a strained attempt at humor. Perhaps Borges' own words, even though they are rather harsh, best describe his method: "falsify and distort" (*HI*, 10).

Inspired by the precedent of Stevenson and Chesterton, governed by his own metaphysical-esthetic formula, Borges rejects all that is overtly psychological in his sources and stresses or injects much that is fantastic. His characters are nonintrospective agents, presented without analysis of motive; their world is intermittently unsubstantial, undermined by flashes of fantasy; their gestures are uncomprehended symbols, exhibited without comment by Borges. Looking first at the plot of one of Borges' sources, for example, and then at his version, we can isolate the specific devices he uses to achieve these ends.

A. B. Mitford's "The Forty-seven Ronins"[17] tells of two noblemen who were obliged to study court etiquette with a certain Kira Kotsuké no Suké in preparation for the visit of a royal envoy. Kotsuké, an avaricious man, mistreated the two noble pupils because their gifts to him were not valuable enough; one of these pupils, outraged to the point of contemplating Kotsuké's murder, was saved from this rash act by his counselor, who procured better treatment from Kotsuké by means of a bribe. The other noble, Takumi no Kami, had no such wise counselor at hand and Kotsuké continued to treat him disrespectfully, finally driving the Lord of Takami to lunge at him with a dagger. Although Kotsuké was only scratched on the forehead, the attack had taken place in the palace, so Takumi no Kami was condemned to death by hara-kiri, his property confiscated, and his retainers disbanded. Among these retainers, now Ronins or knights errant, was Takumi no Kami's counselor, Kuranosuké, who had been absent during his master's fatal conflict but who planned with forty-six other Ronins to avenge his lord's death. While most of the Ronins disguised themselves as craftsmen and sought employment near Kotsuké, Kuranosuké entered upon a life of debauchery in order to throw Kotsuké off his guard, and eventually he succeeded in doing so. Breaking into the palace one night, the Ronins searched for Kotsuké, who fled through a secret door but was at last caught in a little outbuilding. Granting him the privilege of ritual suicide at first, they were finally forced to cut off the coward's head; and having achieved their purpose, they traveled back to the tomb of Takumi no Kami where they offered up the head on their master's grave. It only remained for them to be judged by the Supreme Court and condemned to hara-kiri. After their burial, people flocked to their grave, and among the worshipful mourners was a man from Satsuma who had spat upon Kuranosuké when the faithful avenger was feigning cowardly debauchery. In retribution the Satsuma man committed suicide and was buried alongside the Ronins.

Such is the barest outline of Mitford's narrative. In Borges' rendering, no mention is made of Kotsuké's governing avarice, and Takumi no Kami's fellow pupil is omitted entirely: Borges begins directly with Kotsuké's insulting behavior. The effect of these omissions—they serve to make Kotsuké's demeanor starkly heinous, archetypically infamous—betokens the larger effect Borges seeks in inverting the traditional import of the story. Borges is of course fully aware of the tradition he subverts: he refers to the customary versions in his opening paragraphs, where he mentions that "about a hundred novels, monographs, doctoral dissertations and operas commemorate the deed" (*HI*, 73). He might have added that this story has remained alive to this day in the Bunraku puppet and derivative Kabuki interpretations. But whereas these other accounts, possibly even those dubious "doctoral dissertations," emphasize the nobility of the heroes, Borges abbreviates the narration to focus more powerfully on the villain Kotsuké. The shift in titles reveals all: in Mitford we find "The Forty-seven Ronins"; in Borges, "The Uncivil Master of Etiquette Kotsuké no Suké."

Borges weights the scales in favor of infamy because that is his theme but also because it permits a paradoxical display of transpersonal symmetry. Kotsuké, Borges writes, "is a man who deserves the gratitude of all men, because he awakened precious loyalties and was the black and necessary occasion for an immortal undertaking" (*HI*, 73). The reverse of this paradox is found in the ironic behavior of Kuranosuké, who, to establish his dissolution, "sent his wife and the youngest of his children away, and purchased a mistress in a brothel—a famous infamy that rejoiced the heart and relaxed the fearful prudence of his enemy" (*HI*, 77). The villain as agent of good, the hero as base coward—images dear to Borges, who constantly shows any man as all men and, consequently, heroes and villains as identical. The actions of both Kotsuké and Kuranosuké are symmetrical: both behave villainously, collaborating (or so it would seem, if, like Borges, we set aside personal motive) to bring honor out of infamy. Kotsuké and Kuranosuké are thus prototypes of Borges' many "double" characters, like the identical narrator and Vincent Moon of "The Shape of the Sword," like the executed traitor who is the assassinated martyr in "Theme of the Traitor and Hero." These two stories, a back-to-back diptych in *Ficciones*, demonstrate that acts of bravery and cowardice are necessary adjuncts of each other and that all traitors and heroes are manifestations of the same human mind: once more we see the direction in Borges' stories away from an individual psychology and toward a universal mythology. So, while there is no novelty in speculating that the destiny of Jesus required Judas, Borges implicitly postulates that Jesus and Judas are one. (Later, one of Borges' characters will explicitly argue this point [*F*, 173-75].) We may recall in fact that it is Moon who says, "If one man does something, it is as if all men have done it" (*F*, 133)—the same Vincent Moon who has played the parts of both timorous traitor and strong-willed master, a man who bears, like Kotsuké, the mark of his shameful sins: a sword scar on his face.

Tales of adventure, then, become for Borges the medium of metaphysical speculation. Not yet ready, he says, to create for himself a fictional world that can exist freely in its own terms and as the vehicle of philosophical demonstrations, not yet able, he pretends or believes, to transform completely the world he has borrowed, Borges contents himself with terse intimations of a higher reality. We have previously noted the apparitional world briefly disclosed in "The Uncivil Master of Etiquette"; but, if we look at the model for that passage, we find that Borges himself has interjected that world, without explanation or consequence, by altering the original. In Mitford we read:

Now in the raised part of the room, near the place of honour, there was a picture hanging; taking down this picture, they saw that there was a large hole in the plastered wall, and on thrusting a spear in they could feel nothing behind it. So one of the Ronins, called Yazama Jiutaro, got into the hole, and found that on the other side there was a little courtyard, in which there stood an outhouse for holding charcoal and firewood. Looking into the outhouse, he spied something white at the further end.[18]

In Borges' characteristically condensed version we read:

They searched again and discovered a narrow window disguised as a bronze mirror. Below, from a shadowy little courtyard, a man all in white looked at them. (HI, 79)

We notice the potentially expressive force of "disguised" (*disimulada*) as well as the supplanting of "picture" by "mirror," the latter one of Borges' favorite symbols for a phantasmal reality, but we notice these modifications because they are modifications, not because—as would be the case in Borges' later fiction—they are especially significant. Similarly, in other passages that have no precedent whatsoever in Mitford, we find Borges introducing a mirror—this time a more obvious symbol of the unearthly—and playing cards, a sign and enactment of cyclical repetition in life. For example:

What is certain is that they had to proceed between justified delays and that some of their councils took place not on the difficult peak of a mountain but in a chapel in the woods, a modest pavilion of wood, with no other decorations than a rectangular box that contained a mirror. (HI, 76)

The enshrined mirror is mysteriously evocative, hinting at a supernatural quality, but it is a hint only vaguely fulfilled in Kotsuké's tricky escape. The description of the forest chapel, the kind of scene we are familiar with in medieval romances is at once as simple, as symbolic, and as unexplained as the picture on a Tarot card—but in the context of the story, where it finally matters, what are we to make of it? Or, for that matter, of the scene involving the secret door,[19] or of the description of the Ronins meeting "in a run-down garden in the vicinity of Yedo, near a bridge and a playing-card factory" (HI, 77)? If we accept that Borges' alteration of his sources is not capricious, the only solution is that he is interposing what are at this point in his career almost private symbols in a traditional narrative, with the result that neither narrative nor symbol achieves complete expression, the one falsified by the other. Borges fractures the smoothly glazed surface of his classic Japanese tale and fleetingly reveals other, darker surfaces to our gaze; but he neither creates a new form nor completely destroys the old—the original effect is vitiated and no recognizable new effect is achieved. In a very real way, although in an altogether different tone and mode, Borges' interpolations and modifications affect his originals just as advertising captions placed under well-known paintings corrupt the obvious intention of well-known paintings ("Hasn't scratched yet," for example, under Giorgione's reclining Venus) corrupt the obvious intention of the painting. The principal difference lies in the fact that while on the one hand we know both painting and slogan (or at least have both in front of us) and therefore can appreciate the humorous tension between the two, we cannot fully respond to the new dimension Borges adds because we frequently cannot identify his interpolated symbols with surety, certainly not without benefit of Borges' later works or an intuitive reading of the poems and a close reading of the essays up to the publication of *Universal History*. To our hindsight, at least, the intention of these symbolic intercalations is evident; yet if we want to evaluate their immediate and proper effectiveness, we will not go far wrong in borrowing Borges' own hindsight judgment of these stories: "They are the irresponsible game of a timid man" (*HI*, 10). "Timid" and "irresponsible" assuredly describe the devices he employs in "The Uncivil Master of Etiquette." Fortunately, however, not all Borges' procedures in *Universal History* should be so harshly dismissed, and since some of them are incorporated into his later fiction, they deserve our attention.

On the one hand, Borges taints the reality that his sources describe; on the other, he corrupts the authenticity of those sources themselves. In both cases the motive is to penetrate to the metaphysical world that lies beyond fact and substance, to pass through the covers of nonexistent books into literary landscapes that are equally phantasmal. Therefore Borges deliberately gives the wrong references for some of his sources, cites nonexistent editions for others, and misrepresents the sources for still others. In *Universal History* this kind of falsification mostly trifles humorously and expresses minimally, but the device is there, and it is one Borges made impressive use of in the years to come.

"The Unlikely Imposter Tom Castro" purportedly comes from Philip Gosse's *History of Piracy*, which Borges says was published in London in 1911. Now, Gosse's book was originally issued in 1932 and the verso of the title page is clearly marked "First Edition"; moreover, since it is what it pretends to be, a history of pirates, Gosse's work never mentions Arthur Orton, alias Tom Castro, who was not a pirate. Even Borges does not make Orton out to be a pirate, and one can only guess that he conceived of his reference to Gosse as yet one more "impostor *inverosímil*." Most likely the real source for the story was one of three books: Bram Stoker's *Famous Impostors* (New York: 1910); Joseph Lewis French's *The Book of the Rogue: Studies of Famous Scoundrels* (New York: 1926), which reprints Stoker's thirteenth chapter on Orton; or Edward Abbott Parry's *Vagabonds All* (New York: 1926). Each of these works, ostensibly like *Universal History*, is an anthology of the lives of notorious villains. Any one or combination of them may have inspired Borges to anthologize in *Universal History* stories he had already written for the Saturday supplement of *Crítica* in 1933 and 1934, as he alerts us in the Tom Castro story. Borges might have found one or all three of these books in his search for works about pirates and gangsters; on the other hand, it is entirely possible that none of them is the actual source for Borges' story because the Orton case agitated many controversies and turned many printing presses. However, I am inclined to believe that Parry's volume is the likeliest choice since its manner of presentation is closest to Borges' own.

Borges sees each of the characters in his gallery as an epitome of a particular kind of infamy, and Parry has this to say of Orton:

In the annals of crime, Arthur Orton, the notorious claimant to the rich estates and titles of Tichborne, takes a foremost place; not only as the originator of one of the most colossal attempts at fraud on record, but also from his remarkable success in duping the public.[20]

Furthermore, Parry stresses the mythic quality of Orton's deception, a stress that would have caught Borges' attention:

Arthur Orton, horse-slaughterer, was a myth and a cult, with high priests running the show and acolytes and disciples ready to lay down their fortunes at his feet. . . . The time and cost of destroying the myth were enormous.[21]

In any event, with or without the support of Parry's account, Borges elaborated the myth and introduced his own metaphysical fillip. Parry makes it clear, as do most of the historical and biographical accounts, that Orton hit upon his infamous plan for himself and by accident:

His first introduction to the Tichborne affair was when his friend Dick Slade, or Slate, handed him a copy of the Australian Times *and called his attention to a "funny advertisement." It was one of Lady Tichborne's appeals for her son to return. By way of a joke Tom Castro pretended to be very affected when he read it and Dick Slade, after the manner of his kind, was deeply impressed and asked Tom what he knew about it. Tom Castro only shook his head mysteriously and said nothing. This, of course, deepened the impression already formed in Dick's fertile imagination.*[22]

But Borges' own fertile imagination saw in the situation an opportunity to develop one of his favorite theses: the insignificance of personality, as exemplified in the story of a man who is conceived or dreamed by another mind. Borges takes one of the victims of Orton's real-life duplicity, a Negro servant with the improbable but actual name of Bogle, and transforms him into the originator of the plot, the creator of Orton's Tichborne; thus Orton himself becomes the shadowy creation of Bogle's wit and at the same time a stupid reincarnation of the returning prodigal son, a living myth. By means of this stratagem, Borges illustrates the ephemeral quality of the individual, not only in the negative sense of Lady Tichborne's delusion but also in the positive sense of Bogle's ability to create a character. Here, in contrast to "The Uncivil Master of Etiquette Kotsuké no Suké," Borges does not merely toy with the details of the story but meaningfully and consistently rearranges facts and adjusts characters for the expression of his theme. We may guess that Borges' dissimulation of sources is, in this case, both a provision for maximum freedom and a gauge of the degree to which he has written his own story, not merely dissembled someone else's. Hence, we can say that here Borges has been neither timid nor irresponsible: even the minor changes in the story, like the substitution of *Mermaid* for *Bella* as the name of the ship on which Tichborne went down, serve to reinforce Borges' mythic vision of the characters and their actions.

The extension of sources, not of course in length but in what they suggest about reality—that is the most important aspect of Borges' experiments in *Universal History*. In his later works Borges often accomplishes that extension by the method of packing books within books, stories within stories, a procedure that Ana María Barrenechea has commented on:

Borges has spoken of the surprising effect produced by the map-within-a-map in Josiah Royce's The World and the Individual, *by the play-within-a-play in* Hamlet, *by the novel-within-a-novel in* Don Quixote, *and by the twin inclusions in* The Arabian Nights *and* The Ramayana. *To readers and*

*spectators who consider themselves real beings, these works
suggest their possible existence as imaginary entities. In that
context lies the key to Borges' work. Relentlessly pursued by
a world that is too real and at the same time lacking meaning, he tries to free himself from its obsession by creating a
world of such coherent phantasmagorias that the reader
doubts the very reality on which he leans.*[23]

In his early work Borges had not yet developed this technique, but we see evidence that it had already captured his
attention in the fact that most of his sources actually come
from books within books. A good case in point is the Murrell
story in *Life on the Mississippi*, which Twain introduces by
saying: "Here is a paragraph or two concerning this big op-
erator, from a now–forgotten book which was published half
a century ago";[24] and another is "The Widow Ching, Pirate,"
where Borges gets most of his information from Gosse's
History of Piracy, which in turn depends from Yung Lun
Yüen's *History of the Pirates Who Infested the China Seas*
and Richard Glasspoole's *Narrative of the Capture and
Treatment amongst the Ladrones*, both of which were translated by Karl F. Neumann and appeared in the Oriental
Translation Fund Publications in 1831. Borges' story about
Mrs. Ching, in fact, concludes with a quotation from
Neumann. What is interesting to see, however, is that this
quotation, as it appears in Gosse, is itself a falsification of
the original. If Borges looked at Neumann's translation, the
source of his source, he discovered that Gosse, with no apparent aspiration to fiction, jammed together two passages
that in Neumann occur some twenty pages apart and refer to
events that happened in different years! In Gosse's history
or one like it, Borges may indeed have discovered a precedent for his method of compounding fact and fantasy. When
I asked him in April 1968 if he had been aware of Gosse's
falsification, he replied, smiling: "Yes, of course. What is the
point of rewriting an author if you don't do it differently."
Aware or not, if his method did not come straight from

Gosse, Borges at least responded to the potentially infinite recession of books within books that we so often find in historical or scholarly writing—to the extent of assimilating it into his own esthetic.

Conclusion

To the readers of *Universal History*, as well as to its author, Borges' first collection of stories must have seemed little more than an ephemeral game played with analecta; to us, who have the benefit of a retrospective vision, it must appear the prophecy of a significant new dweller in the house of fiction. There can be no doubt, however, that the book's importance to the critic or student of Borges is vastly disproportionate to its literary merit, and having understood the author's intention and method, we must not neglect to judge its achievement.

Confining our attention to what use Borges makes of his sources, to the nature of allusion in this book, we must say that *Universal History* exists on the lowest or referential level of allusion; that, in modeling his stories on other books and in referring to other authors within the tales, Borges proclaims the referential constitution of his art in this book, but in merely sporting with the conventions of such reference he fails to extract much expressive value from his citations except for an anemic humor. In contrast to his later practice, which exploits the referral as well as the matter referred to, Borges' citations in *Universal History* are virtually meaningless, except to the extent that they document, falsely and therefore facetiously, the themes of Borges' variations, variations scarcely more estimable than their inconsiderable inspirations. Since the reader should not be expected to check out the references—the task is first tedious and ultimately unrewarding—the book exists largely as a joking game between the author and himself. Even supposing that a snooping reader does unmask Borges' deception, he learns something of the work's origin, perhaps something of its procedures, but scarcely anything of the writer's meaning, excluding what can be inferred from Borges' other, elaborated works. Furthermore, such a frustrating investigation points up an inherent danger in Borges' intensive bookishness: the temptation to forge a fantasy world by embroidering textual irregularities leads to a hollow shell of narrative that dryly collapses under the critic's scrutiny or the reader's demand for the pleasure of fiction. The game Borges plays, like the utterance of a trivial pun, may express the author's pixyish humor, but it arouses, at best, the reader's indulgent annoyance. In fact, much of the playfulness of *Universal History* is on a dead level with the kind of invention Addison appropriately labeled "false wit": the changing of Murrell's first name from John to Lazarus, presumably because Murrell planned a demonic uprising, is petty waggery, and the misrepresentation of bibliographical facts, possibly to amuse one or two knowing friends while fooling unknowing readers, is sophomoric frippery. In the context of these slight stories the problem is not overly important; Borges is merely stringing a few carefully cultured pearls along with the certified genuine. Nevertheless, what we see in miniature here becomes a decisive problem in the later works, leading to questions like the one posed by Robert Martin Adams:

There is an interest in the virtuosity displayed, an interest too in running down the books uncovered and tracing out the often subtle blending of Borges' intent with that of the authors. But in fictional terms, does this amount to enough of an interest, or the right kind of interest?[25]

Still, if the pitfalls of Borges' method are evident in his first collection of stories, so are the latent possibilities. The eventual product of Borges' "exercises" in *Universal History* was a potentially viable form in which he could generate his universal metaphysic from a characteristically bookish matrix. He discovered a method for telling a story that in its form as well as in its content expressed the apparitional façade of reality. In the play between the recognizably "fictional" in a book—that is, the characterization, the plot—and the conventionally "real"—that is, the footnotes, commentaries, and bibliography—Borges perceived a metaphysical possibility, a possibility he realized in the first truly important story of his career, "Pierre Menard, Author of *Don Quixote*," which is predictably about a writer and is told by means of a critical bibliography, footnotes, and biographical comments. That Borges first made this discovery in alloying the adventures of his childhood reading with the matter of his adult learning, that both these adventures and these facts came to him, for the most part, in English books, is no accident; for English had been the means of his ingress into that great world of adventure in the first place, and English had been the stepping stone to the possibly vaster and hardly less venturesome realm of erudition in the second. What we should see in the stories of infamy is the intended amalgamation of a subject matter usually reserved for children with a fantasy world extracted from all kinds of books, a veritable synthesis of Borges' earliest, and at that time, most recent literary experience; for Borges discovered a literature of literature—"a literature of literature and of thought" as Bioy Casares later said of "The Garden of the Forking Paths"[26]—based on the pleasure and adventure of reading, on the information and techniques of factual and imaginative writing. In doing so he discovered all the exotic islands and distant spaces he would ever need.

If the actual achievement of *Universal History* is negligible, the exercises in literary dovetailings and symbolic interpolations are foundational, which is also to say that the negligible book presents invaluable prefaces, both literally and prophetically. Lacking a self-propagated stock, Borges took the available one of certain English books and attempted to graft on his own fictional flowers and metaphysical fruits—understandably the scion barely survived. *Universal History* reveals the first stages in this delicate grafting process; *Ficciones* and *El Aleph* display the mature new variety. The important thing is that a graft eventually took.

Notes

1. For a full treatment of this relationship, see Emir Rodríguez Monegal, "Macedonio Fernández y el Ultraísmo," *Número* IV, 19 (April-June 1952).
2. Ana María Barrenechea and Emma Susana Speratti, *La literatura fantástica en Argentina* (Mexico: 1957), ix.
3. Eduardo Mallea, *Historia de una pasión argentina* (Buenos Aires: 1940) 65-80; 81-95.
4. Both essay and translation first appeared in *Proa* 6 (January 1925): 3-6, 8-9 respectively.
5. *Número* 28 (February 26, 1927).
6. Amado Alonso, "Borges narrador," *SUR* 14 (November 1935): 105.
7. Ibid., 111.
8. Hugh Kenner, *Paradox in Chesterton* (New York: 1947), 1.
9. Alonso, "Borges narrador," 106.
10. Ibid., 107.
11. Tamayo and Ruiz-Diaz, *Enigma y clave*, 73.
12. Given Borges' precocious appreciation of von Sternberg's quick cuts, it is fitting that Jean Luc Godard, with his notoriously breathless cutting, should invoke Borges in the epigraph of *Les Carabiners*, to the effect that the old, traditional metaphors are the best.
13. Barrenechea, *The Labyrinth Maker*, 85, 87.
14. Kenner, *Paradox in Chesterton*, 37-38.
15. Bernard De Voto, *Mark Twain's America* (Cambridge, Mass.: 1951), 19.
16. De Voto, *Twain's America*, 311.
17. A. B. Freeman-Mitford (Lord Redesdale), *Tales of Old Japan* (London: 1919), 3-16.
18. Mitford, *Tales*, 12-13.
19. Anticipating my discussion of Borges' self-acknowledged debt to De Quincey, I suggest here that the British writer's "Historico-Critical Inquiry into the Origin of the Rosicrucians and Freemasons" (*Collected Writings* [Edinburgh: 1889-1890] XIII, 404) suggested the iconography to Borges:

    > *Each of the seven sides of the vault had a door opening into a chest; which chest, besides the secret books of the order and the* Vocabularium *of Paracelsus, contained also mirrors, little bells, burning lamps, marvellous mechanisms of music, etc., all so contrived that after the lapse of many centuries, if the whole order should have perished, it might be established by means of his vault.*

20. Edward Abbott Parry, *Vagabonds All*, 1.
21. Ibid., 6.

22. Ibid.
23. Barrenechea, *Labyrinth Maker*, 16.
24. Twain, *Life on the Mississippi,* 244.
25. Robert Martin Adams, "The Intricate Argentine," *Hudson Review* XIX (Spring 1966): 145.
26. *SUR* 92 (May 1942): 60.

THE ACHIEVEMENT OF FORM

Stages of Development

If we assume, as Borges directs us, that the first seven stories of *Universal History of Infamy* were experiments, and if we decide, as I believe we must, that they were largely unsuccessful, then we must either ascertain what advance they marked over "Man from the Pink Corner" or declare them futile trials. Our first impression may well be that they were, if not totally abortive, then at least premature, since Borges' next collection did not appear until six years later. Furthermore, Borges himself has conspired to strengthen this impression by correlating the beginning of his story writing with his recovery from a serious illness in 1939, thus emphasizing the interval between the tentative attempts of *Universal History* and the deliberate achievement of what he wrote in 1939. The impression Borges creates, consequently, is that after having made an encouraging start in one kind of narrative, he made a weak assay of another, recognized the inconclusive result of his later effort, gave up fiction for several years, and returned to it only by force of the extraordinary circumstance of his illness, which impelled him to begin again, this time in an entirely new mode facilitating his literary fulfillment and eventually bringing him international fame.

Since so much of what has been written about Borges proceeds directly from what he says about his own writing, critics have tended to divide his career into these three discrete stages, thereby assuming no real development in his fiction at all, no accretion of skill but, rather, a miraculous metamorphosis marked by two abrupt transformations, one of them no less mysterious than the emergence of the butterfly from a cocoon. In this view, the phases are respectively represented by "Man from the Pink Corner," the seven stories of infamy, and "Pierre Menard, Author of *Don Quixote*," the latter standing as the symbolic primogenitor of all the stories in *Ficciones* and *El Aleph*. Useful as such a schema is, and I do not deny its diagrammatic clarity, it nevertheless distorts the growth of fiction in Borges' oeuvre, especially at the major transitional point, that between the second and third stage.

Even the break between the first two phases is somewhat modified in the reader's eye because Borges chose to collect the *compadrito* tale along with the stories drawn from preexisting books and interrelated them all in *Universal History* by connecting the scandalous hero of "The Terrible Redeemer Lazarus Morell" to Rosendo Juárez, a character in "Man from the Pink Corner": "A fellow distinguished for the use of his knife—one of Don Nicolás Paredes' men, who, in turn, was one of Morell's men" (*HI*, 95). Nevertheless, we would be wrong to group these two types of fiction together, separated as they are by Borges' decision to relocate himself—his literary self, that is—in a library of English books rather than in the "streets" and "visible sunsets" of Buenos Aires. In contrast to the bookish stories about villains, "Man from the Pink Corner" is something like a typical first novel in which the writer tests his narrative skill on materials drawn from the world about him. Although in Borges' case the material is patently less personal, the narrative, in both its style and content, is extracted from real life:

I had met a man from the Palermo district who talked a little like my good fellow; that is to say, who told stories a little like that story. He was an old murderer.

When I wrote this story, my friend was dead. His name was Don Nicolás Paredes. At that time I wrote each phrase very slowly, very painstakingly, because I re-read every phrase trying to read it in his voice. If there was anything too literary, I would erase it. That helped me to really strike out the literary phrases—"literary" in the bad sense of the word.

Then I said to myself: "I can write stories," and I had launched myself a bit. It was rather good for me, because I do not think of myself as a poet. (L'Herne, 379)

Having thus paid a debt to national, even to linguistic ori-
gins, Borges turned to the prose experiments that constitute
the major portion of his second period of fiction, the stories
comprising his history of infamy.

The division between the first two stages is clearly
discernible, not only because Borges points it out but also
because an examination of the works on either side reveals
outstanding differences of style, form, and purpose. This is
not to say, however, that the seven stories improved upon the
techniques of "Man from the Pink Corner"; rather, that they
were a new beginning. In these later stories Borges abandoned early methods for new ones—the same kind of whole-
sale rejection and recommencement on new ground that he
and his critics would have us believe took place early in
1939. But while a radical reorientation and regeneration is
evident around 1933 when the individual biographies of the
infamous began to appear, a closer examination will disclose
that a second revolution of this type did not in fact occur in
1939; that, instead, there is an unbroken line of growth from
1933 to 1941. Such an examination will permit us to draw
the evolution of Borges' fiction in a new perspective, one that
carries our sight lines past the artificial vanishing point established by Borges and accepted by his critics and back to
his earlier attempts at fiction.

Typically, when asked by James Irby how he came
to give up poetry for fiction, Borges responded:

*In 1939 I became very sick with septicemia, just like
Dahlmann in "The South." The fever and the delirium were
such that I thought I was going crazy and I feared that I
would no longer be able to go back to writing. I didn't even
want my mother to read books to me because I was afraid
of not being able to understand them. One night in the sanatorium, when I was already getting a little better, she began
to read from a book by C. S. Lewis*—Out of the Silent
Planet—*which had just arrived from London. Immediately I
found myself crying from happiness, because I truly under-*

stood what my mother read to me. Then I decided to write something, but something new and different for me, so as to be able to lay the blame on the novelty of my undertaking if I failed. I set myself to writing that story which is entitled "Pierre Menard, Author of Quixote."

But you had written stories before that, hadn't you?

Yes, I had written "Man from the Pink Corner," which, in spite of the success it has had, isn't worth much; and I had written those little tales of infamy which are only glosses of other books. Also, I had written a false bibliographical note entitled "The Approach to Almotásim"—a very amusing little work which I inserted in my collection of essays History of Eternity. A friend of mine believed that that detective story really existed and tried to order it from London.[1]

We have already separated "Man from the Pink Corner" from Borges' major fiction. Now his own phrases "little tales of infamy, which are only glosses of other books" ("*cuentitos de infamia, que sólo son glosas de otros libros*") and "a false bibliographical note . . . a very amusing little work" ("*una falsa nota bibliográfica . . . un trabajito muy divertido*") and in particular the diminutives *cuentitos* and *trabajito* serve to disjoin these other works. Nor is it difficult to imagine why Borges should want to associate the beginning of his story writing with his illness in 1939, or why a story written concurrently with his recovery should have seemed the discovery of a new territory of fiction as well as of new health. The birth of an idiosyncratic narrative from the matrix of hallucination, high fever, and near-death; a birth assisted by a literary fantasy that ironically verifies comprehensible reality: these are aspects that Borges might well have invented had they not forced themselves upon him, for they are the conditions of much of his fiction; they make of his illness and recovery profound esthetic and metaphysical as well as psychic and physical experiences, perhaps no less imperative for his development than his earlier intuition of timelessness. Even in my interview with him, where his memory betrayed him for a moment, Borges insisted on his illness as the beginning of all his fiction:

Then I had an accident . . . [and] . . . I spent about a fortnight in a hospital. I had nightmares and sleeplessness—insomnia. After that they told me that I had been in danger, well, of dying, that it was really a wonderful thing that the operation had been successful. I began to fear for my mental integrity; I said, "Maybe I can't write anymore." . . . So I thought I'd try my hand at something I hadn't done; if I couldn't do it, there would be nothing strange about it, because why should I write short stories?—also it would prepare me for the final overwhelming blow: knowing that I was at the end of my tether. I wrote a story, let me see, I think, "Hombre de la esquina rosada," and everyone enjoyed it very much. It was a great relief to me. If it hadn't been for that particular knock on the head I got, perhaps I would never have written short stories.[2]

To derive his fictive impulse from this trauma is altogether appropriate, yet appropriate as things are in his stories; and satisfying as this derivation may be, we cannot accept it. "Pierre Menard" was not wholly "something new and different" for Borges, who had already discovered the method of "Pierre Menard" in pressing onward with the technical experiments of *Universal History*. We have seen him redistribute the forces and directions of his life before; I believe that, in dramatizing the break of "Pierre Menard" with everything that went before it, he does so again, just possibly without total awareness. This writer, who has argued so persuasively that an author creates his own precursors (*OI*, 145-48), has neglected to argue that a writer similarly and no less retroactively creates his own biography. His neglect possibly demonstrates the self-evident truth of the assertion.

There is no doubt that when we get to "Pierre

Menard" we encounter one of what Ana María Barrenechea calls the "strange and lucid narratives" that "have made his stories renowned,"[3] but we must also remember that between the adaptations of *Universal History* and the distinctive "Pierre Menard"—that is, between Borges' protofictions on the one hand and his developed narratives on the other— stands a single story that fully measures the yield of Borges' early experiments and clearly introduces his future experiments, a story in which, as Barrenechea herself says, the characteristics that have made Borges' stories famous are "fully defined."[4] That this story, "The Approach to Almotásim," is, despite what Borges may say, both a story and one that belongs to the later phase of his career even though it was written in 1935, is absolutely demonstrated by his twice reprinting it: first in the collection *The Garden of the Forking Paths* (1941), where "Pierre Menard" first appeared in book form, and then again in *Ficciones* (1944), where it cannot be separated from the other stories either in form or theme. No story from the *History of Infamy* could stand that comparative test and, on this basis alone, even if others were lacking, we must assert that it was in "The Approach to Almotásim" and not in "Pierre Menard" that Borges first came into his own. But since other criteria are not lacking, we can justify this assertion by establishing through comparison just where "The Approach" stands, whether with *Universal History*, with "Pierre Menard," or by itself.

In the year following *Universal History of Infamy*, Borges issued another history with a title even more pretentious and playful than its predecessor. This little volume collected several essays, including the one from which it took its name—"History of Eternity"—and two notes on literature, only one of which corresponds to its appearance. In "The Art of Insult" Borges actually studied "vituperation and mockery" (*HE*, 145) as literary forms, but in what pretended to be the review of a detective story, he continued his experiment in fiction. I say "continued," because the affinities of his so-called note with the seven stories of infamy are both superficial and basic, while the differences are of degree and daring. Both efforts—the seven stories and the spurious note—are placed in heterogeneous collections, menageries really more than anthologies—just as many of his stories are little museums or curio shops of quotation and speculation— where they rise from a seemingly factual foundation and erect a more or less elaborate tension between fact and fiction, between the overt form or locus of their presence and their hidden intention, and finally between apparential and metaphysical reality, for the factual content in both instances—an infamous deed and its consequences—is actually Borges' metaphysic, conveyed in the partially or totally feigned retelling of a narrative. As a matter of fact, in "The Approach to Almotásim" Borges delineates the line from infamy to metaphysics with sharp, explicit clarity:

It is impossible to trace the changes of fortune in the nineteen remaining chapters. There is a vertiginous pullulation of dramatis personae—not to speak of a biography that seems to exhaust the movements of the human spirit (from infamy to mathematical speculation) and a peregrination that takes in the vast geography of Hindustan. (HE, 139)

Here are the themes of his speculation: infinity of persons, of places, and hence, implicitly, of times, all contained in a single imaginary book; there is the range of his life's reading.

The accountable superiority of "The Approach to Almotásim" lies primarily in the degree to which Borges has energetically and confidently pursued his conceit: he is still falsifying and joking, for Enrique Anderson Imbert has shown that the imagined novel *The Approach to Almotásim* bears some resemblances, chiefly in the circumstances of its publication and the nature of its genre, to the little known detective story entitled *The Mystery of Años Street*.[5] Borges is still extracting literature from literature, but now he has

stopped inserting disquieting snippets into recognizable versions of other narratives and has instead concocted his own
source, which he passes off as the legitimate subject of a
note. Not only does he thus fabricate the dream of every reviewer—a book that elicits all the comments and observations the reviewer stores for the proper moment; a book the
reviewer cannot deal too sparingly or too expansively with—
he also succeeds in his self-appointed task of revealing the
phantasmal nature of conventional reality, at least to the extent that his friend tried to buy the imaginary novel. This
success, one may argue, is hardly more encouraging than the
"irresponsible game" of *Universal History*; yet, first of all,
this story can stand on its own once the joke is known, a fact
Borges himself proved by his double reprinting of it in purely
fictional contexts; and second, it measures the strength of
Borges' fictional impulse, for not even he could call "The
Approach to Almotásim" the work of "a timid man."

For the other part of our comparison, we see that if
"Pierre Menard" had something new, it was in the order of
its brilliant conceit and not of its form, which is fundamentally similar to that of "The Approach." Both pieces can be
described by the phrase Borges applied to "Pierre Menard,"
"something that was not always a story" (*L'Herne*, 379),
since they both take the form of a literary note such as we
find in journals: the one a "review" augmented in the established manner with citations or allusions and parallels to
other works; the second a literary-biographical sketch augmented with the equally well-established procedure of a descriptive bibliography. In both instances, Borges relies
heavily on reference to existing authors and books for an
effect of circumstantiality; but whereas in *Universal History*
Borges timidly introduced false tonalities into preexisting
composition, he now intrepidly introduces a false book into
an assemblage of real ones, and a false author into the company of past and present writers. Granting that these intro-
ductions take us to the world of literary fantasy, we see that
this world is hardly contiguous with that of science fiction,

so it does not matter whether after his illness his mother read to him from *Out of the Silent Planet* or from *The Martian Chronicles* as *L'Herne,* perhaps mistakenly, quotes Señora Borges as saying.[6] Neither "The Approach" nor "Pierre Menard" has anything to do with science fiction except that all three rely on the fantastic; but even this element in Borges' stories, as we shall see later, is more closely related to the formula of the detective story than to that of science fiction. Therefore while Borges' emphasis on his illness and the summoning power of the fortuitously chosen page—an echo of Kabbalistic, medieval, even Augustinian experience—no doubt has a basis in fact, the episode has more to do with the creation or invention of precursors and sources than with the unfolding of Borges' career in fiction, which is rendered incoherent when we view "Pierre Menard" as the originator rather than as the result of a cumulative series beginning with *Universal History of Infamy.*

The progress from *Universal History* to "The Approach" is not, then, what it appears—the progress from parasitism to symbiosis—but actually the transition from parasitism to independent existence. Accordingly, the achievement of "Pierre Menard" is the creation of life itself: from interpolating and arranging passages in the early 1930s, to the invention of an author and his oeuvre in 1939, the advancement is chronological, sequential, progressive—if we grant the logic, absolutely inevitable. In fact, so inexorable is this logical progression that the next step, obviously the fabrication of an entire world, was completed with "Tlön, Uqbar, Orbis Tertius" in early 1940, and the corollary establishment of a mythology for this newly informed universe in the sequent "The Circular Ruins" and "The Lottery in Babylon," published respectively in December 1940 and January 1941. We can even go on to say that in 1942, with the collaboration of Adolfo Bioy Casares, Borges completed the development by introducing to the world not only six more fantastic tales, *Six Problems for Don Isidro Parodi,* but also, by the device of a pseudonym, a completely fantastic living author: H. Bustos Domecq, whose character and career Borges and Casares have continued to elaborate over the years. While Pierre Menard exists only within the framework of the story about him, H. Bustos Domecq exists outside his several books—he continues to write and continued to be written about. With the introduction of this humorous specter, we can see that the work is whole, the line unbroken.

Unity of Oeuvre

In reassessing "The Approach" as the missing link in the evolution of Borges' fiction, we establish one meaningful line of continuity and imply another, for this story not only serves to draw together earlier and later stories, but also focuses our attention on the essential unity of Borges' oeuvre. Along with Emir Rodríguez Monegal, almost every writer on Borges has noted the interrelation of poetic, essayistic, and narrative forms in which his work is embodied: "The three are forms of a single esthetic creation notable for its concentration and unity."[7] The concentration, we already know, is a desired effect in Borges' writing, but the unity is a no less consciously desired effect, so successfully achieved in distinguishable ways that in one sense the development of Borges' art can be traced in the gradual dissolution of boundaries between the genres in which he works. The highest accomplishments of his career—his best stories—exert their force upon us as much through the novel mixture of recognizable literary forms as through the handling of strange material.

PARALLELISM AND RECIPROCITY The effect of unity in Borges' oeuvre is primarily achieved through recurrent parallels (narrative, verbal, ideational) and an apparent reciprocity of works. Whether we are reading within a genre or cutting across generic lines in Borges' writing, we frequently encounter passages that echo one another in thought and expression. For example, if first we read the poem "The Card Game" in *Fervor of Buenos Aires* that begins "Forty cards have displaced life" (*P*, 23), we may come with a certain surprise upon the prose section in *Evaristo Carriego* also entitled "The Card Game," which begins: "Forty cards want to displace life" (*EC*, 106). Further along in both poem and biography we find: "Amulets of painted cardboard"; and, once again, in the poem we see: "Within the borders of the table lingers common life," while in the prose: "They are sufficient to conjure up common life." The nearly identical subject of each passage—a subject that in itself points to the way in which Borges' mind returns to fundamental concerns, in this case the game of cards, which acts as token of the repetitive, symbolic nature of life—seems to demand nearly identical verbal expression. But even in poems or essays on markedly different subjects, the same images, the same conceits are frequently brought to play so that opposites, like traitor or hero, or contrasts, like the following couplets from two different poems, resolve themselves, showing how Borges mints contraries, like different sides of the same coin, from a single metal:

> *The vague chance or the precise laws*
> *That rule this dream, the universe* (*P*, 81)

> *The clear chance or the secret laws*
> *That rule this dream, my destiny* (*P*, 87)

When seen in conjunction with the repeated use of certain adjectives and symbols and the reductive nature of Borges' metaphysical thought, such parallels emphatically demonstrate that the concentration and unity Rodríguez Monegal describes are really reflections of each other.

Beyond parallels such as these, which lead us to become aware of a static relationship between many of Borges' works, indeed to view some of them as siblings or even twins, there is a determinant parent-offspring relationship between others, and it is to this connection that I shall apply the label "reciprocity." Frequently it is nearly impossible to determine which is the engendering work, but Borges' habitual reflex from expression to analysis, or from speculation about the possibility or necessity for a given type of literature to the production of such a work, is clearly demonstrated at the very start of his career where his two earliest volumes of verse were quickly followed by two volumes of essays. The close appearance of these four books established the junction of creative and critical act that has marked Borges' career at every stage. Not all the essays in these books are about poetry, but they tend to be about writers and writings or about topics that sometimes bear directly on the subjects of Borges' own poems. Hence poems like "The Streets," "*La Recoleta*," and "Unknown Street," to take the first three poems in *Fervor de Buenos Aires*, can be seen as a direct response to the following passage in *The Extent of My Hope*:

More than a city, Buenos Aires is now a country and it must be discovered by the poetry and music, the painting and religion and the metaphysic which accord with its greatness. That is the extent of my hope, which invites us all to be gods and to labor in its incarnation. (*TE*, 9)

It is as if, to cite the famous parallel in our own literature, Borges were both Emerson demanding the national bard and Whitman fulfilling the imperative prophecy. The parallel is not weakened by the fact that the poem was published first and the plea afterward, for both spring from the same mind, and it would be impossible to determine the cause or result from the expression of either; besides, we already have, in the case of Borges' petition for a literature of pure fantasy and his writing of such fiction, an instance where the cause and result conform to logical, chronological order. In any case, what is truly important here is the spectacle of a mind in vital commerce with itself, a mind simultaneously winding and weaving with the same shuttle.

Such interrelation implies interdependence. Undeniably, each of Borges' works breathes deeper and more fully to the extent that it exists in the atmosphere created by its neighbors; some of his works, like the story "The Man in the Doorway," or many of the short essays cannot survive meaningfully without support from other of his works, and as James Irby has noted, at least one volume of essays, *Other Inquisitions*, "forms a necessary complement to the stories of *Ficciones* and *El Aleph*."[8] To the reader with a wide experience of Borges' writing this characteristic may yield the continuing pleasure of making connections; but to the uninitiated reader, it must reveal an insufficiency, a fundamental limitation in certain compositions. Furthermore, the reciprocal relationship that develops between the stories, poems, and essays, leads us, finally, away from the works themselves and toward the mind that created them. This, of course, is not in itself bad—we are not here concerned with a simple-minded distinction between biographical and purely formal criticism—but it does seem to suggest that perhaps the final effect of Borges' writing, the end to which the unity of his oeuvre is a means, is the creation of a fictive author whose personality informs the given works, each of which is to be read, like the productions of Pierre Menard, as facts toward the biography of a single mind. Hence, I presume, the task has devolved on Borges of creating on the one hand, of extracting on the other, the literary history of his works' author and, for the same reason, the writing of prefaces and notes that seldom reveal much about the works in comparison to what they tell us of the author, and of pieces, like "Borges and I," which goes further than any other of Borges' writing toward the fabrication of an author for his writings. The perspective of time—along with a more adequate edition of his writings—is needed before we can see properly the relationship of this authorial personality to his works, but certainly the suggestion is there that the "impersonality" of Borges' writing is in reality the dramatization of an autobiography, and that his youthful pronouncement is more relevant to his work than has heretofore seemed possible: "All literature is autobiographical, ultimately" (*TE*, 146).

HYBRIDIZATION The properties of unity I have pointed to thus far have been the conditions of Borges' work, seemingly natural and necessary conditions: that Borges should choose common themes and similar modes of expression in his poems, stories, and essays is, after all, not surprising, even if the frequency with which he makes that choice is. In contrast, however, and demanding distinction from the parallelism and reciprocity I have described, is the amalgamation of essay and short story which, since it led to the invention of a fictive form that virtually precludes narrative and emphasizes instead the discursive and speculative, is the most astonishing and productive gesture toward unity that he ever made. Once discovered, this form permitted the solidification of Borges' literary effort and predicted the greatest triumphs of his art; in its very first manifestation—"The Approach to Almotásim"—the form encapsulated both modes of fiction Borges was to pursue in the following years at the same time that it sustained the essay style he had developed and demonstrated the diminishing need for verse, which he almost completely abandoned in the ensuing years. So significant in its achievement and so different in kind from other indications of unity in Borges' work, "The Approach" deserves separate notice as the first and fundamental realization of a formal unification answering esthetic and metaphysical ends.

"The Approach to Almotásim"

Because of the scrupulous self-awareness in Borges' attempt to create connections between his own writings and those of other writers—even long after the fact, as in the preface to *Ficciones* (*F*, 12), where he cites a correspondence between "The Approach" and *The Sacred Fount* although he read James' novel years after he wrote the story—it is not surprising that Borges should also indicate resemblances between the writing and thinking of his characters and his own work, between the fictive and authorial worlds. Occasionally, therefore, we encounter passages that erupt from the context with the power of revelation and force us to recognize a counterpart of Borges' own production. In such instances, the awareness of a relationship is our own, and Borges' art is working in us, not merely *on* us. If we choose to lessen the effect of such an awareness with an all too simple autobiographical explanation, it is not the work but our own appreciation that is appreciably diminished.

One such example occurs in "Examination of the Work of Herbert Quain":

He perceived with absolute lucidity the experimental nature of his books—books admirable, perhaps, for their novelty and a certain laconic probity, but not for the virtues of passion. (F, 77)

Another in the first paragraph of "Tlön, Uqbar, Orbis Tertius":

Bioy Casares had dined with me that night and we prolonged a vast polemic about the execution of a novel in the first person, whose narrator would omit or distort the facts and involve himself in various contradictions that would permit a few readers—a very few readers—to guess the atrocious or banal reality. (F, 13)

And still another, of more specific applicability, on the first page of "The Approach" where Borges summarizes two points of view on the novel he is pretending to review:

Essentially, both writers concur: both point out the detective story mechanism of the work and its mystical undercurrent. That hybridization can lead us to imagine some resemblance to Chesterton; we shall soon prove that there is no such thing. (HE, 135)

Here the analogy—and it is just that, and not a one-to-one correspondence—reveals the essential form of Borges' story:

two writers have agreed upon "hybridization" and implied a similarity to Chesterton that does not really exist in the novel; Borges' story itself proceeds upon the principle of hybridization and also raises the question of a similarity to Chesterton. In other words, the analysis of the novel suggests an analogical analysis of the story where we shall find, first, a mechanism, apparently not that of the detective story, but one as discernible, formal, and rigid, which is the literary vehicle of Borges' subject matter; second, a mystical undercurrent distinguishable from the overtly mystical subject; and, concurrently, a merging of mechanism and undercurrent inappropriately suggestive of Chesterton.

MECHANISM   The mechanism of "The Approach" is easily identified, especially if we refer to its original appearance in *History of Eternity*, where Borges calls it a note or review and thereby categorizes it as nonfiction prose. In the usual classification of his works this category is rather loosely labeled "essay," and it includes such divergent modes as the polemic of "The Alarms of Dr. Américo Castro," the literary criticism of "Vindication of *Bouvard et Pécuchet*," the metaphysical speculation of "New Refutation of Time," and the movie reviews of "Films." Of course, "The Approach" is almost entirely fictitious, so that when Borges called it a "*nota*" he was ultimately referring to the procedure of the piece, not to its content, and we must ask ourselves why Borges adopted this essayistic form and what are its characteristics.

In the decade, roughly from 1933 to 1944, when Borges seriously turned to the short story for the first time, it is clear from what we already know that he was trying in more than one way to approach narrative without sacrificing too much of the ground he had gained for himself in other genres and without exposing himself to the possible criticism of those who thought of him primarily as poet or essayist. Consequently, much of the work he produced in those years masquerades as one thing while attempting to be something else. We already have the example of *Universal History*, and whether we choose to believe the psychological motive of timidity, as given by Borges, or the esthetic-metaphysical intention of creating a fantastic literature, as revealed by an analysis of the stories, or even if we choose a combination of the two, our conclusion must be the same: *Universal History* demonstrates a crossing of literary forms. A similar crossing, this time of lyric and narrative, is evident in the group of pieces entitled "Confessions," which first appeared in *Crítica* between the publication of *Universal History* and *History of Eternity*.[9] Although the experimental nature of these compositions, e.g., "Dreamtigers" and "My Nails," was originally obscured by their appearing under the pseudonym of "Francisco Bustos" and subsequently by their inclusion in the 1960 volume *El Hacedor*, where their brevity and personal bent appear the externally enforced result of Borges' need to compose short pieces, such works, when examined in the context of what Borges was attempting in the 1930s, show an attempt to combine an impulse that ordinarily found its expression in poetry with the newly tried prose narrative.

Once we see the works in this light, we realize that "The Approach" is not an isolated piece but the culmination of a sustained effort and the very best of Borges' early experiments, a judgment supported by his pursuit of the form in subsequent fiction. Too timid to write a straightforward narrative under his own signature, but recognizing that fiction by name and nature as the perfect medium for his metaphysic, Borges hid his story in "The Approach" in the middle of what passes for a review. We can imagine that he said to himself something like: "I can write essays and reviews; I have written them. Therefore I will take the situation I have in mind and write an essay about it, pretending that I have already composed the tale I hesitate to publish." Whatever his rationalization or motivation, the device allowed him to exercise his discursive and analytic powers at the same time that it nourished his growing narrative impetus: the embryonic narrative is incubated in the matrix of an essay. Moreover, the scheme masked his timorousness by attributing the story he imagined to another writer, thereby evading his responsibility for trying something new, at least insofar as his unsuspecting readers were concerned. As for his friends, who might well suspect the trick, he could reply that it had been a joke, nothing but a joke. Any or all of these explanations may be valid— there is surely some truth in each—but we would be wrong to think of the device of an invented novel reviewed with mock and real seriousness as purely compensatory on Borges' part, because while he may have been afraid, Borges sacrificed nothing to his fears in writing "The Approach." To produce a concentrated, essential literature expressing a metaphysical apprehension of the fundamental and fantastic unity of life had been the basic goal of his major efforts, and that goal is achieved in this early story; to work more directly from literature and books in general than from experience of life, to use as the basic metaphor for the illusive quality of our existence the imaginary reality of the characters and events we read about, had been a defined objective of his writing and that objective also is clearly realized in "The Approach."

In order to understand what Borges accomplished in "The Approach" and how he managed it, we must recognize the basic qualities of his essay style, which are fully implied in the titles *Discussion* and *Inquisitions*. His major essays are most often the rapid and highly rational résumé of metaphysical notions or the application of a metaphysical notion to a literary theme. If the topics are frequently what he would call "fantastic," his prose has no kinship with the whimsical essays, say, of Lamb, for to investigate or examine means, for Borges, to present a theme in the significant context of its analogues and recurrent manifestations, while to discuss means to propose a subject and then to offer complementary or conflicting arguments possibly without the need or desire for resolution. Until the end of an essay, it sometimes seems that Borges' prose simply provides the medium of *rapprochement*, but the last part is usually his own point added as the logical conclusion, the final fillip that forcefully adjusts the preceding quotations and allusions to the peculiar angle of his vision. Whatever his subject, however, we can say that the general technique and goal of Borges' essays is the linking of writers and thoughts, the demonstration of connections where none apparently existed—in a word, the exhibition of a partial unity implying a universal unity. By skillful allusion and quotation he constructs atemporal forums where his own voice can be heard as Plato, Marcus Aurelius, and Nietzsche all comment on the same subject, or where Chesterton disagrees with Croce while Borges is unable to decide who is right.

Like Montaigne's essays, Borges' essays aspire neither to formal didacticism nor to exhaustive methodical analysis, so that, despite the immense erudition that has often been attributed to him, we must remember that he has not produced, nor even tried to produce, a learned study on any of the subjects he knows best—the Kabbalah, for example, or English literature. Borges' writings are not those of a scholar; his essays are precisely that and not studies: the personal expression of insight, interest, and enthusiasm, the logical, rational counterpart of the lyric metaphysicality we find in his verse. Nevertheless, the bulk of each essay is largely nonpersonal in the sense that Borges is mostly quoting or paraphrasing other writers. Of course it is Borges who chooses the passages for quotation or paraphrase even though he appears to be simply displaying the thinking of others, and we may see in this technique another way of dealing with his own modesty; but the effect, the intended effect, is to lead us away from the writer to an apprehension of a thematic continuity.

This characteristic trend is visible in "The Approach" when we move from specific quotation about a given novel at the beginning to a summarized myth at the end, but then even the skeletal structure of the story conforms to the pattern of essay and can be schematically represented:

I Background	II Summary	III Judgment	IV Analogues
1. Criticism	1. Chapters 1-2; situation	1. Criteria	1. Possible sources
2.Bibliography	2. Chapters 3-21; succeeding events and underlying argument	2. Evaluation	2. Underlying myth

Because of the scrupulous organization of the story, such a diagram does less injustice to the story than might be expected: while only one division is indicated typographically in the text (by an asterisk in the middle of the page) and another independent section is set off as a footnote, the parts and their subdivisions are in fact clearly defined by the paragraphing. Once the story is broken down according to the pattern in the chart, there is no difficulty in seeing how little of "The Approach" is devoted even to the retelling of a story: the plot-summary section is only one of four basic parts, and it fills about four pages while the other sections fill about one and one-half pages each, the rendered narrative with its adjunctive argument thus comprising only about one-half of the total composition as it appears in the *Complete Works*. "The Approach" is not narrative in the ordinary sense, unless one is willing to apply the term to plot summary with comment and annotation. It is true that much of what went into the making of "The Approach" also goes into the writing of fiction: the invention of a plot with episodes embodying the action of a central character in a specific environment. But to this skeleton Borges attaches no flesh except for a few phrases that serve, like the peeled-back flesh on a chart in a biology classroom, to reveal the nature and function of the innards. The rest of Borges' story consists of the analytic labels, descriptive commentary, and table of comparisons that surround such drawings: we do not have the presentation of a story here but the dissection of one. In other words, "The Approach" is an experiment in inquisition, as Borges' previous essays had been miniature inquisitions; only this time all the inquisitorial, essayistic apparatus is drawn up against an imagined book, so that we have neither legitimate investigation nor actual story, but, as Borges was to appropriately label it at a later time, a *fiction*, literally, a *feigning* on both sides.

Bioy Casares was the first to point out to Borges that some of his stories are really halfway houses between fiction and essay.[10] But in "The Approach" Borges has in truth written something much closer to essay than to fiction. Hence it might prove useful to amplify Bioy Casares' observation and classify Borges' stories in three categories: (1) stories that take their form predominantly from the essay; (2) those that indeed are "halfway houses" between essay and fiction; and (3) those that have little or no essayistic quality. But even this is not enough: in order to understand these apparently simple formulations we must distinguish still further what, in Borges' work, constitutes fictional and essayistic elements.

Beyond the rudimentary distinction that his stories employ fictitious as well as actual events and characters, we should observe that Borges' fiction can be differentiated from his essays primarily on the basis of plot—the concatenation of events as outlined in "The Approach" or as evidenced in "The Dead Man"—or on the basis of a mental biography of an imaginary character as in "Three Versions of Judas." A story like "El Aleph" balances both elements, and almost no story is completely free from the admixture; but some do not fit easily into either category: "The Library of Babel," "The Cult of the Phoenix" and, to a lesser degree, "The Zahir," each of which is the prose elaboration, without presentation of plot or character, of a situation that could in conventional ways be worked into a story. Contrasted with the two previous groupings, this last group of stories demonstrates that we are dealing less with different types of writing than with different stages of expression, namely: *conception, development, embodiment.* In the first category we are exposed to an almost naked presentation of what Henry James would have called Borges' *donnée,* so that in "The Approach" we read of the imagined novel:

The general argument is now glimpsed: The insatiable searching for a soul through the delicate reflections it has left on others: at the beginning the tenuous sign of a smile or of a word; at the end, diverse and increasing splendors of reason, of imagination, of virtue. (HE, 140)

In the other categories, the *donnée* is by degrees more thoroughly homogenized with the narrative form until in some instances ("Emma Zunz" or "The South" for example) the inspiring notion is entirely implicit in the words or deeds of the character. Thought of this way, the progress from "The Approach" to "Pierre Menard" and "Tlön, Uqhar, Orbis Tertius" to "The Circular Ruins" is the progress from the conception of a possible plot expressing metaphysical ideas and a discussion of its values, to the development of a possible character and place expressing certain metaphysical-literary notions, to the embodiment of a metaphysical notion, a character, and a place in a genuine narrative—the progress, in effect, to use an analogy from another art, from low relief to high relief to sculpture in the round.

If nothing else, such an analysis serves to reaffirm that Borges' fiction develops ultimately from metaphysical notions that are described in nearly pure abstraction in the essays; that in adapting the essay mechanism in his first successful story, Borges was not only taking advantage of a form that would make it possible for him to tell stories at all but also imitating the very procedure of his mind that gave rise to fiction in the first place. Consequently, we see that such curious pieces of fiction as "The Approach" or "Herbert Quain" are examples of the formal unity in Borges' oeuvre, which is, finally, a unity of process rather than of stasis: these works present the emergence of fiction in a form where the writing of a story has not been divorced from the writing about a story. As such they look forward to the writings of at least one of our most important authors—Nabokov, whose *Pale Fire* extends and elaborates Borges' mechanism in "The Approach."

UNDERCURRENT The radix of all of Borges' important writings, whether they be verse, essay, or narrative, is the fantastic, a mode of thought, perception, and description broad enough in his formulation to include literature (*Out of the Silent Planet* and *Green Mansions*), philosophy (Plato and Berkeley), theology (Erigena and Swedenborg), or any other extension of the intellect on nonverifiable, essentially imaginative subjects. In particular, Borges' attention focuses on the immanence of the fantastic in the real world, and it is the goal of much that he writes to awaken our awareness to that immanence, to stimulate and reveal it. Therefore he seldom writes what can be described as pure fantasy, like Tolkien's *The Lord of the Rings* or Maeterlinck's *Blue Bird:* in the manner of Wells' science fiction and in the tradition of Poe's fantasies, Borges discovers the extraordinary under a stairway, in a dark cellar, or within the pages of a reference work. For him the fantastic is not the characteristic of another world, but the covert essence of this one. His is not, then, simply a fascination with the supernatural, nor a belief in the ascendency of the immaterial, not even the single intention of revealing our ultimate "unreality"—to use Barrenechea's word—so much as the desire to show an absolute belief in a substantial, personal, empirical reality and concurrently either an astonishing suspicion, often fleeting but occasionally nagging or overwhelming, of another order of reality that is immaterial, impersonal, unknowable, or the theoretical exposition of such a reality. To commit oneself exclusively to either phase of perception is to commit oneself to a literature of pure fantasy or to one of unrelenting

material realism, and Borges has invoked the writings of
Conrad to support his belief that reality is itself fantastic:

He [Conrad] wrote—and that struck me because I write fan-
tastic stories myself—that to deliberately write a fantastic
story was not to feel that the whole universe is fantastic and
mysterious; that it meant a lack of sensibility for a person
to sit down and write something deliberately fantastic. . . .
Conrad thought that when one wrote, even in a realistic way
about the world, one was writing a fantastic story because
the world itself is fantastic and unfathomable and
mysterious.[11]

And so Borges' use of certain literary conventions—the casually discovered manuscript describing an incredible event
for instance —corresponds to his deepest intention of leading us by way of the familiar or recognizable to a perception of the mystery inherent in the familiar.

In this latter sense Borges is close to Chesterton for
whom, as Hugh Kenner points out, the central fact of life is
the metaphysical paradox of the Incarnation; and also like
the Chesterton whose "real concern," in the words of Kenner,
"is with the metaphysical art of wonder,"[12] Borges' fiction
turns again and again upon the point of "astonishment"
(*asombro*), arising from a detection of the indwelling marvelous. But whereas Chesterton is declarative and dogmatic,
Borges is tentative and speculative. The fantastic truth, for
Chesterton, has been satisfactorily expressed for all time in
the mystery of the Incarnation and only requires attention
called to it; the incredible intuition, for Borges, has been
periodically felt by many men, but hardly stands up against
the certainty of individual experience. Chesterton's spiritu-
alized fiction is a confident celebration of a preexisting sal-
vation; Borges' metaphysical fiction is an attempt to construct a possible redemption. Of course, Borges had before
him the influential example of Macedonio Fernández, whose
fiction, as described by Ana María Barrenechea, "denies
matter and the 'I' and along with them, space, time and cau-

sality. Instead it affirms being: what I feel and am now, in an eternal present, that blots out past and future."[13] But Borges, who employs the same denials, differs from Fernández, differs from Chesterton and Conrad too, because the solution is tempting but finally unsatisfactory for him:

Our destiny is tragic because we, irreparably individuals, are restricted by time and space. There is nothing, therefore, more gratifying than a belief that eliminates circumstances and declares that each man is all men and that there is no one who is not the universe.[14]

The crucial word in this passage is "gratifying" (*lisonjero*), which unites the pitiful vanity of such a faith and its esthetic, psychological appeal, a union that is frequently evident in Borges' thought, as in "New Refutation of Time," where he admits:

In the course of a life dedicated to literature and (sometimes) to metaphysical perplexities, I have barely perceived or intuited a refutation of time that I myself disbelieve but that customarily visits me at night and in the weary dawn with the illusory force of an axiom. (*OI*, 237)

The two conflicting states of mind described above are congruent, and from this congruency arises the need in Borges' fiction to establish both phases of thought; and also from this congruency arises both the mournful tone when the opposition is experienced as a destructive, traumatic corruption and infection of our existence, and the comic manner when all that is at stake is our decorum and sense of life as convention.

Expressed in its most general terms, the conflict Borges deals in is that between body and soul, and in this ancient dialogue he places himself with those who know they have bodies and suspect they have souls, but souls that exist simultaneously, indistinguishably from their bodies:

I think I'm Aristotelian, but I wish it were the other way. I think it's the English strain that makes me think of particular things and persons being real rather than general ideas being real.[15]

The conflict between wish and recognition, invention and belief, destiny and faith is the conflict upon which his fiction is based: the tension is between the material surface of life and the mystical undercurrent. The expression of this tension has led Angel Flores to place Borges' work in the category of "magic realism," and, in fact, to date the beginnings of that movement in Latin America from the appearance of *Universal History of Infamy* in 1935.[16] The term has the advantages of preserving the seeming contraries in Borges' fictional world at the same time that it accents his commitment to reality, but its application, even in the fine arts, is vague. In its place I would prefer to use an oxymoronic phrase from Borges' own writing: "*naturaleza fantástica*" (*F*, 81).

If Borges' attempts to embody the apparent chaos of reality and a secret order of metaphysics, his work is ultimately realistic in the sense that it tries to present the world both as it appears—that is, as we register it with our senses—and as it may be understood—as we can artfully organize it in our mind. It is finally wrong to call his work anti-realistic because he never denies our sensation of multiple, or as he would say *vertiginous* reality. Rather, he says that we know another reality—either by guess or desire—and it is this reality, hidden in the muddle of our sensations, that his work tries to reveal. He attempts to extract an inexorable (but incredible) order from the nightmare; he is very much in tune with the modern feeling that the only reality left to us is that of the dream; that we feel most real in recognizing what has traditionally been called unreal. In this view, Freud and Jung are our guides to what is ultimately real in our lives, an attitude that Susan Sontag epitomizes in the epigraph to the first chapter of her novel *The Benefactor: "Je rêve donc je suis."*[17] No less than Freud or Jung, Borges tries to see the secret order of our lives, our literature, our history. His stories often enclose a concealed, an intellectual mystery that even the characters are unaware of but that is manifested to us, in part, by the allusions. Such is the case with "The Approach to Almotásim."

The mystical undercurrent of "The Approach to Almotásim" is a function of the hybridization of literary forms and cannot be discussed without reference to that hybridization. Since Borges chooses to represent not merely the conflict of reality and fantasy but their subtle interpenetration, as is evident even in *Universal History of Infamy*, where he infiltrates the historical biographies with fantastic elements, what he had to find was a way of representing that commingling. The most available rhetorical device, the one he made most frequent use of in *Universal History*, was paradox; but paradox, with its inevitable dependence on an antagonism of terms, is not completely adequate to Borges' purpose, and we see that verbal paradox, frequent to the point of mannerism in those early stories, diminishes in importance in the subsequent books until it no longer disturbs the stylistic texture. Nearer the mark, although not so successfully handled in *Universal History*, was the technique of interleafing one type of literature, the factual or historical, with another, the fictional or fantastic. Combining the two modes, Borges came close to suggesting a cubistic sense of life that passes beyond the experience of a solid reality observed from a single point in time and space to an ideal vantage that, by its integrated multiplicity, denies the absolute validity of any one angle. Cubism exhibits simultaneously the fact of the object perceived and the fiction of its unseen extension, thereby establishing a hypothetical viewer who is an equivalent of the all-seeing God of Berkeley; Borges, in "The Approach," combines two literary modes in order to establish factually the phantasmal reality of a total fiction, which, once perceived, implies the possible phantasmal nature of the reader.

The core of Borges' story, the plot summary of Mir Bahadur Alí's novel, is overtly metaphysical, and in fact succinctly abbreviates the substance of Borges' literary-metaphysical system. By recounting, instead of actually writing the novel, Borges distills narrative form to essential plot, and beyond that reduces plot to its most rudimentary outline at the same time that he compresses narrative content into its basic mythic form. The pressure of reduction is so great that we are apt not to recognize how much significance is being squeezed out of so few words, but the plot summary is really another universal history—"a biography that seems to exhaust the movements of the human spirit" (*HE*, 139)—and the events referred to so briefly are tokens of Borges' cosmic myth: for "the story begun in Bombay . . . closes its orbit of leagues and years in that same Bombay" (*HE*, 139), we must read "Cyclical history ('begun in Bombay' and 'closes . . . in . . . Bombay') circling ('orbit') through space and time ('leagues' and 'years'), returning always to the same point ('same')." Here then is the heart of Borges' metaphysic, except for "the insignificance of personality," which is expressed both in the total absence of characterization—a device Borges permits himself to ironically comment on in his evaluation (*HE*, 141)—and in the concluding myth of the Simurg, the key to both Borges' composition and Bahadur Ali's novel.

The imagined novel seems to end ambiguously:

After years and years, the student reaches a gallery "in whose depth there is a door and a cheap reed curtain with many beads and in back of it a radiance." The student claps his hands once and then twice and asks for Almotásim. The voice of a man —the incredible voice of Almotásim—urges him to enter. The student draws the curtain and advances. At this point the novel ends. (HE, 141)

It is easy enough to see that the mystical search of the pointedly unnamed student has led him to the final goal of all mystics, the point where the veil is parted, the splendor revealed, and the word spoken; however, the novelist withholds this final vision. Borges, on the other hand, makes perfectly clear what the student will discover by appending a note about the *Coloquio de los pájaros*:

The remote king of the birds, the Simurg, drops a magnificent feather in the middle of China; sated with their ancient anarchy, the birds determine to search for him. They know that his castle is on Kaf, the circular mountain that surrounds the earth. They undertake the almost infinite adventure; they surmount seven valleys or seas: the name of the penultimate one is "Vertigo," the last is called "Annihilation." Many of the pilgrims desert; others perish. Thirty of them, purified by their labors, set foot on the Simurg's mountain. At last they contemplate him: they perceive that they are the Simurg and that the Simurg is each one of them and all of them. (*HE*, 144)

The search of birds and student is equivalent: the latter, like the former, will move from vertigo as he passes through the curtain to annihilation of self upon seeing Almotásim, upon realizing that he is what he searches for and, therefore, is not just himself, but, like the Simurg, *todos*, all: the murderer, the murdered, "the man from whom that radiance proceeds" (*HE*, 140), Almotásim himself. We are not told exactly what it is that the student sees behind the curtain, but since it is a reflection of himself, he probably encounters a kind of celestial mirror (the English subtitle of the supposed illustrated edition is *A Game with Shifting Mirrors*; the student has been searching for Almotásim by seeking his reflection in others) and the confrontation that is meaningfully augmented when Borges takes "The Approach" out of *History of Eternity* and prints it in *The Garden of the Forking Paths* and again in *Ficciones,* thereby forcing us to continually readjust our expectations between what we demand of fiction and what we rely upon in criticism—that conflict stimulates unaccustomed fluctuating reflexes in the reader's mind that finally create a literary *mal de mer* or vertigo, a sign of incipient revelation experienced by so many of Borges' characters, including the student in "The Approach." The continual re-adjustment of our mental eye—a readjustment that can never cease because of the cleverly superimposed planes of fact and fiction, review and story, appearance and reality—is close to the effect of Op art, where our intellect and our vision, our mind and our body, are at odds over the simple intelligibility and the vibrating ambiguity of what we see, an opposition that shakes our very sense of being. The disquieting effect of both modes of expression is sharpened by the homogeneity of means: in many Op paintings there is only one color interacting with a common ground and only a single, repeated shape; and in Borges' story there is an analogous uniformity.

The principal reason for this uniformity in "The Approach" is a consistency of fictive texture achieved through an ever-expanding allusive gesture that permits him to manipulate the book-within-the-book device so as neither to violate his rules for a concentrated literature nor to extend himself beyond the literary world while, at the same time, introducing the fantastic element of his metaphysic. Since there is nothing in "The Approach" that is not a concentrated allusion, we can say that literary allusion is both the substance and the medium of his expression in that story, a unified expression as well as a consistent means for achieving his characteristic brevity.

As for the fantastic, we need look no further than the story's first page to see how Borges suggests it by means of allusion:

Philip Guedalla writes that the novel The Approach to Almotásim *by the lawyer Mir Bahadur Alí of Bombay "is a rather uncomfortable combination of those Islamic allegorical poems that rarely fail to interest their translator and of those detective stories that inevitably surpass John H. Watson and heighten the horror of human life in the most irreproachable boarding houses of Brighton." (HE, 135)*

This sentence, another instance of self-description anticipating the passage about hybridization at the bottom of the page, is itself "a rather uncomfortable combination" of the authentic and spurious: Philip Guedalla is the name of a real, almost forgotten writer, and John H. Watson is the fictional Dr. Watson, Sherlock Holmes's friend;[18] while Mir Bahadur Alí and the novel attributed to him as well as the critical piece ascribed to Guedalla are imaginary. The entire sentence is therefore a cleverly contrived fiction bearing the semblance of actuality, a mixture of apparent fact and real fantasy, an imitation of life as Borges had earlier described it: "Life is true appearance" (*I*, 94). The significant thing is that Borges does not hold his mirror up to "life" at all, but to literature and to one specialized form of literature whose conventions are familiar and unpretentious. The appearance he tries to keep up is literary to begin with—at one remove from "real life" and admittedly apparitional in nature—and whereas other writers resort to pseudobiography (compare the opening of *Gulliver's Travels*) or to a heavy peppering of imagery (compare the opening of *The Time Machine*) to establish a correspondence between their books and life as we experience it socially and sensuously, Borges relies on the established custom of literary procedure to establish a literary verisimilitude. It is only by analogy that "The Approach" deals with life, only when we look at the story and our experience of it as implying something about the fantastic nature of existence.

I have frequently pointed to the pervasiveness of reading and writing in all Borges' fiction: I should add here that he has consistently built up a picture of himself as a man who has devoted his life to those pursuits rather than to living, almost as if in conscious conformity with the myth that has been perpetrated about Henry James and Flaubert. Characters in Borges' stories are frequently literary figures—like Pierre Menard, Herbert Quain, Nils Runeberg, Carlos Argentino, Stephen Albert, Averroës, and Borges himself—

whose lives, to the extent that we know them, are defined in and by their literary pursuits. Literature is for Borges not an activity in one's life, not even a *way* of life, but an acceptable metaphor for life itself. He has considered the ancient topos of the world as a book, as Ana María Barrenechea points out,[19] and has found in it a metaphorical truth confirming and demonstrating the validity of his metaphysic. Not just a book, however, that is to be read, but one that is to be written by our lives, he has believed, following Carlyle. The majority of his stories are either centered in the effort of writing, as in Pierre Menard's attempt to write *Don Quijote*, the effort of criticism and interpretation, as in "Three Versions of Judas" or in the effort of reshaping life from literary principles, as in "Tlön, Uqbar, Orbis Tertius." Some of his fiction, most notably "Death and the Compass" poise the effort of criticism—Lönnrot's unraveling of the text—against the effort of the creation—Scharlach's weaving the net of clues. But whatever the balance of these activities in his fiction, there is the constant demand that we recognize the acts of reading, writing, and elucidating as basic metaphors for the metareality Borges tries to represent. *Not* to lull us, *not* to induce "the willing suspension of disbelief" in the work as verbal construction; but to emphasize the bookishness, to emphasize the surface we have become accustomed to accept unawares; indeed, to reveal that surface, that acceptance as incredible, fantastic—this is a driving force in his writing. As Tamayo and Ruiz-Díaz have rightly said of Borges' frequent quotations:

To quote is equivalent to interrupting the syntactical direction with the interpolation of a foreign fragment. Interrupting and distraction are two qualities inherent in citation.[20]

That very interrupting and distancing, or the equivalent fragmentation and deflation produced by footnotes and appendices, is a calculated effect, which, as Tamayo and Ruiz-Díaz make clear, is handled so that the citations and annotations "come together . . . inflexible and mysterious friendship with a confident personal style,"[21] but that nevertheless is constantly working to break through our conventional response to literature and is, in fact, the source of much of the astonishment we experience in reading Borges. Every time another book is cited, another footnote appended, another quotation inserted, we are caught up short, the spell is broken; and we realize that we are *reading*: the illusion is destroyed. Yet because of our awareness we believe more, not less, in the reality of what we read, and from that tension Borges develops his theme, insinuating that we too are phantasmagoric.

Ultimately we must understand that the union of allusive essay and mystic fiction to form the fictionalized essay in "The Approach" is the formal, structural expression of Borges' design announced in his earliest volume of essays:

One must show an individual passed through a mirror, one who perseveres in his illusory country (where there are shapes and colors, but all controlled by the immobile silence), one who feels the shame of being nothing more than a shadow whom the nights obliterate and the glimmering lights allow to exist. (I, 29)

The striking thing is that in "The Approach," as in some of the best of Borges' fiction, the individual is not only the character but the reader as well: it is *we* who are pitched into that mirror world described by Ana María Barrenechea:

a phantom universe where passion and lucidity can co-exist, as well as precision and mystery, the fact of living in the clouds of a dream and of knowing that one is dreamed.[22]

The same world Borges himself describes in *Otras Inquisiciones*:

Why does it disturb us that Don Quixote is a reader of

Quixote, *Hamlet a spectator of* Hamlet? *I think I have discovered the cause: such inversions suggest that if fictional
characters can be readers or spectators, we, their readers
or spectators, can be fictitious.* (*OI*, 68-69)

The underlying theme of "The Approach" is then a variation
on *la vida es sueño*, the radical theme in all Borges' writing,
most notably and explicitly expressed in "The Circular Ruins" where the magician-priest is ultimately led to a perception that runs directly counter to Tom Castro's development
in "The Unlikely Imposter Tom Castro." Whereas Castro
began by knowing that his identity was a dream of that dark
Bogle and ended up by believing he was what Bogle had
imagined, the priest is led, no less disastrously, to an opposing conclusion:

*With relief, with humiliation, with terror, he understood that
he too was an apparition, that someone else was dreaming
him.* (*F*, 66)

The student learns the same thing when he penetrates the
mystical veil, and the reader experiences the dizzying insinuation when he tries to achieve a balance between the fact and
fiction in "The Approach." There can be no doubt that for
Borges the perception is extraordinarily moving—the periodic construction of the sentence just quoted sufficiently emphasizes that by placing all the rhetorical weight on "relief,"
"humiliation," and "terror"—and the responsive reader feels
something too as he tries to navigate the story; and if it is
not humiliation, not terror or relief, there can be no doubt that
it is a real sensation. Borges' fiction, once again like Op art,
does not attempt to evoke a specific emotion—pity, wrath,
joy—but demonstrates that exciting sensation wedded to an
apparent clarity of vision is still possible. Both modes lead
us to a threshold of feeling where the thrill, the exciting sense
that we are responding at all, is the dominant thing. To say
that Borges' story is cold, impersonal, is to say that the

shapes of many Op paintings are angular, square; what the Op artist and Borges recognize is that the response must be, can only be, in the eye of the beholder.

SIMILARITY TO CHESTERTON   If, in retrospect, it seems strange to find the narrator of "The Approach" rejecting a possible similarity between the imagined novel and Chesterton's fiction—strange if only in the light of Borges' often repeated fondness and admiration for Chesterton—it is even stranger on first reading of this particular story, to find the question of similarity brought up in the first place. Metaphysics are indeed present in the story but they hardly seem to be of Chesterton's Roman Catholic cast; and the crime is at best shadowy, perhaps nonexistent. Moreover, there is no apparent detection in the Chestertonian sense at all, but only a search in which the hero-criminal finds himself, more in the manner of Oedipus than of either Father Brown or Gregory Syme. We can only ask ourselves, then, why Borges has his fictive critics propose the resemblance merely to have his narrator dismiss it when in all probability the analogy would never have occurred in the first place. In the answer to that question lies a clue to the source and direction of Borges' fiction.

Within the story, the allusion directs our attention to the mystery—both metaphysical and criminal—that is central; but in a wider view the feinting allusion to Chesterton first of all tells us as much about the literary background from which the story emerges as it does of the narrative's form and technique: it is an allusion, therefore, that establishes a context and defines a departure. The simple fact is that "The Approach" is not so much cast in the mold of a detective story as it is the embodiment of Borges' own concern with that genre. In fact the periodical format of "The Approach" and consequently its non-narrative, pseudocritical quality reflects an important phase of Borges' own career as well as an important period in Argentine literary history when Borges' himself was acting as the medium, once more, of the introduction of foreign literary notions. This time, however, in stimulating interest in the detective story, Borges' concern was with narrative prose not lyric poetry, his models were chiefly Anglo-American not Spanish, and his influence was inspiriting not exemplary. All these characteristics are discernable in "The Approach" but since they are playfully refracted there, as in the veiled reference to Argentina's first detective story, we are not likely to realize that Borges, in the words of Donald Alfred Yates, "served as a sort of patron to the detective story" in Argentina;[23] or that in addition to writing reviews of detective novels, commenting on their theory and practice in essays, and keeping readers informed of what the best authors were doing in this line by means of his series "Foreign Books and Authors" in *El Hogar*, Borges was editing the literary supplement of the newspaper *Crítica* and encouraging the production of detective fiction. Alfonso Ferrari Amores has explained:

Even before 1935 some of us were publishing detective stories in the supplement to the daily Crítica. *We were inspired by Jorge Luis Borges, who was familiar with the genre since he could read the world's outstanding specialists in their original language.*[24]

With this background in mind, however, we can see that the form that "The Approach" assumes is the fictional embodiment of Borges' critical and editorial endeavors in the early 1930s.

Narrowing our concern from the detective form in general or a specific resemblance to Chesterton, we can see most easily, at first, why after suggesting the similarity, Borges' narrator rejects it. The customary "detective story mechanism" of the Father Brown stories is not present, and as for doctrinal likeness to Chesterton, there is none. Quite on the contrary, Borges' story propounds a metaphysic that is antagonistic to everything Chesterton and his *raisonneur* stand for:

"You do believe everything. We all believe everything, even when we deny everything. The deniers believe. The unbelievers believe. Don't you feel in your heart that these contradictions do not really contradict: that there is a cosmos that contains them all? The soul goes round upon a wheel of stars and all things return; perhaps Strake and I have striven in many shapes, beast against beast and bird against bird, and perhaps we shall strive for ever. But since we seek each other, even that eternal hatred is eternal love. Good and evil go round in a wheel and that is one thing and not many. Do you not realize in your heart, do you not believe behind all your belief, that there is but one reality and we are its shadows; and that all things are but aspects of one thing: a centre where men melt into Man and Man into God?"

"No," said Father Brown.[25]

All that the villain quoted above says is representative of Borges' metaphysical system as expressed in "The Approach" and elsewhere; but even in his most Chestertonian piece, about which he has said, "I wrote 'Death and the Compass' following Chesterton a bit. It is possible that in adding that detail of the straight line, I was thinking of his story called 'The Horsemen of the Apocalypse',"[26] even in that story, Borges ends on the very note discredited by Father Brown:

"There are excessive lines in your labyrinth," he said finally. "I know of a Greek labyrinth which is a single, straight line. So many philosophers have lost themselves on that line that a mere detective could easily lose himself. Scharlach, when in another incarnation, you hunt me, imagine (or commit) a crime at A, then a second crime at B, 8 kilometers away from A, then a third crime at C, 4 kilometers from A and B, at the midpoint on the road between the two. Afterwards, wait for me at D, 2 kilometers from A and C, again at the midpoint of the road. Kill me at D, as you now are going to kill me at Triste-le-Roy."

> *"As for the next time I kill you,"* Scharlach replied,
> *"I promise you that labyrinth consisting of one straight line
> that is invisible, incessant."* (*F*, 158)

Both writers admit, therefore, a metaphysical concern to their
fiction, but their respective tenets are opposed. In other re-
spects, the approach Borges takes in " The Approach" is still
more fundamentally Chestertonian, in a literary way, than
any kinship of belief could have been. Furthermore, it is in
noting this approach, not peculiar to Chesterton alone but
basic to Poe and all masters of the detective genre whom
Borges admires, that we come closest to seeing what Borges
extracts from these writers.

The basis of the detective formula, and surely the
basis of the formula's attraction for Borges, is an esthetic,
purely formal view of its subject matter. Murder—as De
Quincey wrote, Chesterton and Poe understood after him,
and Borges stressed still later—can be considered as one of
the fine arts; and when it is, the author creates an abstract
intellectual-esthetic problem whose solution is the narrative
we read. One apologist for the detective genre, Marjorie
Hope Nicolson, writing shortly before the period in Borges'
career that we are now considering, emphasized this quality
by way of justifying the form's value:

*As every connoisseur knows, the charm of the pure detective
story lies in its utter unreality. This is a point the untrained
reader does not comprehend. He wonders at our callousness,
at our evident lack of sensitiveness; he cannot understand
how we can wade eagerly through streams of blood, how we
can pursue our man even to the gallows with the detachment
of Dr. Thorndyke himself. He is tortured by visions of blood-
stained rugs; he shudders at the smoking revolver, the knife
still sticking in the wound. "I dreamed all night of people
lying in pools of blood," declared my unsympathetic friend
at breakfast this morning. "How* can *you read those things
and go to sleep at all." And she will never believe me quite*

a human being again because I assured her that after five murders I can put out the light and sleep like a child until morning, the reason being that whereas she has seen, with horrible distinctness, an old man lying in pool of his own blood, I had seen—a diagram.[27]

The detective story in its classic form is, then, an esthetic problem in logic—"a pure analytic exercise" as Dorothy Sayers called it[28]—quite formal and lucid without necessary commitment to its subject matter. And it is precisely this ability to focus on the argument or "diagram" behind the facts that Borges finds everywhere in Chesterton, even in that man's obviously engaged defenses of Christianity:

The certainty that none of Christianity's attractions can really compete with its boundless improbability is so notorious in Chesterton that his most edifying apologies always remind me of "Defense of Insanity" or "Murder as One of the Fine Arts." Now, those paradoxical defenses of indefensible causes call for critical readers convinced of the absurdity of those causes. "Murder Considered as One of the Fine Arts" will not be pleasing to a consistent hard-working murderer. If I should essay a "Vindication of Cannibalism" and demonstrate that it is blameless to eat human flesh since all man's food is, potentially, human flesh, no cannibal would concede even a smile to me, no matter how pleasant he might be. I am afraid something like that happens to sincere Catholics with Chesterton's vast games. I am afraid his stance as a witty defender of lost causes bothers them.[29]

Most of us would not follow Borges in his explanation of what Chesterton does—nor should we—but it is obvious that what he points to in Chesterton is the manner of thinking and writing Borges himself refers to in the preface of *Discussion,* where he declares "his incredulous and persistent affection for theological difficulties" (*D*, 9), and again in the epilogue to *Other Inquisitions,* where he states his tendency "to evaluate religious or philosophical ideas for their esthetic value, and even for what they contain of the unique and marvellous" (*OI*, 259), the manner he exhibits most purely in the indicatively titled "Argumentum ornithologium" (*H*, 17) but also displays in many of his most important essays, like "New Refutation of Time." It is a quality he too finds intrinsic to detective fiction:

*The genuine detective story—shall I be compelled to say it?—rejects with similar disdain physical dangers and distributive justice. With calmness it eliminates prisons, secret stairways, remorse, gymnastics, false beards, duels, the bats of Charles Baudelaire, and even chance. In the first examples of the genre ("The Mystery of Marie Roget," 1842, by Edgar Allan Poe) and in one of the latest (*Unravelled Knots *by Baroness Orczy) the story is limited to the discussion and the abstract resolution of a crime, perhaps at many leagues from the incident or at many years.*[30]

Complementary "discussion" and "abstract resolution," with "abstract" equaling Nicolson's term "unreality," are the essential operations, for Borges, of the detective story; he makes that even clearer when he comes to summarizing Herbert Quain's detective story *The God of the Labyrinth*, a book whose abstract plan closely resembles that of "The Approach":

There is an undecipherable murder in the opening pages, an idling discussion in the intermediate ones, and a solution in the concluding pages. Once a mystery is cleared up, there is a long retrospective paragraph. (*F*, 78-79)

But these operations are also, as we know, the essence of his essays collected in volumes whose titles now take on added meaning: *Inquisitions, Other Inquisitions, Discussion.* Furthermore, these operations are the basis of what I have called the reciprocity of Borges' art, and in this light "The Approach" appears to be the combination of both phases of the reciprocity; it marks, therefore, the beginning of Borges' significant application of the procedures of the essay, which are also those of the detective story, to the literary themes he develops in his narrative. Thus, his interest in detective fiction gave Borges, first of all, not so much a subject for fiction as a way of telling a story, a method of implementing the basic modes of his thought in narrative; or as Yates says of Borges and his fellow practitioners of the form, Bioy Casares and Peyrou: "These writers produced fiction in much the same way as did Poe—using its structure as an external form which conveniently lent itself to the expression of a certain set of ideas or vision."[31] For Borges the detective story became the medium of exchange between the matter and manner of his essays and the management of his fiction, a function amply illustrated by the form and the substance of "The Approach."

At first the identification in Borges' writing of detection with speculation and of argument with fantasy does lead us to make comparisons with Poe—comparisons supported by the brevity of Borges' stories as well as by their metaphysical content, not to mention his long interest in Poe—but the way Borges more specifically develops the analogy that itself projects the formal quality in detective stories, forces us to see another affinity, remotely with De Quincey, deeply with Chesterton.

The analogy, implicitly epitomized in the phrase "murder considered as one of the fine arts," is developed at length in the Father Brown stories. "The Blue Cross," the first of those stories, expresses the theme with epigrammatic clarity: "The criminal is the creative artist; the detective only the critic."[32] Chesterton's balanced sentence imitates the ratio forcefully; but, while for Father Brown the comparison of detective and critic is chiefly a comparison, as in "The Dagger with Wings," where he likens the murderer to a novelist, for Borges the comparison becomes literal statement, so that each work of art, each metaphysical system, each literary career is seen as a conscious creation obeying formal laws defined and discerned by the critical intelligence of the literary detective. In this way he frees himself of the "physical dangers and distributive justice" and opens the way to the largest kind of abstract or "unreal" puzzle making and solving. In "The Approach," for example, the emphasis on detection is displaced from the criminal act to the literary act—the student-murderer is clearly not functioning as much in the role of a detective as is the narrator, who gathers factual evidence at the beginning, states the problematic situation in the second part, examines the problem by precedent and law in the third, and abstractly solves the puzzle in the fourth. Here Borges' shifting of the criminal deed from "real life" to a novel is indicative of his tendency both to view subjects esthetically and to operate on the proportion of *criminal: artist:: detective: critic.* Of course Borges was not alone in seeing this potentiality in the mystery story, and we can turn again to Nicolson's essay for a kindred point of view. By way of justifying her statement that "scholars are, in the end, only detectives of thoughts," she asks:

After all, what essential difference is there between the technique of the detective tracking his quarry through Europe and that of the historian tracking his fact, the philosopher his idea down the ages?[33]

We come full circle, then, from essay as detective story to detective story as essay—a circularity demanded by Borges' esthetic and metaphysical motives. We see, ultimately and paradoxically, that for Borges the "mechanism of the detective story" and the "mechanism" of the essay are identical.

But even when Borges more amply invests the detective process with the narrative form and locates it in "life," the situation assumes a literary nature. In "The Garden of the Forking Paths," for example, the problem that is discussed and resolved, quite abstractly, is the literary one of deciphering a text, and that problem is in turn enclosed in the narrative situation of sending and decoding a verbal message. In "Death and the Compass" the crime is treated by criminal and detective alike as an artifact, and it is revealed as having not only the intellectual rigor we expect in a formal composition but also the cohesive imagery, in this case hieroglyphic: Red Scharlach constructs his pattern of crimes from the chance inspiration—"The first letter of the name has been articulated," a literary inspiration—and he builds his masterpiece carefully by rhyming the recurring rhombs of the walls with the costumes of the harlequins and the windows at Triste-le-Roy.[34] These images of shape and color delineate a structural unity, and their diamond form, reinforced by the numerically significant dates, is a clue to the mystery. Lönnrot is the detective-critic whose mind "functions in the *sense* that the murderer foresees and directs."[35] The process of the story corresponds to the process of Borges' writing—discussion or presentation, and resolution—as well as to fundamental aspects of his mind, as Yates suggested:

But in the final analysis both Scharlach and Lönnrot are of Borges . . . each one is Borges. Borges the intellectual, the philosopher, the erudite fashioner of logical fantasies is Lönnrot. Borges the restless, self-tortured intellect who knows that intellect can reach far beyond the most seemly perfection, Borges the super-intellectual, Borges the perverse is Scharlach.[36]

That Borges had in fact searched for a narrative technique and that he had found inspiration in the Chestertonian detective story can be inferred from two of his essays that deal with the nature of narrative and the code of detective fiction. The first of these, "Narrative Art and Magic" was published in 1932, showing that, before he wrote any notable fiction, Borges was already laying the esthetic foundations of his narrative production; the second, "Labyrinths of the Detective Story and Chesterton" was published in 1935, the same year as "The Approach," further indicating that Borges' fiction developed concurrently with his interest in detective literature. The two essays answer each other, the first being exploratory and analytic, leading to general statements about the proper conduct of narrative, and the second being definitive and dogmatic, culminating in a formulary for the writing of detective stories. Both depend on the stories of Chesterton.

In "Narrative Art and Magic" Borges makes some preliminary deductions by analyzing William Morris' *The Life and Death of Jason*, which he finally characterizes as a basic type of narrative: "the natural, which is the uninterrupted effect of uncontrollable and infinite operations" (*D*, 91). Then he goes on to describe and quote from Poe's *Narrative of A. Gordon Pym*, which leads him to say:

One induces, correctly, from the foregoing that the main problem of the novel is causality. One of the varieties within the genre, the lengthy novel of character, feigns or constructs a concatenation of motives which are proposed as being no different from those of the real world. Its case, nevertheless, is not usual. In the novel of constant vicissitudes, that motivation is inappropriate, just as it is in the short story of only a few pages and in the infinite, spectacular novel that Hollywood composes with the silvery images of Joan Crawford and that the cities re-read. (*D*, 88)

As Borges presents the problem, it is, typically, esthetic–philosophic, the question of causality; and he searches for a logic of fiction that can replace psychological motivation and at the same time be applicable to the mythic, essential literature he contemplates. Borges discovers what he wants, fittingly, in the ancient and supernatural "clarity of magic" (*D*, 88), which he describes as:

the coronation or nightmare of the causal, not its contradiction. The miracle is no less of a stranger in that universe than in the universe of the astronomers. It is ruled by all the natural laws, and still other imaginary ones rule it too. For the superstitious person, there is a necessary connection, not only between a gun shot and a death, but also between a death and a mistreated waxen effigy or the prophetic breaking of a mirror or the salt that is spilled or thirteen terrifying dinner guests.

That dangerous harmony, that frenetic and precise causality, takes charge in the novel as well. . . . That suspicion that a feared event can be brought about by mentioning it, is nonsensical or useless in the Asiatic disorder of the real world, but not so in a novel, which ought to be a precise game of vigilances, echoes and affinities. (D, 89-90)

In his essay Borges refers to Frazer's *Golden Bough* for anthropological support of his theory of magic, but more pertinent and no less convincing for us is a passage in Lévi-Strauss's *The Savage Mind*, where he first says that "magic postulates a complete and all–embracing determinism," and then writes:

One can go further and think of the rigorous precision of the magical thought and the ritual practices as an expression of the unconscious apprehension of the truth of determinism, the mode in which scientific phenomena exist.[37]

Such apprehension, although hardly unconscious, exists in Borges' "magic" narration, in his "lucid, limited narrative," where details are prophetic. In such narratives, it is the formal control of the artist that Borges admires. For him "the only honesty possible" (D, 91) is in the employment of such technique; and he points once more to the "teleology of words and episodes" (D, 90) in the early films of von Sternberg—to *Showdown*, *The Underworld*, *Dishonored*—and for "the most perfect illustration of an autonomous orb of correspondences, omens, monuments" he gives "Joyce's predestined *Ulysses*" (D, 91). But von Sternberg's is another medium, and Joyce's intention is obviously beyond Borges' scope, so the most important reference in the essay—the most important for the development of Borges' own writing—is what he has to say about Chesterton:

Every episode in a painstaking story is projected previously. Thus, in one of Chesterton's phantasmagorias, an unknown person attacks another unknown person so that a truck may not hit him, and that necessary but alarming violence prefigures the final act of declaring him insane so that he may not be executed for the crime. In another story, a dangerous and huge conspiracy comprised of a single man (by means of beards, masks and pseudonyms) is first announced with obscure exactitude in the couplet

> *As all the stars shrivel in the single sun,*
> *The words are many, but The Word is one*

which later comes to be deciphered, by a permutation of the capital letters:

> *The words are many, but the word is One.*

In a third, the initial maquette—*the mere mention of an Indian who hurls his knife at another man and kills him—is the strict reverse of an argument: a man knifed by his friend with an arrow at the top of a tower. Flying knife, arrow gripped in the fist. Words have an extended repercussion. (D, 90)*

"Prefigures," "later comes to be deciphered," "repercussion"—these are the key words here, indicating the magical process Borges is discussing. They betoken a two-part structure—prediction and fulfillment—united by the correspondence of small details. The narrative device they designate is one Borges employs frequently, as in "The Garden of Forking Paths," where what Borges has called "worked-in, inlaid" details[38] are to be seen in that scene where the spy bids goodbye to himself in the mirror (*F*,100) and thus prefigures his own death (we may also recall his shrinking away from the glass in the train window), or in the phonograph record ("disco de gramófono") near "the bronze phoenix" (*F*,

104)—both solid manifestations of cyclical time hinting at the reincarnation of Ts'ui Pen in the form of Albert. Even Albert's name is an "inlaid" detail: "Albert" means "illustrious hero," which fittingly opposes him to the Chinese spy, and "Stephen" further reinforces the noble suffering of that last name by recalling St. Stephen, not merely a martyr but the protomartyr. Then, too, "Stephen" etymologically signifies "wreath" or "crown," another symbolic circular shape that points to Albert's repeating Ts'ui Pen's destiny in having his secret die with him. The figures of the record, the statuette, the name, and, beyond them, "the vivid circle of the lamp" (*F*,107), the halo, around Stephen Albert's face should serve to remind us that the narrative procedure Borges finds esthetically satisfying is one that expresses his metaphysic: cyclical time is evinced in the portentous detail. Hence, it is not simply the internal logic of significant, related imagery Borges makes reference to with his term "magic," but meaningful particulars that explicitly, if somewhat mysteriously, present the essence of his metaphysic. The perfect example of what I mean occurs in the story Borges himself has described as "perhaps my best story" (*F*, 116), "The South."

The bipartite structure of this story was first indicated by Borges himself when he wrote in the prologue to the "Artifices" section of *Ficciones* that "it is possible to read it as straightforward narration of novelistic facts, and also in another way" (*F*, 116); and later elucidated when he told James Irby: "Everything that happens after Dahlmann leaves the sanatorium can be interpreted as an hallucination of his at the moment of dying from septicemia, as a fantastic vision of how he would have wanted to die."[39] The two readings are not therefore the result of superimposed levels as might be imagined at first, but the response to two halves of the story arranged in a spatial and chronological sequence. The first half foretells the later half, and the two are united by a series of prognosticating details. To give just one example: in the first part of the story, Dahlmann is struck in the head by the edge of the door as he rushes up a flight of stairs, and then, in the hospital, suffering from this wound, "a man stabbed a needle into his arm" (*F,*189); in the second half, Dahlmann is hit in the head with a "pellet of dough" (*F*, 194) and finally leaves the general store to be stabbed by his opponent, to be freed from the hallucination of this life just as there had been "a liberation for him, in the first night at the sanatorium when they stabbed him with the needle" (*F,*195).[40]

What "Narrative Art and Magic" demands, then, and what "The South" provides, is a narrative based on a reasonable relationship of cause and effect embodied in a closely worked web of significant detail; what it clarifies and, to an extent, even predicts is Borges' exploitation of the detective formula in constructions ostensibly unlike Chesterton's murder story: in narratives such as "The South," whose form and meaning are revealed in concatenate clues, and in essays, such as "Circular Time," which meaningfully link writers and ideas by searching out antecedents and parallels. Looking at the essays in this way, we see that allusion, in both story *and* essay, is frequently a function of "magic" correlation. The epigraph tersely indicated at the beginning of "The Intruder" and the passages alluded to in "Kafka and His Precursors," to take basic examples from fiction and essay, present the two-part pattern we have discerned: the biblical paradigm foretelling the national mythos in the first case, the neoteric writer actualizing older authors in the second. In both instances, Borges' work establishes a repetition that, as we have come to know, denies succession or time. The justification for Borges' use of this allusive instrument is expressed with axiomatic clarity by the narrator of "The Library of Babel" in another of those revelatory passages: "To speak is to involve oneself in tautologies" (*F*, 94); and the intended effect of this device is also discovered by that narrator: "The certainty that everything has been written annuls us or makes phantoms of us" (*F*, 94). Literary history, like human experience, is thus seen to operate on the same principle, manifested by symmetrical circumstances in the one case, by antiphonal allusions in the other. Sometimes Borges goes so far as to suggest the future, as in "Death and the Compass" and "The Dream of Coleridge," but usually his prose fulfills the function of "prophetic memory" (*OP*, 251)—to borrow one of his own phrases—a phrase that suggests a union of simultaneous forward- and backward-directed activity in a synthetic present, a complex movement that he accomplishes most often by means of literary allusion.

The classic detective story, which complies with Borges' necessary logic of verbal magic, and more particularly the Chestertonian kind of detective story that resembles Poe's *Narrative of A. Gordon Pym* in having both a superficial and a hidden argument, is clearly suggested by "Narrative Art and Magic." Science fiction might have been another possibility, but the causal pattern of prophetic proposition and echoing, complementary resolution is not essential to that genre, and we see that this pattern becomes fundamental in Borges. One illustration is the clearly discerptible story "The South." And another is the late poetry in which Borges cultivates the sonnet. We often hear that Borges' predilection for the sonnet is based on its brevity, on its memorability (since he cannot write poems down because of his blindness); but the sonnet, as María Esther Vázquez reminds us, also provides Borges with the familiar logical formula:

A sonnet has two parts. Borges likes to to repeat: the first part or proposition, which is made up of two quatrains, and the second or resolution, which is comprised of two tercets, where the initial movement is completed, either badly or well.[41]

On the other hand, Borges did not implement the theory of fiction presented by "Narrative Art and Magic" in recognizable detective format until the early 1940s; but, in the meantime he wrote "Labyrinths of the Detective Story and Chesterton," which made possible the execution of the type of fiction adumbrated in the earlier essay by assimilating the "magic" necessity into the rigorously logical apparatus of Chesterton's type of story.

In "Labyrinths of the Detective Story and Chesterton" Borges formulated the implicit rules of the detective story from the example, once again, of Chesterton; however, he was also anticipating the devices of his own fiction, enunciating a fictional credo comparable to his earlier poetic one. He separated the kind of fiction he had in mind—the kind he would write—from the literature based on character or psychology.

The detective story of some length borders on the novel of character or the psychological novel. . . . The nature of the brief story is problematic, tight.(D, 93)

And then he offered six precepts for the management of such fiction, precepts deduced from Chesterton's latest volume, *The Scandal of Father Brown.* Borges' primary distinction, quoted above, and his six-part codification— "a) discretionary limit of six characters; b) declaration of all the terms of the problem; c) avaricious economy of means; d) primacy of the 'how' over the 'who'; e) decorum in treatment of death; f) necessity and amazement in the solution"—take us back, first to "Narrative Art and Magic" and then to his Ultraistic dictates. In the process we see anew the fundamental coherency in Borges' thinking.

Two of Borges' precepts develop from what I previously called his esthetic of compression: "Discretionary limit of six characters"; "avaricious economy of means." And in commenting on the latter, Borges says: "The final discovery that two people in the plot are one can be pleasurable" (*D*, 94), which recalls the conclusion of "The Shape of the Sword" and the premise of "Theme of the Traitor and the Hero" as well as reminding us of "the insignificance of personality." Thus Borges reaffirms the association of literary economy and an emphasis on transpersonal experience, a stress deepened by the fourth of his rules: "primacy of the 'how' over the 'who.'" Marjorie Hope Nicolson had already spoken for the professional intellectuals in hailing the detective genre as:

a return to the novel of plot and incident—that genre despised these many years by littérateurs. *The appeal of the detective story lies in its action, its episodes. . . . Character— so worshipped by the psychological novelists—troubles us little, though characters we have in abundance. Characters addicted to dependence upon the subconscious or upon the glands need not apply; men and women need all their conscious wits about them in the detective yarn. One brooding moment, one pluperfect tense, one conditional mode, may be fatal. We grant that our characters are largely puppets, and we are delighted once more to see the marionettes dance while a strong and adept hand pulls the strings cleverly. Our real interest is not in the puppets, but in the brain which designed them.*[42]

And Borges, too, had seen in the manipulation of plot according to an ineluctable logic, yielding, nevertheless, a surprising conclusion—"Necessity and amazement in the solution"—a means for escaping from psychology, from individualism, to something more formal and impersonal. In his treating subjects esthetically, in his dependence on a rational process in his fiction, in his use of vatic details, Borges testifies to the similarity between his fiction and that of Chesterton, and at the same time classifies himself as part of that "escape" of which Nicolson wrote:

Yes, the detective story does constitute escape; but it is escape not from life, but from literature. We grant willingly that we find in it release. Our revolt—so mysteriously explained by the psychologists—is simple enough: we have revolted from an excessive subjectivity to welcome objectivity; from long-drawn out dissections of emotion to straight-

*forward appeal to intellect; from reiterated emphasis upon
men and women as victims either of circumstances or of their
glands to a suggestion that men and women may consciously
plot and consciously plan; from the "stream of consciousness" which threatens to engulf us in its Lethean monotony
to analyses of purpose, controlled and directed by a thinking mind; from formlessness to form, from the sophomoric
to the mature; most of all, from a smart and easy pessimism
which interprets men and the universe in terms of unmoral
purposelessness to a rebelief in a universe governed by cause
and effect. All this we find in the detective story.*[43]

On the other hand, but by the same token, Borges seems to
anticipate the experimental fiction of such writers as Robbe-
Grillet who flee from a novel of characters, a novel of transcription, to one of construction, of internal necessity, recognizing all the while, along with Swift, that "nothing is
more fantastic, ultimately, than precision."[44] If such a comparison makes us see Borges in something of a new light, as
a prophetic innovator in the world of fiction, it inevitably
forces us, precisely because of the literary genealogy he has
drawn up, to see Chesterton, and consequently both Poe and
De Quincey, in something of a new light: it necessitates a
reevaluation of the detective story's force in the twentieth
century and justifies Borges' wholehearted participation in
that genre.

 Starting from the hint in "The Approach," we come
to see that Chesterton is important to Borges in providing
exemplary fiction from which Borges deduces his principles
and against which he justifies his practice; and setting aside
for the moment other possible influences of Chesterton on
Borges' work, we can see that at an early stage Chesterton
furnished an esthetic disposition, a fundamental metaphor,
a necessary logic, and a minimal esthetic. To be more precise: the disposition to view subjects analytically, esthetically; the metaphor of the criminal as artist, the detective as
critic; the logic of deterministic word and event, that is, of

"magic" causality; the minimal esthetic of the detective story. What we are left with, finally, is the understanding that the similarity to Chesterton, as it is presented in "The Approach," is indeed quite as inappropriate as we are told, but that the relationship that it directs us to is fundamental, an understanding equivalent to the one supplied by our analysis of the "detective-story mechanism" in "The Approach": though the essay-story is not inherently a detective story, for Borges the forms become one. If we couple the detective process as we have come to comprehend it in Borges with that erudite subject matter we have seen revealed in his early fiction, then we can properly call the author of "The Approach" the scholar detective. In relation to Borges the word "scholar" does not point to his profession, but to the temper of his mind and to the single most important source of his subject matter—his library, which includes, among other volumes, the entire collection of the Biblioteca Nacional of Buenos Aires. This extraordinary reflection causes us to recall that his greatest inquiries, somewhat paralleling the narrator's in "The Library of Babel," have been in that universal library through which he winds his way, an indefatigable investigator of evidence both hypothetical and circumstantial, a plotter and solver of the single mystery that is his subject.

Notes

1. *"Encuentro con Borges,"* appendix to "The Structure of the Stories of Jorge Luis Borges" (University of Michigan, 1962) 313.
2. *Paris Review* (Winter-Spring 1967): 124. Reprinted at the end of this volume.
3. *Borges the Labyrinth Maker*, 14, 15.
4. Op. cit., 14.
5. *"Nueva contribución al estudio de las fuentes de Borges," Filogía* VII (1962, pub. 1964): 7-13.
6. *L'Herne*: 11. Señora Borges could not have read from *The Martian Chronicles* or any part of them, because the *Chronicles* did not begin to appear until 1945, and Bradbury has stated that he was "unsold as

a writer" at the time of Borges' illness (letter to author, dated September 14, 1965). Señora Borges explained that the editors of *L'Herne* "made a mistake with author and title, perhaps, because the theme was Martian people" (letter to author dated September 2, 1965). Whatever the explanation, the confusion, which in relation to almost any other writer's work would appear a simple error, here seems to show life imitating art—perhaps even a contrived example.

7. *"Borges: teoría y práctica," Número* VI, 27 (December 1955): 124.

8. Jorge Luis Borges, *Other Inquisitions*, trans. Ruth L. C. Simms, intro. by James Irby (Austin: University of Texas Press, 1964), ix.

9. September 18, 1934. Reprinted under title "Inscriptions," *Destiempo* I, 1 (October 1936): 3.

10. *Paris Review,* 160.

11. Op. cit., 40.

12. *Paradox in Chesterton*, 68.

13. *La literatura fantástica en Argentina*, 38.

14. Prologue to Emerson's *Representative Men* (Buenos Aires, 1949), xiii.

15. *Paris Review*, 62.

16. Angel Flores, "Magical Realism in Spanish American Fiction," *Hispania* XXXVIII, 2 (May 1955): 187-92.

17. Susan Sontag, *The Benefactor* (New York: Farrar Straus & Giroux, 1963), l.

18. Originally, on the basis of an identical name I had found in a card catalogue, I listed Watson as a nearly forgotten writer too; but Evelyn Fishburn and Psiche Hughes, authors of the useful *A Dictionary of Borges* (London: Duckworth, 1990), noticed my error by way of a scholarly inquiry.

19. Ana María Barrenechea, *La expresión de la irrealidad en la obra de Jorge Luis Borges*, 54.

20. *Borges, enigma y clave*, 18.

21. Ibid.

22. Ana María Barrenechea, *La literatura fatástica en Argentina*, 54.

23. Donald Alfred Yates, "The Argentine Detective Story," unpublished dissertation (University of Michigan, 1960), 26.

24. Op. cit., 17.

25. G. K. Chesterton, "The Dagger with Wings," *The Father Brown Stories* (London, 1963), 418.

26. James Irby, *"Encuentro con Borges,"* 309.

27. Marjorie Hope Nicolson, "The Professor and the Detective," *The Art of the Mystery Story*, ed. Howard Haycraft (New York, 1947), 117-18.

28. Dorothy L. Sayers, "The Omnibus of Crime, *The Art of the Mystery Story*, 101.

29. Jorge Luis Borges, *"Modos de G. K. Chesterton," SUR* 10 (July 1935): 92.

30. Jorge Luis Borges, "*Los laberintos policiales y Chesterton,*" *SUR* 22 (July 1935): 92.

31. Yates, "The Argentine Detective Story," 82.

32. Chesterton, *The Father Brown Stories,* 12.

33. Nicolson, "The Professor and the Detective," 125.

34. The rhombic shapes and particularly the rhomic, multicolored windows are a recurring image in Borges' writing, and they are usually traced to real windows in Borges' life, windows he saw as a child or as an adult in Buenos Aires architecture. (For an example of the latter tracing, see María Esther Vázquez's essay "Everness.") But it is appropriate to find a reinforcing literary precedent for this lozenge pattern, and I offer the following from Sir Thomas Browne's "The Garden of Cyrus, or the Quincuncial, Lozenge, or Net-work Plantations of the Ancients, Artificially, Naturally, Mystically Considered," *Religio Medici and Other Writings,* 202:

> *And, beside this kind of work in Retiarie and hanging textures, in embroideries, and eminent needle-works; the like is obvious unto every eye in glass windows. Nor only in Glass contrivances, but also in Lattice and Stone work, conceived in the Temple of Solomon; wherein the windows are termed* fenestrae reticulatae, *or lights framed like nets.*

Besides Borges' love of Browne's prose, an obvious advantage of tracing the windows to this source is that Browne makes a labyrinth (net) of the lozenges. (The whole essay as well as the whole of Browne is pertinent to Borges, though my study makes relatively few comparisons in that direction.)

35. Tamayo and Ruiz-Díaz, *Borges, enigma y clave,* 34.

36. Yates, "The Argentine Detective Story," 152.

37. Claude Lévi-Strauss, *The Savage Mind* (Chicago, 1946), 11.

38. Irby, "*Encuentro con Borges,*" 305.

39. Op. cit., 310.

40. Alexander Coleman pointed out to me that the stabbing is "a doubling back or refraction of a famous moment in Argentine literature": the chapter in *Don Segundo Sombra* "where an innocent is goaded into a knife fight in a cheap bar by the so-called hero, Don Segundo, who reappears in Borges' 'El Sur' as '*el viejo gaucho extático*' [the old esctatic gaucho]."

Following Coleman's lead, one can find many Borgesian elements in Güiraldes (many Güiraldesean elements in Borges), including labyrinths, limitless nights, nightmares, and vertigo. There also may be another descendent from this novel in Borges: early in *Don Segundo Sombra* we learn that the half-breed named Burgos sold his twelve-year-old daughter to a whoremaster for twenty pesos; surely this girl is reflected in the silent Juliana Burgos of "The Intruder," who was also sold to a madam of a brothel.

41. María Esther Vázques, *"Everness"* (Buenos Aires, 1965): 15.
42. Nicolson, "The Professor and the Detective," 116.
43. Op. cit., 113-114.
44. Alain Robbe-Grillet, *For a New Novel: Essays on Fiction*, trans. Richard Howard (New York, 1965), 22, 162, 165.

THE LITERARY FIGURE

Categories

The importance of Chesterton to Borges' fiction, even under the limited aspect in which I have presented it, suggests
the necessity of considering in some larger way Borges' use
of other writers as a means to establishing ourselves in the
broadest context of his allusions. I say "use of other authors"
rather than "influence on him" because that is the most meaningful way to consider the topic in Borges' work, where we
should not only remember Gide's dictum that "*L'influence
ne crée pas, elle éveille*,"[1] but add to it the implicit disclosure of "Kafka and His Precursors," namely, that Borges'
writing aims at creating in us an awareness of his sources,
or *fuentes*. For these reasons, we should distinguish two categories of authors: those whom we principally think of as
stimulating Borges' productivity and those his stories cause
us to reconsider. Naturally, the two categories cannot be
entirely separated, and the second inevitably will be more
important in relation to the allusiveness of Borges' writing;
but we may postulate the following subdivisions that lead us
from the first into the second group: the period of the late
nineteenth and early twentieth century; the class of factual
and informative writing; and the type of the literary figure.
These demarcations rest on fundamental distinctions I made
previously, and they are not offered as an index to Borges'
sources but as a flexible guide to an understanding of his
allusive technique.

PREMODERN The first two subdivisions are really a matter of emphasis—the reader's and Borges'. I have already
proposed the consequence of what Borges read as a child, but
now I want to lay stress on the fact that literature from the
period just before his birth and through the years of his early
manhood—dominated by the triumvirate of Stevenson,
Chesterton, and Wells—constitutes the bedrock of his ac-
quaintanceship with English literature. The writers named

typify the uncommon quality of Borges' particular interests. For Borges the case is, in fact, comprehensible enough: he was responding to famous authors who were still writing at the time, or to writers like Stevenson, who were still current; and he was reacting as they had, naturally, against the dominant form of the spacious, social, and psychological novel exemplified in English by *Middlemarch*. His dependency, clearly, is on the writers who first mattered to him; but to the Anglo-American reader the situation is not so evident: we first come upon Borges as an unmistakably new, modern writer—even though the best of his work is already decades old—and yet we find him deeply involved with writers who for us are largely dead or only partially resurrected: William Morris and Herbert Spencer, for example, or even Chesterton and Stevenson. For us there is something distinctly nineteenth century, something quaintly old fashioned in his reading preferences; and it might well have seemed so even to his youthful contemporaries. Moreover, the writers he favored served to open up even more unusual areas of literary exploration; for example, Borges discovered Teutonic literature by means of Morris' sagas. That Borges has ranged far from the writers of this period and their concerns is obviously true, but we can find the beginnings of almost all his literary wandering in his favorite writings from this period, and to it we must inevitably return for a basic understanding of what he attempts. A striking case in point is Borges' preoccupation with Old Norse and Anglo-Saxon literature, a major concern of his starting in the late 1950s and one that accordingly isolated him even further from most current literature. Did that preoccupation not originate much earlier in his reading of *Song of the Volsungs*, and is not his best-known late story, "The Intruder," an effort to do in his own way and with his own material what Morris did with the Norse? The point is worth noting because it shows Borges, as ever, true to his own past both as he lived it and as he constructed it; moreover, the awareness serves to rectify or at least modify our natural tendency to consider him in relation to strictly contemporary writers. There is more to be learned by weighing Chesterton's (or even Browning's) importance to Borges than in pursuing the comparison implicit in the Prix Formentor awarded to Borges and Beckett simultaneously. In fact, it would be more appropriate, despite the tardiness of their composition—a delay explained in part by the considerations of previous chapters in this study—to set Beckett aside and think of Borges' stories as the idiosyncratic but contemporaneous production of the intermediate generation, of Joyce's *Ulysses*, and of Eliot's *Waste Land*, than as the product of the 1960s, which they must seem to many readers in English-speaking countries who know them only in their relatively recent translations. This backward thrust is not at all unfair or deprecating to Borges' production, which has aimed at the eternal and has followed a course of turning upon itself, so that his most recent compositions in prose and poetry are, ironically, more nearly the perfected achievements of his earliest efforts than are his most successful stories of the 1940s and 1950s.

INFORMATIVE WRITING Premodern also defines Borges preferences in the factual and informative writings that provide the skeleton and erudite flesh for many of his works from *Universal History of Infamy*. He has admitted his love of reading encyclopedias and confirmed that it is the older ones—the tenth, eleventh, and twelfth editions of the *Encyclopaedia Britannica*, for example—that he has preferred, ever since he was too timid as a young man to ask for a book in the Biblioteca Nacional and would take a volume of the *Britannica* from the shelf and read the entries on various writers and religions. Since then his reading of such books has not slackened, as we can easily see from his statement in a review of still another "nonliterary" book, *Mathematics and Imagination*:

Looking over the library again, I see with awe that the works I have re-read most and overwhelmed with marginalia are

Mauthner's Dictionary of Philosophy, *Lewes's* Biographical History of Philosophy, *Liddell Hart's* History of the World War, 1914-1918, *Boswell's* Life of Samuel Johnson *and the psychology of Gustave Spiller:* The Mind of Man *(1902). (D,* 165)

Or, just as easily, we can turn to his fiction, where "Tlön, Uqbar, Orbis Tertius," itself the miniature encyclopedia of an imaginary world, memorializes Borges' discovery of the marvelous in the factual:

I owe the discovery of Uqbar to the conjunction of a mirror and an encyclopedia. The mirror disturbed the end of a corridor in a villa on Gaona Street in Ramos-Mejía; the encyclopedia is deceptively entitled The Anglo-American Cyclopedia *(New York, 1917) and is a literal as well as outdated reprinting of the* Encyclopaedia Britannica *of 1902. (F,* 13)

Or we may recall the opening of "The Garden of the Forking Paths," which shows Borges operating out of an historical background, grafting his fiction, once again, on the stock of fact:

On page twenty-two of Liddell Hart's History of the European War, *we read that an offensive of thirteen British divisions . . . against the Serre-Montauban line had been planned for the twenty-fourth of July in 1916, and had to be postponed until the morning of the twenty-ninth. (F,* 97)

In "The Garden of the Forking Paths" Borges uses an historical work for his point of departure; in "Tlön, Uqbar, Orbis Tertius" he acknowledges his debt to the encyclopedia with facetious formality; but even in his poetry, where he renounces footnotes, Borges shows how his work does grow from scholarly explorations. His poem "The Golem," for example, contains the lines:

> *Scholem relates these truths*
> *In a learned place in his book. (OP, 170)*

The reference is to Gershom G. Scholem's *Major Trends in Jewish Mysticism*, first issued in New York in 1941, the year before Borges published "Death and the Compass." In that story two names stand out: Yarmolinsky and Ginzberg. Borges admits that the first fascinates him for its sound alone, and he may have encountered it in a library, for Abraham Yarmolinsky is the author of a book entitled *The Wandering Jew* and Avraham Yarmolinsky is a noted student of Russian literature. Ginzberg, which in the story is an assumed name of the murderer who tricks the detective by means of an elaborate web of clues depending upon Hebraic learning, is a name referred to by Scholem. In *Major Trends in Jewish Mysticism* Louis Ginzberg, a Hebraic scholar who wrote a seven-volume work called *The Legends of the Jews* (Philadelphia, 1909-1938), is frequently cited.[2] But then Borges could have gotten the name, along with the story of the Golem, from another book he read, namely Trachtenberg's *Jewish Magic and Superstition*, which appeared in 1939.[3] Apparently we have a case where the focal event of one poem and the detail of a character's name in another story are derived from a work or works of no literary pretensions, works, in fact, of proper scholarly anonymity. The instance, in both its larger and smaller dimensions, is typical and reminds us of the pervasive bookishness of Borges' production. In this particular category of reference, however, we should remember that the individual facts—the borrowing of a name or episode from Scholem or Trachtenberg—are matter only for our curiosity; such awareness on our part cannot change our responses to the poem or story or alter our appreciation of Borges' work except to reaffirm our understanding of him as a learned, deeply read man who conducted his researches on the alert for the odd or fantastic, whether it be the occurrence of a female pirate, an artificial man, or a striking name. In reference works as in metaphysics and theology he is looking for the esthetic, the shock of the beautiful and strange. The important thing, then, is to note the high incidence of inspiration and information Borges extracts from such unlikely books, remembering that in general the sources themselves are valueless in relation to his work except as sources, and that they add nothing to our comprehension of Borges' writing and only little to our knowledge of the man.

THE LITERARY FIGURE In contrast, to such instances of referential allusion is the type of the literary figure, that abstraction whose names are many but whose nature is constant:

For many years, I believed that the almost infinite body of literature was in one man. That man was Carlyle, was Johannes Becher, was Whitman, was Rafael Cansinos Asséns, was De Quincey. (OI, 23)

For Borges, a classicist by his own definition, authors are Author (just as characters or men are Man), and their works are single and repeated (like Time). For Borges, as for the citizens of Tlön, "the notion of plagiarism does not exist: it has been established that all works are the work of one author who is atemporal and anonymous" (*F*, 27). For Borges, as for Emerson, belief in a literary over-soul is possible:

I am very much struck in literature by the appearance that one person wrote all the books; . . . there is such equality and identity, both of judgment and point of view, in the narrator that it is plainly the work of one all-seeing, all-hearing gentleman.[4]

Therefore Borges searches out those congruences of expression and thought that point to this archetypal identity and works them into his fiction, analyzes them in his essays:

The Pantheist who declares that the plurality of authors is illusory finds unexpected support in the Classicist, according to whom the plurality matters very little. For classical minds, literature is the essential thing, not individuals. George Moore and James Joyce have incorporated pages and opinions from other authors in their works; Oscar Wilde used to donate arguments so that others would execute them—both procedures, although superficially contrary, may evidence the same sense of art. An ecumenical, impersonal sense. . . . Another witness to the profound unity of the Word and a denier of the limits of the subjective was the illustrious Ben Jonson, who having engaged himself in the task of formulating his literary testament and the favorable or adverse opinions that his contemporaries deserved, confined himself to assembling fragments from Seneca, Quintilian, Justo Lipsio, Vives, Erasmus, Machiavelli, Bacon, and the two Scaligers. (OI, 22-23)

What seems startling and peculiarly Borgesian in this passage from an essay published in 1945[5] takes on a suitably traditional appearance when we align it with the following excerpt from an essay written in 1919 by another classically minded author, who tells us that the poet

must be aware that the mind of Europe—the mind of his own country—a mind which he learns in time to be much more important than his own private mind—is a mind which changes, and that this change is a development which abandons nothing en route, which does not superannuate either Shakespeare, or Homer, or the rock drawing of Magdalenian draughtsmen . . .

and that

what is to be insisted upon is that the poet must develop or procure the consciousness of the past and that he should continue to develop this consciousness throughout his career.

> *What happens is a continual surrender of himself as he is at the moment to something which is more valuable. The progress of an artist is a continual self-sacrifice, a continual extinction of personality.*[6]

To be sure, T. S. Eliot is not so eager as Borges to identify a notion of literature (classical, traditional) with a metaphysic (pantheistic); but Eliot does recognize the kinship, and in doing so establishes the context of Borges' subsequent statement. Eliot actually writes:

> *The point of view which I am struggling to attack is perhaps related to the metaphysical theory of the substantial unity of the soul: for my meaning is, that the poet has, not a "personality" to express but a particular medium, which is only a medium and not a personality, in which impressions and experiences combine in peculiar and unexpected ways.*[7]

Eliot is legislating what ought to be ("The poet must . . . ") and Borges is describing what he thinks the situation really may be; both offer explanations and satisfactions for their own methods. Or, to put it another way, we can say that what Eliot's "tradition" is to his "individual talent," Borges' "Verbo" is to his "autor." And we can add to that the following proposition: as Eliot's allusions and appropriations embody the tradition that Eliot commends and demonstrate the classicism that Borges describes, so do both their allusions indicate "the profound unity of the Word." For this reason, when we consider Borges' reference to the type of the literary figure either as the paradigmatic *Hacedor* whom Borges calls God or as any of the archetypally mimetic dreamers like Shaw or De Quincey, we are at the intersection of "the insignificance of personality" and "circular time" in a point of allusion: we are concerned with what Eliot calls "the present moment of the past,"[8] and we are dealing no longer with influence, reference, information or anything of that sort but, rather, with meaning.

The literary figure is not always abstract in Borges' fiction, just as tradition is not always general in Eliot's poetry. In *The Waste Land* we read phrases and thoughts—at times annoyingly precise in view of our ignorance—that impale and specify generality, phrases obviously meant to do just that; in Borges we find, more often than not, the name of an author, sometimes in conjunction with the title of his work, which is used as a definite example in a universal series. As we read through Borges' works, certain of these names (and works, like the *Arabian Nights*) recur with marked frequency. What is more, the most frequently repeated of these names, as I noted in another connection, do not include the typical ones—typical, that is, if we are looking for the essential or even the predictable in a canonical tradition of literature. Now Eliot's allusions have a good deal that is eccentric about them too, and may even lead us away from the individual importance of the writer. In Eliot's poetry there seems to be no intention in referring to any particular writer's work beyond the specific appropriateness of the passage in question, which is to say that, if we collect his allusions to Shakespeare or to Lancelot Andrewes, we will not be able to decipher a pattern of meaning. In Borges' writing, on the contrary, the repetitive references—and this very sense of repetitiveness is lacking in Eliot—force upon us an awareness of writers as exemplars, while the choices Borges makes among writers and then—finer distinction still—among portions of their work, suggest the possibility of our constructing the archetypal writer inductively. The effort, however, is unnecessary since, as always in the case of Borges, the key is already in the lock: the early essays tell us what we need to know.

The Borgesian literary archetype—that figure whose mythic reality is found in the mirrors of his nature: Shakespeare, De Quincey, Borges—is defined in an essay from the 1920s on Sir Thomas Browne, where a single word, by implying a repetition and therefore a state of atemporality and unity of personality, insinuates the archetypal into a discussion of individuals. The word is "prefigured":

The literary man and the mystic are united in Sir Thomas Browne: the vates *and the* gramaticus *to express it with Latin solidity. The type of the literary man—prefigured by Ben Jonson, in whom converged all the signs of his kind: the striving for glory, the reverence for and preoccupation with language, the prolix weaving of theories in order to justify the work, the man aware of himself as the embodiment of an epoch, the study of languages, and even the leadership of a literary circle and the organization of factions—is manifest in him. The beauty of his work is learned and consummate.* (*I*, 32)

With only the adjustment of "prolix," the passage describes, first of all, Borges himself and then the writers he admires; or, really, what he admires most in the writers he admires. It is the epitome of the literary figure, both as Borges imagined that figure and as he has tried himself to approximate it. The leading concerns of Borges' life—literature, learning, metaphysics—are here ascribed to Browne, but we can go a step further by seeing that as Jonson prefigured Browne, so Browne prefigures Borges; and therefore that it is exactly the triunity of roles—*gramaticus, vates, poeta doctus*—that defines the literary figure for Borges, whether that man be called Sir Thomas Browne, Pierre Menard, Herbert Quain, Paul Valéry, or Jorge Luis Borges. Writers evincing a predilection for any one of these three roles always interest him; writers combining all three stimulate him most and are what we would ordinarily call "influences" on him. For my purpose it is enough to see that this last group provides the largest source of all his allusions.

Gramaticus. All the qualities of the *gramaticus* have been Borges' at one time or another, and his writings uncover the same traits in others. As a young man, already expert in several languages, he led the Ultraists; and as for a concern with language, that has been Borges' since his earliest days; but since none of his early essays, which are largely concerned with style and idiom, has been translated into English, and since Borges has even suppressed them in the Spanish edition of his works, this aspect of his early "reverence for and preoccupation with language" has received little attention here. We thus see him as a writer fully in charge of an odd but finished style, never witnessing his struggles with dialect, phonetic spelling, and compound words, which are marks of the *gramaticus* in him. Yet his book *The Language of Buenos Aires*,[9] published first in 1952 and revised and reissued in 1963, testifies to his continuing attention to fundamental problems of expression. This attention accounts for his imagining of a Berkeleyan language, complete with Swiftian nonsense words like "hlor u fang axaxaxas mlo" in "Tlön, Uqbar, Orbis Tertius" (*F*, 21), which he later ironically cites as a book titled *Axaxaxas mlo* in "The Library of Babel" (*F*, 93-9), as well as for his inquiries into the nearly forgotten Bishop Wilkins' universal language in "The Analytic Language of John Wilkins" (*OI*, 139-44). But the essay on Wilkins suggests a significant distinction: we are implicitly reminded of the difference between narrower and broader responses to language, between those (like Wilkins) who are devoted only to words and those (like Borges) who are concerned as well with the reality words classify. The distinction is made clear by De Quincey, in whom Borges may have found the repeated encouragement for use of the term *gramaticus*:

gramatici, *as I have explained some scores of times, did not express so limited a notion as that of* grammarians, *but was the orthodox mode of indicating classically those whom the French call* littérateurs, *and we English less compactly call men of letters.*[10]

Wilkins is not a *literato*, a "man of letters," so that Borges is not concerned with Wilkins' style as the extension of his grammatical preoccupations, but while Borges has gradually developed his own mode of lucid writing and es-

teemed it in others, he has never lost his admiration for or
interest in writers who employ elaborate forms of expression.
In fact, we might guess that as a writer's style becomes substantially richer, as he comes to consider language an organ
to be played with all the stops out, the greater is Borges' interest; or, to shift the metaphor, we may say that Borges,
himself writing chamber music, is still a lover of opera and
symphonies. Certainly the list of his favored writers includes
some of the richest, most self-conscious stylists known: Sir
Thomas Browne, Jeremy Taylor, De Quincey, and in a somewhat different mode, Chesterton and Stevenson. So great,
both as a personal commitment and a studied belief, is
Borges' devotion to the writer as stylist that it can lead him
to ignore almost everything else in an author's work. As he
can treat philosophy and theology esthetically, so Borges can
see literature purely as effort toward or achievement of style.
It is usually Stevenson's *prose* that he praises; and setting
aside the bullying, tendentious, sectarian Christianity of
Chesterton—the aspect that attracts a few readers and repels
most—Borges usually focuses on Chesterton's manipulation
of language and metaphor, singling out a baroque element
in his writing. The focus is uncommon and salutary for most
of us, but surely, in the end, it tells us more of Borges' interest in style than it does of Chesterton's achievement as a
writer.

The second basic aspect of the writer as *gramaticus*
that appeals to Borges and corresponds to his own literary
character is the poet or novelist in the role of critic or theoretician whose work is "the prolix weaving of theories in
order to justify the work" (*I*, 32). "To think, to analyze, to
invent . . . are not anomalous acts; they are the normal res-
piration of the intellect" (*F*, 56), wrote Pierre Menard, describing admirably the flux and reflux, the inspiration and ex-
halation, in the mind of Borges and the writers he values. The
full display of an intelligence expressing and reflecting upon
itself in creative, speculative, and critical modes—the spectacle of a mind in the roles of author, thinker, reader—obviously fascinates Borges and many of his citations in essays

and epigrams come from the theoretical or critical portions of such authors. Given this preference, we see why the writers in whom Borges has the most lasting interest tend to be, like himself, *literatos*, men of letters in the fullest, even most professional sense. Chesterton, once again, is a good example, as are Wells, Stevenson, Emerson, Shaw, De Quincey—all lovers of words, poets, or storytellers, weavers of theories: all manifestations of the writers as *gramaticus*.

Vates. Looking over the list of Borges' favorite English authors, one would hardly call them mystics; yet it is the power and nature of Borges' art to find the mystical element in these writers and make us see it too. What he means by *místico* or *vates* is the writer who looks through the solidness of our reality and reveals another world and perhaps a secret scheme or logic that controls our world. Emerson is clearly such a writer; his transcendentalism is explicitly vatic in the Borgesian sense; more surprisingly, both Shakespeare and H. G. Wells, in the way Borges presents them, are also types of the *vates*.

That Borges sees Wells not as a great writer (*gramaticus*) yet still as an irreplaceable author because fantastic seer (*vates*) is the explicit judgment of his encomium in "The First Wells":

Like Quevedo, like Voltaire, like Goethe, like many another, Wells is less a man of letters, than a literature. . . . From the vast and diverse library he left us, nothing pleases me more than his narration of some atrocious miracles: The Time Machine, The Island of Dr. Moreau, The Plattner Story, The First Men in the Moon. *They are the first books I read; perhaps they will be the last. . . . I think that they shall be incorporated, like the formula of Theseus or of Ahasuerus, into the general memory of the human species, and that they will multiply themselves within their realm beyond the boundaries of fame of the one who wrote them, beyond the death of the language in which they were written.* (*OI*, 128)

The portion of Wells most important to Borges is the fiction based on the confrontation of two worlds, a confrontation that reveals a new order of reality. In this respect, Borges urges us to the awareness that *The War of the Worlds* is not merely a title of one Wells novel, but the fundamental pattern of Wells' perception. What would seem to underscore Wells' vatic quality is that many of these confrontations take place in a time that is the possible present or near future; but the real vatic quality in Wells is precisely the disposition of reality and circumstances along fantastic new lines. Read the following passage from a Wells novel in which the narrator, Sarnac, dreams a past life where he was another man, one Mortimer Smith:

"It was a life," said Sarnac, "and it was a dream, a dream within this life; and this life too is a dream. Dreams within dreams, dreams containing dreams, until we come at last, maybe, to the Dreamer of all dreams, the Being who is all beings."[11]

That is the true Borgesian *vates*, even if it is, at first glance, the unusual Wells: it introduces us to "the landscape of a dream"[12] and leads us to a revelation, which, as Bedford, another of Wells' narrators expresses it, is "a pervading doubt of my own identity."[13]

Strangely enough, Borges isolates exactly the same vatic quality in Shakespeare, responding to Shakespeare both as figure and as author. Except for Homer, Shakespeare is a type of the literary figure without equal because his very existence demonstrates the vatic element in literature. Shakespeare, like Homer, is a complete individual because he is no individual at all; he is the transparent eyeball through which so many personalities are permitted to view the world. But when we search out the references to Shakespeare's works in Borges, we find that they are surprisingly few. *Lear, Macbeth, Julius Caesar*, and the sonnets are mentioned, it is true, but it is only to the "Murder of Gonzago" in *Hamlet* that Borges frequently returns. He does this not because he thinks it a great scene in Shakespeare, but because it demonstrates the fantastic in literature and the vatic in Shakespeare.

El Hacedor provides typical instances of Borges' references to Shakespeare, principally four: (1) the essay fiction "Everything and Nothing" (*H*, 3-5), which celebrates Shakespeare's resemblance to God in being everything and nothing, everybody and nobody; (2) a brief reference to Shakespeare's recalling Caesar's last words (*H*, 28); and (3,4) two references to the play scene in *Hamlet*:

The story is incredible but it happened and perhaps not once but many times, with different actors and in different places. It contains the perfect summation of an unreal epoch, and it is like the reflection of a dream or like that play within the play that we see in Hamlet. (*H*, 20-21)

> *Claudius, king of an afternoon, dreamed king,*
> *Never felt he was a dream until that day*
> *When an actor mimed his treachery*
> *With silent art on a stage.* (*H*, 62)

The emphasis on Shakespeare in Borges' work, then, is almost exclusively "mystical": we hear little about Shakespeare as *gramaticus*.

The particular emphasis Borges places on each of these disparate writers typifies the idiosyncratic stress he places on most writers in the middle and later periods of his career when his own style is perfected. Over the years he increasingly turned to writers—at least he wrote about them as if that were his motive—for illustrations and expressions of the mystic or fantastic. In "The Approach to Almotásim" there was at least the sample quotation; in "Pierre Menard" there was the subtle verbal analysis of Cervantes' and Menard's texts; but in the greater portion of Borges' fictions, when we are introduced to one or another of his gallery of writers, it is to encounter an astonishing notion, a bizarre twist of thought. In "The Immortal," for example, which is the longest, most complex piece about the literary figure, there is virtually no notice of the *gramaticus*, all attention being subverted to the hallucinatory nature of death. Understandably, then, we hear most about Borges himself as the fantasist, the mysterious systematizer, rather than as the stylistic innovator or even the leader and organizer of literary movements, his chief roles when he prepared his entrance to that community of writers that includes Sir Thomas Browne and Ben Jonson.

Poeta doctus. The *gramaticus* and *vates* meet in the *poeta doctus* to give Borges' writing its singular bookishness. Reading is the principal subject of his writing, and reading principally in works by writers appropriately labeled *gramaticus* or *vates*: *littérateurs* and theologians, philosophers and poets. The result of such material, the result Borges has made inevitable, is apprehension of common themes, similar notions, identical insights, all reflected in his own work by references and allusions that are the province of the *poeta doctus*. Here again Borges is closer to Joyce and Eliot than to Beckett or Robbe-Grillet, but a conspicuous difference is the way in which he asks the reader to share his view of previous learned writers as cynosures. Eliot directs us to Jessie L. Weston's synthesizing book, but Borges leads us to writers whose production is encyclopedic in extent and form as well as in intention—writers as widely separated as Pliny and De Quincey, whose subjects, like his own, are largely forms of acquired knowledge. So when Borges qualifies the beauty of Sir Thomas Browne's writing as "learned" (*docta*), he is pointing to a value—the astonishment, the esthetic sense of awe produced in the reader by a display of incredibly vast learning (surely this is another manifestation of "agreeable horror")—*and* a method—the construction of a literary work with purely, or almost purely, literary elements. He is pointing to the prevalent type of the literary figure in his own works, who, next to himself, is best seen in De Quincey.

Thomas De Quincey

An imaginary still life composed of two principal objects can, by his own choice, represent De Quincey's spirit and evoke his presence: marking the visual horizon, the arm of an easy chair nudges a small tabletop where, in the foreground, we see the ingredients of De Quincey's spiritual communion—a large decanter of red laudanum and an open book of German metaphysics. Placed side by side, these iconographical objects will, De Quincey tells us, "sufficiently attest my being in the neighborhood" (II, 18). Both instruments of imagination and high fancy, the bottle and the book, nevertheless, exhibit two strains of mental activity in De Quincey. On the one hand, the container of laudanum represents the personal and subjective, the internal scene of nightmare and dream, the activated individual memory creating unending corridors, vast ruins, and dramas of frustrated search from its own store of images; in a word, the psychologically *autobiographical*, which in De Quincey always takes us back to what he called "the dream-theatre of my childhood" (XIII, 30). On the other hand the book may stand for his externalized intellect fixing on studies and occupations that support and extend, nurture and develop that private world. If the former is childlike and fanciful, a form of mental play—terrifying—yielding image and scene, the latter is adult and learned, a mode of employment—necessary and inevitable—producing information and argument. The laudanum expresses the *vates*, the book tokens the *gramaticus* (that it is a book of German metaphysics may be a sufficient indication of *doctus*); but only in conjunction—it is a book of metaphysics after all—do they typify that writer who, in so many ways, is the prototype of the curious combination we find in Borges.

Borges first read De Quincey around 1917. He was about eighteen, and the effect, apparently, was immediate, while the affect, certainly, has been chronic. De Quincey, of course, is famous for two things: first, an elaborate style, and second, descriptions of opiate, visionary experience—the respective signs of *gramaticus* and *vates*. Although it may have been that famous style alone that first attracted Borges, there can be no doubt that the metaphysical, and thus, for Borges, concomitant erudite quality in De Quincey's works, held Borges' attention and issued in his writings. Here as almost everywhere, Borges' concern with the mystic or metaphysical takes precedence, total or final, over the writer's value as stylist, as *literato*. So when we come to describing the actual influence, or more accurately, the real presence of De Quincey in Borges, we are by and large able to pass over stylistic influence and concentrate on two phases of what may be called, with Borgesian license, mysticism— the learned, symbolized by the book, and the personal, symbolized by the decanter.

ERUDITION Dividing his writings according to subject into the matter of autobiography and the matter of literature (far from an exact division), one finds that the latter accounts for the bulk and the former for the best of De Quincey's work. His writing is largely the product of reviewing and explaining, translating and editing, abridging and reworking other people's books, so that Albert Goldman, who probably knows more about the question than anyone else, is convinced "that De Quincey's dependence on printed sources is the key to his literary career."[14] We could say the same thing of Borges and re-apply Bioy Casares' phrase by noting that De Quincey's essays, like all of Borges' prose, are "a literature of literature," adding with emphasis Casares' next phrase: "and of thought,"[15] for De Quincey, like Borges, chiefly pursues poetry, history, philosophy, and theology. Both men contemplate vast synthesizing projects—*History of Eternity*, "Prolegomena to all Future Systems of Political Economy"—and write essays that digest the enormous breadth of their reading. In fact De Quincey's peculiar use of the essay form may have served to determine Borges' own. Both employ the essay in the way David Masson ascribes to De Quincey:

An "Essay," in his definition of it (which, however, may not be universally accepted), is a paper addressed purely or primarily to the understanding as an insulated faculty,—i.e. distinguished from other papers by containing a good deal of the speculative element. It does not merely give information by presenting in a compact shape all the existing knowledge on any subject; nor is its main object that of delight to the reader by dreams and pictures of the poetical kind; nor does it seek merely to rouse and stimulate the feelings for active exertion of some sort; but, without any of these aims, or while perhaps studying one or other of them to some extent, it has in view always the solution of some problem, the investigation of some question, so as to effect a modification or advance of the existing doctrine on the subject. (VI, 1-2)

Both share an intense interest in the written past that enters their works in many ways, none more persistent or revelatory of their bookishness than the etymologies that trail along the bottom of De Quincey's pages and tense Borges' prose. The hallmark of this bookishness in De Quincey, the footnote, carried to its baroque extreme of footnoting footnotes,[16] is also stamped on Borges' work. De Quincey's comprehensive and idiosyncratic scholarship, matched by Borges' own peculiar erudition, is a continuing source of discovery for Borges, who writes:

The work that endures is always capable of an infinite and plastic ambiguity; it is everything for everyone, like the Apostle; it is a mirror that manifests the traits of the reader and it is also a map of the world. (OI, 126-27)

This is precisely the effect of De Quincey's *Works*—infinite and encyclopedic, but precise and individual as well. In a word, an Aleph, as Borges' works strive for alefdom. De Quincey is himself a mirror of the world, a collection of possibilities for essays, stories, poems, quotations. His work is a seeming *Britannica* that implies and substantiates a world of literature and thought; De Quincey the writer is reader and dreamer.

In De Quincey, as in Borges, the metaphysical and the erudite are seldom separated; they are, in fact, aspects of each other, since books of abstruse doctrine are, after all, abstruse themselves. De Quincey recognizes this when he describes his reading:

I will assert finally that, after having read for thirty years in the same track as Coleridge—that track in which few of any age will ever follow us, such as German metaphysicians, Latin schoolmen, thaumaturgia, Platonists, religious Mystics. . . . (II,147)

The Coleridgean series proposed by De Quincey prophetically includes Borges as a subsequent term, if not as the terminus itself; but there is this difference: Borges self-consciously exploits this train of reading to elicit the fantastic undercurrent in life. Abstruseness is a positive value in his writing. Working, as he usually does, on the explicit or implicit equation of life and literature, the world and a library, Borges asserts the possibility of a hidden key (like the volume searched for in "The Library of Babel") that necessarily must exist in a remote place. Literature, like life, is a mystery and a dream; they are both fundamentally recondite, and the purpose of his work, the procedure of his mind, is always to pierce to that secret meaning:

Epictetus ("Remember the essential: the door is open") and Schopenhauer ("Is Hamlet's monologue the meditation of a criminal?") have vindicated suicide with a multitude of pages; the prior certainty that those defenders are right makes us read negligently. That is what happened to me with the Biathanatos *until I perceived, or believed that I perceived, an implicit or esoteric argument beneath the notorious argument.* (OI, 130)

The negligence of our acceptance of these arguments is the same negligence with which we accept the surface of literature (the point, remember, of "The Approach"); it is, in fact, the same negligence that leads to our acceptance of apparential reality: we receive life itself with "previous certitude." Borges shocks us with the weird and marvelous from his fund of knowledge in order to destroy that easy negligence and force our attention to an awareness of our existence that he discovers or imagines ("I perceived, or thought I perceived"), one that is both intrinsic and esoteric. The uncommon, the supernatural, the fantastic all serve his end: to demonstrate the esoteric, he depends on the esoteric. Hence he intends the Coleridgean strain in his works to give us the content of that mystery as well as a key or kind of solution, just as it is in De Quincey; while he intends the means of its entry, in allusions to obscure authors or to little-known passages of well-known ones, to give us a real sense of discovering the inherently occult nature of literature and life itself. Borges cultivates fantastic literature because life is fantastic; he is erudite, similarly, because "meaning" is erudite. What, then, is the implicit quality or character of De Quincey's writing becomes the very point of Borges'.

Forms of Interchange

De Quincey's polymathic writing suggest Borges' fictions and essays; Borges' writings discover De Quincey's compositions: the commutual relationship is carefully and consciously elaborated by Borges for personal reasons and esthetic ends. The interchange assumes various forms, of which I want to consider four: the documented debt, the congenerous story or essay, the method of construction, and the fundamental image or symbol.

Emblematic of the first form is the opening sentence of Borges' essay on Donne's "Biathanatos":

To De Quincey (to whom my debt is so vast that to specify one part seems to repudiate or to silence the others) I owe my first awareness of the Biathanatos. (OI, 129)

The debt acknowledged here is one of information, perhaps knowledge, and it is almost always for surprising thought or stimulating information that Borges cites De Quincey. Unlike Wells, who is recognized in the epilogue of *El Aleph* (*A*, 172) to have impressed the central, inspiring images of two stories on Borges' imagination, De Quincey is usually recognized, most often with unusual specificity of volume and page number, to have supplied material from what David Masson, De Quincey's editor, calls "his budget of carefully acquired erudition, often most curious and out of the way" (VI, 3). Therefore it is not strange to find De Quincey referred to only a few times in the stories, many times in the discursive writings. In "The Immortal" he is credited with having contributed a descriptive passage (*A*, 26), and more typically in "Three Versions of Judas" (*F*, 170) he is quoted for a theory about Judas. But even more usual expressions of the one writer's thought working through the other occur in terse references like the epigraph to *Evaristo Carriego*; the anecdote in *Discussion* about a pastor who swore from the pulpit by the *Iliad* and *Odyssey* (*D*, 15); a footnote to "The 'Biathanatos'" (*OI*, 132); a passing reference in "From Allegories to Novels" (*OI*, 211); or the brief reminder of De Quincey's own reminder that "the true name of Rome was secret" (*OI*, 22). De Quincey appears, overtly at least, in Borges' works as an item in the stock of erudition, much as many authors figure in De Quincey's own essays, and it would seem that the major appeal of De Quincey for Borges is the way in which his works (*both* their works, to be sure) proceed from "libraries that stretch into infinity, like the armies of Xerxes" (VI, 295). But the references to De Quincey are only clues to the profound connection between their imaginations. What Borges got from De Quincey in the way of useful information—useful to him, that is—he could have gotten finally from numerous other sources, from De Quincey's own sources. A case in point is the theme of Achilles and the tortoise, which Borges presents in "The Perpetual Race of Achilles and the Tortoise," and in "Avatars of the Tortoise," briefly returns to in "Kafka and His Precursors," and mentions, in a slightly different form, in "The Lottery in Babylon." Borges knew De Quincey's treatment of the same conundrum in the biographical sketch of Sir William Hamilton (V, 330-32), and he was no less familiar with De Quincey's proffered solution, yet De Quincey is never mentioned in either of Borges' essays on the subject, where authors from Aristotle to Lewis Carroll are cited. The two men travel the same rivers of knowledge, right to their sources, so that the many referential allusions to De Quincey in Borges' writing really take us very little of the way toward appreciating what Borges ultimately found in De Quincey.

There is this to be learned from the explicit references to De Quincey: Borges' referential allusions, especially those that indicate a borrowing or a "debt," seldom tell the whole story. They point us in the right direction, but as to real information, they are apt to ignore more than they avow. A good example occurs in the reference to De Quincey in "The Immortal," cited in the preceding paragraph. As we shall see later, the description of the ruinous city that Borges admits borrowing from De Quincey, is by no means the whole of his obligation nor even the most important part. There is, then, in addition to the strikingly explicit quality of Borges' listing sources for his fiction, a secret property: the appearance of scrupulous, almost scholarly acknowledgment does not correspond to the real basis in other writings. If nothing else, a recognition of this property should guide the reader to a sense of these references as selected, controlled statements rather than as expressions of literary *politesse* or pedantry.

The case of "The Perpetual Race of Achilles and the Tortoise" is typical in that Borges often makes no reference to De Quincey's essays, even when he is writing on a theme that De Quincey developed at length. In my first chapter I mentioned "The Cult of the Phoenix"; other examples are "The Secret Miracle" and "The Immortal." To prove that Borges actually found his inspiration in De Quincey's essay

"Secret Societies" for the first story and in the essay called "Miracles as Subject of Testimony" for the second story may indeed be possible, while the case for his having lifted his theme for the third from De Quincey's "Homer and the Homeridae" is circumstantially, at least, beyond a doubt. But, especially in the first two examples, I have neither sufficient evidence nor the inclination to make such an ascription and prefer, instead, to look at these similarities in another way, namely, under the heading of congeners.

By "congeners" I mean to describe the parallel or sibling status of the works in question rather than the origin-outcome status that is so often the conclusion in studies of influence. This label is legitimate, because in each case what Borges finds in De Quincey is information, perhaps even knowledge, but knowledge that itself is funneled from immense reading, which in turn becomes or already is part of Borges' own vast store. The debt therefore is not so much *to* De Quincey as *through* De Quincey, to previous and even subsequent sources. De Quincey, like Sir Thomas Browne and Pliny, is a repository of erudition to which Borges returns again and again, only to be sent out to the same and other quarries from which these writers gathered their supplies of matter. In turn, Borges' own work becomes a new repository, more selective, more concentrated, more synthetic, but fundamentally the same.

Borges' story "The Cult of the Phoenix" is a brief, nonnarrative fiction in the form of an unstated riddle—still another indication of Borges' sense of mystery. The story describes a sect or secret society and refers to an enigmatic rite that guarantees immortality to the sect's members. By claiming that the mysterious rite "does not require description" (*F*, 183) Borges leaves the reader with a puzzle. Those readers I have talked with all suggest that the answer is propagation by sexual intercourse, a way of guaranteeing the immortality of species rather than of individuals. At first this seems a properly Borgesian interpretation, but it finally is unacceptable and explicitly denied by "The Nightingale of

Keats," which argues that "the individual is in some way the species " (*OI*, 167) and is supported in turn by Emerson's essay "Nominalist and Realist," to which Borges alludes on several occasions and which states that "We fancy men are individuals; so are pumpkins; but every pumpkin in the field goes through every point of pumpkin history."[17] Then there are those perplexing ingredients of cork, wax, gum arabic and, sometimes, slime or mud. One may choose to stop short of seeing a sexual implication in those. I think Borges has a rather more typically metaphysical answer in mind. The rite that is celebrated by the sect of the Phoenix is the last rite, that of death. We die in order to be reborn, a point illustrated by "The Immortal"; and as for the cult's emblem, Sir Thomas Browne says about the Phoenix in *Pseudodoxia Epidemica*: "So have holy men made use hereof as far as thereby to confirm the Resurrection."[18] I must admit, however, that I owe my solution of the puzzle to a reading of De Quincey's essay "Secret Societies," which could well have inspired Borges' story.[19]

In "Secret Societies" De Quincey speaks of those he has read about and offers several bits of information that are apposite to Borges' story. De Quincey's startling point about the most famous of secret societies—the Eleusinian Mysteries and Freemasonry—is that they have no secret: the rite they guard is nonexistent or vulgarly commonplace and therefore cannot be revealed because no one would believe it to be a mystery. In this account, one can see an impetus for the form of "The Cult of the Phoenix." The second fact is that most such societies are concerned with immortality. On the one hand we have the frauds, whom De Quincey sarcastically whips:

He (Bishop Warburton) knew, he could circumstantially reveal, what was taught in the Eleusinian shows. Was the Bishop ever there? No; but what of that? He could read through a milestone. And Virgil, in his 6th Aeneid, had given the world a poetic account of the Teletai, which the Bishop *kindly translated and expanded into the truth of absolute prose. The doctrine of immortality, he insisted, was the chief secret revealed in the mysteries.* (VII, 198)

But, in contrast, De Quincey had read of societies that meet

in secret chambers at the noontide of night, to shelter, by muffling with their own persons interposed, and at their own risk, some solitary lamp of truth—sheltering it from the carelessness of the world and its stormy ignorance; that *would soon have blown it out—sheltering it from the hatred of the world;* that *would soon have made war upon its life: all this was superhumanly sublime.* (VII, 181)

De Quincey goes on to describe the immortality of such societies and specifically to introduce the Phoenix:

But another feature of sublimity, which it surprises me to see so many irreflective men unaware of, lies in the self-perpetuation and phoenix-like defiance to mortality of such societies. . . . Often and often have men of finer minds felt this secret spell of grandeur, and laboured to embody it in external form. (VII, 182)

One of these "men of finer minds" was De Quincey; another is Borges, whose story is precisely a response to this "secret spell of grandeur," and whose imagination seems to have been stirred by De Quincey's history of such societies:

There was a Phoenix Club once in Oxford (up and down Europe there have been several), that by its constitution grasped not only at the sort of immortality aspired after by Phoenix insurance offices— . . . far more faithful, literal, intense, was the realization in this Oxford case of undying life. Such a condition as a "sede vacante," which is a condition expressed in the constitution of all other societies, was impossible in this for any office whatever. That great case

*was realised which has since been described by
Chateaubriand as governing the throne of France and its
successions. "His Majesty is dead!" shouts a voice; and this
seems to argue at least a moment's interregnum. Not at all—
not a moment's: the thing is impossible. Simultaneous (and
not successive) is the breath that ejaculates "May the King
live for ever!" The birth and death, the rising and the setting, synchronise by a metaphysical nicety of neck-and-neck,
inconceivable to the bookkeepers of earth. . . . Now this
Oxford club arose on these sublime principles: no disease
like intermitting pulse was known there. No fire but vestal
fire was used for boiling the teakettle. The rule was that, if
once entered upon the* matricula *of this amaranthine club,
thence-forwards, come from what zone of earth you would
. . . instantly you are shown in to the sublime presence. You
were not limited to any particular century. Nay, by the rigour
of the theory, you had your own choice of millennium.* (VII,
182-83)

The secret of the society at Oxford is not the same as that of
Borges' sect, but the underlying principle surely is. In fact,
this underlying principle is the theme and goal of Borges'
thought and imagination:

*The same principle in man's nature, the everlasting instinct
for glorifying the everlasting, the impulse for petrifying the
fugitive and arresting the transitory, which shows itself in
ten thousand forms, has also, in this field of secret confed-
erations, assumed many grander forms. To strive after a
conquest over Time the conqueror, to confound the grim
confounder is already great, in whatsoever direction.*
(VII, 18)

We can imagine the response such passages, with their refu-
tations of space, time, and individuality, evoked in Borges.
We can point with confidence to these same passages and
declare them the source or origin of his conundrum, but just

a brief look at the manuscript page reproduced in this book will indicate the broader base of Borges' information.

The important thing to remember is the foundation in reading for both De Quincey and Borges. The one begins, in the section I quoted:

But in Barruel I had heard only of Secret Societies that were consciously formed for mischievous ends. . . . Soon I read of other societies, even more secret (VII, 181)

And the other:

Those who write that the Sect of the Phoenix had its origin in Heliopolis and derive it from the religious restoration that followed the death of the reformer Amenophis IV, allege texts from Herodotus, Tacitus, and the Egyptian monuments, but they are ignorant of the fact that the denomination by the Phoenix is not anterior to Hrabano Mauro and that the oldest sources (the Saturnalia *or Flavius Joseph, let us say) speak only of the People of the Custom or of the People of the Secret. (F, 181)*

Borges' sources are apparently wider than De Quincey's— in one point they are definitely more inclusive in that De Quincey himself figures—but both the essay and the story derive from other works and are developed according to each author's individual intention. The manuscript page confirms what his notes, prefaces, and epilogues assert: Borges writes by a process of accretion. Certainly this is the obvious practice of his essays, which add reference to reference and summary to summary in a sequential order that seems to reflect the final organization of a complex note-taking system. De Quincey's system is different, but no less contingent on other books.

Much recent study of De Quincey, culminating in Albert Goldman's book, *The Mine and the Mint,* emphasizes this aspect of De Quincey's work. *Rifacimento* is what

Goldman appropriately terms the procedure, and while that is not Borges' method, one explanation Goldman offers for De Quincey's adopting this method is curiously similar to an aspect of Borges I described earlier:

For it is one of the peculiar traits of De Quincey's character that he must invariably work as though behind a mask; and even when he has expended the most enormous effort in recasting some wretched piece of historiography or biography, he must perforce claim that his original and highly imaginative work is an authentic and scholarly document. This strange and perverse passion for truth—or at least for an appearance of truthfulness—can be ascribed . . . either to his practical sense that a romanticized version of historical fact would not be acceptable to his English readers, or else to some deep peculiarity in his nature which made the act of creation something secret and furtive, something that must never be openly avowed.[20]

De Quincey's claim is the fictional basis of "Pierre Menard," of "The Approach," and of portions of other Borges' stories; and De Quincey's "deep peculiarity" may correspond to Borges' timidity about writing fiction in the first place. It is entirely possible that Borges is familiar with De Quincey's literary methods (after all, Goldman tells us nothing really new about De Quincey; he merely documents the extent of what De Quincey himself alerts us to). On the other hand, it may be the principle Borges announced in "Kafka and His Precursors" that leads us to see a Borgesian quality in De Quincey's deceptions. I shall offer two examples to support respectively and simultaneously my alternative surmises.

The *Walladmor* hoax is one of the minor, forgotten scandals of literary history.[21] A German writer, taking advantage of Sir Walter Scott's popularity, wrote an imitation Waverly novel, which he claimed merely to have translated from English. De Quincey translated sections of the book and summarized the rest in an abusive review that also laid bare the imposture, but he ended by translating the novel, in abridged form, into English. The title page of De Quincey's English translation of the German translation of a nonexistent novel epitomizes an authentic Borgesian artifice-within-artifice revealing a central nullity which is the source of all: "'Freely translated into German from the English of Walter Scott and now Freely Translated from the German into English." Did Borges take the cue for some of his literary high jinks from De Quincey's behavior? I do not know, but there is a good chance that De Quincey's less startling though no less metaphysically potent bluff did come to his attention. Goldman summarizes nicely:

At first sight there would not appear to be any need to demonstrate a source for De Quincey's series of papers on the Homeric question "Homer and the Homeridae." The reason for this is that in his introductory remarks in the first of these three articles, De Quincey states quite frankly that he intends to seat himself in the chair of the foremost German authority on this subject, a certain Nitzsch, and expound the views of that scholar, which are inaccessible to most readers, locked up as they are in the remote fastness of an enormous German encyclopedia bearing the forbidding title Allgemeine Encyklopadie der Wissenschaften und Kunste. *This unaccustomed show of ingenuousness, however, proves to be a blind, for when one consults the dusty volumes of the* Universal Encyclopedia, *one finds that the article entitled "Homeros" was not written by Nitzsch, who is in fact the author of a well-known commentary on the* Odyssey, *but by an obscure person named Grotefend; and there is no reason to believe De Quincey consulted this article.*[22]

We know that Borges followed De Quincey's leads—read the books De Quincey named; we know that Borges read German encyclopedias for pleasure; we know that he wrote a story entitled "The Immortal" that deals with Homer, fulfills suggestions made by De Quincey, and even explicitly cites De Quincey as a source; but if we lacked all this information, we could be fairly certain that Borges, a man who reacted to the fascinating strangeness of the name Yarmolinsky, could not pass up the temptation of that monosyllable—*Nitzsch* (especially since De Quincey quips: "Nitzsch's name is against him. It is intolerable to see such a thicket of consonants with but one little bit of a vowel amongst them; it is like the proportions between Falstaff's bread and his sack" [VI, 16]). But all such speculation aside, the fact remains, even if the motive and methods are different, that Borges and De Quincey fabricated their writings from other writings and often freed themselves of obligations to factual accuracy by disguised and distorted references. The similarity is unquestionable, the difference indicative: Borges saw a metaphysical possibility where none seemed to exist. Whether he learned the procedure of building literature out of literature from De Quincey or not, and whether he hit upon his special device of the phantom book-within-a-book from De Quincey or not, the opportunities to do so were there, so that if we choose not to see De Quincey as the source of Borges' inspiration on these points, we must see, even more inevitably as a consequence, a kinship of mind and intellectual disposition that is perhaps more important than any specific influence could have been.

After these similarities of intellectual content and artistic strategy and form have been suggested, we are in a position to approach what from my point of view is the most significant aspect of Borges' relationship to De Quincey— the sharing of a common worldview expressed in common imagery. As we read through the diffusive volumes of De Quincey's *Works* after the trenchant brevity of Borges' essays and stories, what strikes us first is the frequency with which we encounter, not only the same idea, but twin formulations in striking images. We are, given the situation I have set up, attuned to Borges' imagery and therefore supersensitive to any similarities in De Quincey; that is, we are apt to notice things that would not have struck us previously—the tiger or the mirror, for example—but, as these resemblances mount and intensify, we are unable to ignore them.

I mentioned the tiger—I mentioned the mirror too, but a discussion of that would not be complete without extensive mention of other writers, Chesterton, for example, and that would take me far from my appointed subject. The tiger, then, is one of Borges' favorite animals and the subject of a two-paragraph autobiographical piece called "Dreamtigers," where he explains how as a child the ferocious Asian tiger captured his imagination and how it still haunts his dreams. He returns to the tiger in "The Writing of God," in "The Circular Ruins," and particularly to Blake's tiger (that the title "Dreamtigers" is in English matters) in *Evaristo Carriego* and again in *Other Inquisitions*:

The infinite nightingale has sung in British literature: Chaucer and Shakespeare, Milton and Matthew Arnold celebrate it, but to John Keats we inevitably link its image, as to Blake that of the tiger. (OI, 169)

It must have been with some satisfaction, therefore, that he encountered passages like the following in De Quincey:

with eyes glaring like a tiger's . . . (XII, 27)

Now, terror there may be, but how can there be any pity for one tiger destroyed by another tiger? (XIII, 7)

the tiger's heart was masked by the insinuating and snaky refinement . . . (XIII, 78)

The tiger that slept in Catalina wakened at once. (XIII, 182)

Death the crowned phantom, with all the equipage of his terrors and the tiger roar of his voice. (XIII, 318)

bounding with tiger's leaps . . . (XIII, 368)

A very small point of correspondence, surely, but sufficient to show that as well as providing a stock of metaphysical topics and information that activate and nourish Borges' mind, De Quincey provided images or concretions of metaphysical intuitions, which no less meaningfully stimulated Borges' imagination and corroborated his own responses; and as long as we are talking of these two men as writers, there can be little more important than the verbal pictures they have in common.

Symbol and Image

In the course of his writings, De Quincey records three epiphanic experiences that expose the core of his thought and emotion while revealing, at the same time, the imagery that informs his language. These three experiences—a panoramic opium vision, a moment of confusion when he first found himself alone in the streets of London, and an uncomprehended discovery on reading a passage in *The Arabian Nights*—furnish the opportunity for an incisive rather than general comparison with Borges.

(1) The first passage occurs in *Confessions of an English Opium-Eater*, and I ask the reader, as he follows De Quincey's account, to recall Borges' "Feeling in Death," which constitutes the key passage in "New Refutation of Time."

At that time I often fell into such reveries after taking opium; and many a time it has happened to me on a summer night— when I have been seated at an open window, from which I could overlook the sea at a mile below me, and could at the same time command a view of some great town standing on a different radius of my circular prospect, but at nearly the same distance—that from sunset to sunrise, all through the hours of night, I have continued motionless, as if frozen, without consciousness of myself as of an object anywise distinct from the multiform scene which I contemplated from above. Such a scene in all of its elements was not unfrequently realised for me on the gentle eminence of Everton. Obliquely to the left the many-languaged town of Liverpool; obliquely to the right, the multitudinous sea. The scene itself was somewhat typical of what took place in such a reverie. The town of Liverpool represented the earth, with its sorrows and its graves left behind, yet not out of sight, nor wholly forgotten. The ocean, in everlasting but gentle agitation, yet brooded over by dove-like calm, might not unfitly typify the mind, and the mood which then swayed it. For it seemed to me as if then first I stood at a distance aloof from the uproar of life; as if the tumult, the fever, and the strife, were suspended; a respite were granted from the secret burdens of the heart—some sabbath of repose, some resting of human labours. Here were the hopes which blossom in the paths of life, reconciled with the peace which is in the grave; motions of the intellect as unwearied as the heavens, yet for all anxieties a halcyon calm; tranquility that seemed no product of inertia, but as if resulting from mighty and equal antagonisms; infinite activities, infinite repose. (III, 394-95)

The similarities between this description and "Feeling in Death" as well as the passage from Emerson's "Nature," which I introduced in the first chapter, are obvious: each scene embodies "the best clarity of metaphysics" (*OI*, 27); in each, the beholder is suspended in a mystical, visionary tranquility where the scene, literally, is only what is seen, and the "I" is the "eye."[23] In their works both Borges and De Quincey return to such encompassing moments, to points in space or time or mind that are all inclusive.

In the epilogue to *El Aleph* (*A*, 172) Borges traces an influence on both "The Zahir" and "El Aleph" to H. G. Wells' story "The Crystal Egg," in which "a mass of crystal, worked into the shape of an egg and brilliantly polished"[24] occupies two points in space at the same time—one on Mars, the other in London—and permits a view of each locale "as if from the other side of a mirror" (*A*, 77) as another Borges story has it. He could as easily have pointed to another Wells narrative he regards highly, "The Plattner Story"; but then, just as correctly, Borges could have suggested the influence of De Quincey, for even closer to the matter and form of Borges' cataloging vision is De Quincey's description of Walking Stewart's mind:

On the whole, Walking Stewart was a sublime visionary. . . . His mind was a mirror of the sentient universe—the whole mighty vision that has fleeted before his eyes in this world: the armies of Hyder Ali and his son Tipoo, with oriental and barbaric pageantry; the civic grandeurs of England; the great deserts of Asia and America; the vast capitals of Europe; London, with its eternal agitations, the ceaseless ebb and flow of its "mighty heart"; Paris, shaken by the fierce torments of revolutionary convulsions; the silence of Lapland; and solitary forests of Canada; with the swarming life of the torrid zone; together with innumerable recollections of individual joy and sorrow that he had participated by sympathy;—lay like a map beneath him, as if eternally co-present to his view, so that, in the contemplation of the prodigious whole, he had no leisure to separate the parts, or occupy his mind with details. (III, 115-16)

Crucial to each of the De Quincey descriptions is the vantage point: Walking Stewart's vision is "like a map *beneath* him," and in his own opium vision, De Quincey looks down from a position that is at once higher than and remote from the scene: "*overlook*," "contemplate from *above*," "at a distance *aloof*," all establish De Quincey's withdrawn omniscience. For De Quincey, this position is a pleasure and triumph that he wins or regains through opium, so he follows his description with a paean beginning: "O just, subtle, and all conquering opium!" (III, 395). The conquest for De Quincey is one of self and of space, just as it is for Stewart, who sees the "prodigious whole"; but it is a conquest of time as well, because Stewart's vision is "eternally co-present" and De Quincey's ode to opium explains that the drug

*"from the anarchy of dreaming sleep," callest into sunny
light the faces of long-buried beauties, and the blessed
household countenances, cleansed from the "dishonours of
the grave."* (III, 396)

Keeping the parallel of "Feeling in Death" in mind, we see
that here is De Quincey's refutation of time; and by induc-
tion we can see that all his work aims at such a refutation and
triumph: "To strive after a conquest over Time the conqueror,
to confound the grim confounder, is already great, in whatsoever direction" (VII, 18). De Quincey, like Borges, aspires
to membership in the Cult of the Phoenix. At times, as in
"Feeling in Death" and the Everton vision from the *Confessions*, the goal is reached; but, as we have noted, in Borges
there is an underlying disbelief in the achievement, and in
De Quincey, an overwhelming despair of not being able to
reach or maintain the transcendental eminence.

(2) The one major element of De Quincey's opium
dreams missing from the paragraphs I have been speaking
of is, in many ways, the most important because it gives
drama and pathos to De Quincey's experience. That element
is the search. Quite naturally it is missing because in those
paragraphs De Quincey is in possession of himself, of the
entire scene. Seeing all, he is all. But such moments of tranquil exaltation are by their nature transitory. "Our faith
comes in moments," wrote Emerson in "The Over-Soul,"
speaking of moments like De Quincey's vision and Borges'
discovery,

*And this deep power in which we exist and whose beatitude
is all accessible to us, is not only self-sufficing and perfect
in every hour, but the act of seeing and the thing seen, the
seer and the spectacle, the subject and the object, are seer
and the spectacle, the subject and the object, are one.*[25]

More usually, however, "We live in succession, in division,
in parts, in particles";[26] and when De Quincey fails to main-

tain the lofty point of view and all that it means, he finds
himself not above, but in the scene with his horizons cut off,
his way lost, and the twisting lines of Stewart's map now
describing the routes of a labyrinth:

No man ever was left to himself for the first time in the
streets, as yet unknown, of London, but he must have been
saddened and mortified, perhaps terrified, by the sense of
desertion and utter loneliness which belong to his situation.
No loneliness can be like that which weighs upon the heart
in the centre of faces never-ending, without voice or utter-
ance for him; eyes innumerable, that have "no speculation"
in their orbs which he can understand; and hurrying figures
of men and women weaving to and fro, with no apparent
purposes intelligible to a stranger, seeming like a mask of
maniacs, or, oftentimes, like a pageant of phantoms. The
great length of streets in many quarters of London; the con-
tinual opening of transient glimpses into other vistas equally
far-stretching, going off at right angles to the one which you
are traversing; and the murky atmosphere which, settling
upon the remoter end of every long avenue, wraps its termi-
nation in gloom and uncertainty; all these are circumstances
aiding that sense of vastness and illimitable proportions
which for ever brood over the aspect of London in its inte-
rior. (I, 182)

Here, in the interior, there is no panoramic vision, and the
sense is all of one cut off from but exposed to the weaving
of people and streets, which is the scene. Deprived of transcendental vision, De Quincey's interrupted spatial vistas
become terrifying, just as extension of time becomes a horror in the other passages. In such scenes De Quincey usually
finds himself searching for the way, for a lost woman, but
with no hope of success; at one time he envisions the confusion by reversing the image and imagining the labyrinth
from the inside out:

*Was the honourable reader ever in a real labyrinth, like that
described by Herodotus? We have all been in labyrinths of
debt, labyrinths of error, labyrinths of metaphysical nonsense. But I speak of literal labyrinths. Now, at Bath, in my
labyrinthine childhood, there* was *such a mystery: viz. in
what were then called the Sydney Gardens, opening upon
Great Pulteney Street. This mystery I used to visit; and I can
assert that no type ever flashed upon my mind so pathetically
shadowing out the fatal irretrievability of errors in early life.
Turn but once wrong at first entering the inextricable jungle,
and all was over; you were ruined; no wandering could recover the right path. Or suppose you even took the right turn
at first, what of that? You could expect to draw a second
prize; yet five turnings offered very soon after: your chance
of escaping error was now reduced to one-fifth of unity; and,
supposing, that again you drew no blank, not very far had
you gone before sixteen roads offered. What remained for
you to do* now? *Why, if you were a wise man, to cry like a
girl. None but a presumptuous fool would count upon drawing for a third time a prize, and such a prize as one among
fourteen. I mention all this, I recall this image of the poor
Sydney Labyrinth,—whose roses, I fear, must long ago have
perished, betraying all the secrets of the mysterious and
pathless house,—simply to teach the stranger how secure,
how impregnable, is the central cell or* heart *of a labyrinth.
Gibraltar is nothing to it. You may sit in that deep grave-like
recess; you may hear steps of the Avenger approaching, but
laugh at them. If you are coining, and have all the implements of coining round about you, never trouble yourself to
hide them. Nobody will in this life reach you. Why, it is demonstrable by the arithmetic of combinations, that, if a man
should so end the flower of his age as a police-officer in trying to reach your coining shop, he could not do it; you might
rest as in a sanctuary, hidden and inaccessible to those who
do not know the secret of the concealment.* (VII, 203-20)

In the Everton and London passages are, respectively, the
high triumph and deep despair of De Quincey's vision; and

if the moment of metaphysical clarity corresponds to Borges' intuition and consequent imagining of a timeless, spaceless impersonality, then De Quincey's entrapment in the labyrinth corresponds to the plight of Borges' characters: to Lönnrot caught in Triste-le-Roy, to Marcus Flaminius Rufus lost in the tunnels and chambers of the Immortals' new city, to the dwellers in the Library of Babel, to that Borges who disbelieves his own refutation of time. Most specifically of all, the plight corresponds to Borges' Homer, who, as we shall see later, is the crucial meeting place for De Quincey in Borges. In the *Confessions*, De Quincey talks of his search through London for a woman named Ann:

If she lived, doubtless we must have been sometimes in search of each other, at the very same moment, through the mighty labyrinths of London; perhaps even within a few feet of each other—a barrier no wider, in a London street, often amounting in the end to a separation for eternity! (III, 375)

Borges, who has "wandered through the red and tranquil labyrinth of London" (*OP*, 257), writes of Homer in"The Maker":

A woman, the first one the gods supplied him, had waited for him in the shadow of a hypogeum, and he had sought her through galleries that were like nets of stone and down slopes that sank into shadow. (*H*, 11)

"There is no writer of universal fame who has not coined a symbol" (*OI*, 56), writes Borges in his essay on Quevedo. His own writing has unremittingly defined the symbol that has, apparently without his will, become the title of his work outside Argentina—the labyrinth. Borges and the labyrinth are synonymous; but, in characteristic fashion, he has carefully pointed to many other writers who have used this image. To Chesterton, for example, who employs the metaphor with startling frequency, startling, that is, once we are aware of Borges' debt to Chesterton. Just a sampling from the *Father Brown Stories* gives us:

That labyrinthine ambition, in chamber within chamber of that palace of lies that we built up around Mary Queen of Scots. (78)

He lived almost entirely in a little room that was in the rooms, and even in this erected another sort of central cabin or cupboard, lined with steel like a safe or a battleship. (306)

Prince Otto looked down with something of a grim smile at the bright, square labyrinths of the lamp-lit city below him. (311)

It was under the latter circumstances that I found a maze of subterranean passages which led at last to a heap of rich refuse, broken ornaments and scattered gems which I took to be the ruins of some sunken altar, and in which I found the curious gold cross. (390)

But no other of his self-acknowledged sources is so labyrinthine as De Quincey. For Chesterton, the labyrinth is a significant symbol of life itself—particularly of urban life—as well as for the confusions of the mind. He enlists the metaphor frequently but rather inflexibly and traditionally. De Quincey, however, not only employs the metaphor with greater frequency but also develops it more elaborately; for him it is *the* metaphor, just as it is for Borges. A clue to De Quincey's thoroughgoing vision of our existence as a labyrinth can be found in the following passages, which display the metaphor in an unusual way:

Wordsworth, therefore, enjoyed this labyrinth of valleys in a perfection that no one can have experienced since the opening of the present century. (II, 262)

A guide-post—always a picturesque and interesting object, because it expresses a wild country and a labyrinth of roads (II, 309)

When Charles and Sophia Lloyd . . . first dawned upon me, coming suddenly out of rain and darkness; then—young, rich happy, full of hope . . . and standing apparently on the verge of a labyrinth of golden hours. (II, 01)

The labyrinth or maze as an architectural setting that reflects the loss of mental or spiritual direction, the chaos of civilization—these are usual and familiar images: we have met them already in De Quincey; but the labyrinth as a fitting description for the untouched lake country, for the intertwining lives of a happily married couple—that is extraordinary. "Labyrinth" for De Quincey is not so simply a word of judgment as it is for Chesterton; instead, it can be a descriptive word that permits us to penetrate from the immediate and apparent to the remote and secret.

Here we enter upon a curious paradox, implicit in De Quincey, explicit and developed in Borges: the labyrinth is the opposite of metaphysical clarity, and its primary qualities are perplexity, disorder, frustration, and inevitable defeat—"a labyrinth is a house constructed in order to confuse men" (*A*, 15); yet the labyrinth is also a kind of order—"its architecture, prodigal with symmetries, is subordinated to that purpose" (*A*, 15). In this quotation from "The Immortal," the key term is "to confuse," an infinitive expressing purpose, not, significantly, "confused," an adjective denoting condition; and the words that point to the accomplishments of that purpose are esthetic, formal: "constructed," "architecture," "symmetries," "subordinated." The resistance to disorder is heroic in Borges; it is the effort of his work. In De Quincey the opposition is weaker yet sometimes successful just the same. De Quincey's view of a landscape, as a labyrinth, for example, is necessarily an overview: the imaginary point of vision is above the scene looking down and discovering a pattern, a pattern that is grasped as labyrinthine.

The same is true of the maze of hours: to see them as a maze they must have, in the mind the describer, run their course; the view is omniscient, retrospective. If the reader doubts my argument, let him try the following experiment. Draw a labyrinth or imagine one. Now consider the vantage point from which you see your labyrinth. Undoubtedly, you drew a floor plan or saw something very like it. You looked down at your labyrinth and grasped it as a total plan—exactly what one cannot do when inside such a structure. The view of a labyrinth from eye-level reveals only passageways and the possibility of one or more exits or entrances: a ground-level photograph of the Hampton Court maze shows only an obstructing wall or hedge. Now consider a different situation. Entering a Gothic cathedral, one looks toward the altar, taking in the view of the long nave corridor, and glimpses the distant openings onto what are apparently other enclosures. That is the view from eye-level, from the vantage point of everyday life. But looking down at the same cathedral from a helicopter, or better yet in an architectural floor plan, one now sees the same corridor and recognizes that the openings give out onto the arms that form the transept; it now becomes clear that the cathedral is cruciform. The cross is not only the pattern of the building; it is its meaning as well—that is the vatic view. The labyrinth is a similar pattern, and its confusing, frustrating complexity is similarly *its* meaning. The labyrinth is useful for presenting chaos in an orderly image, for seeing a pattern that underlies and ties together. In the labyrinth, of course, one is tormented, like De Quincey in London; outside or above it, one has the freedom of perception. Typically, De Quincey's work presents a view from within the labyrinth, where the pattern or totality is unrevealed, while Borges' fiction usually describes an internal view but embodies an overview in which the plan of chance is grasped as the meaning and order of the situation. Ultimately, Borges demands that we make a distinction between the labyrinth in the story and the labyrinth *of* the story. However, De Quincey can speak of "the mazes of religious choral dances" (VI, 35) and "the mingled yarn of human life"

(VI, 251), images that match Borges' "a strumming of a guitar, a kind of impoverished labyrinth that entangled and uncoiled itself infinitely" (*F*, 177) and the "perplexing web of his story" (*F*, 177). Nowhere is the paradoxical order of the labyrinth more apparent than in Borges' story "Examination of the Work of Herbert Quain," and this example is particularly illuminating because it employs a mathematical metaphor as De Quincey did in describing the Sydney Gardens. De Quincey had once planned to express "some important truths" of economics "briefly and elegantly by algebraic symbols" (III, 32); but the general direction of his work is away from abstract compression, whereas Borges, sharing De Quincey's view of mathematics as another language, frequently relies on the formulaic idiom with success. Of Quain's novel, *April March*, he writes:

Thirteen chapters comprise the work. The first relates the ambiguous dialogue of some strangers at a train station. The second relates the events on the eve of the first chapter. The third, also retrograde, relates the events of another possible eve of the first; the fourth, the events of another. Each one of these three eves (which rigorously exclude one another) ramifies into three other eves, of very diverse nature. The whole work consists, then, of nine novels; each novel of three long chapters. (The first is common to all of them, naturally.) Perhaps a diagram may help to understand the structure:

$$
z \left\{
\begin{array}{l}
y^1 \left\{ \begin{array}{l} x^1 \\ x^2 \\ x^3 \end{array} \right. \\[2ex]
y^2 \left\{ \begin{array}{l} x^4 \\ x^5 \\ x^6 \end{array} \right. \\[2ex]
y^3 \left\{ \begin{array}{l} x^7 \\ x^8 \\ x^9 \end{array} \right.
\end{array}
\right.
$$

By analogy with De Quincey's description of the Sydney Gardens, *April March* is a labyrinth, but it is also an esthetic creation informed by the most rigorous, algebraic logic. Reading from left to right, the eye follows the amplifying, forking paths of Quain's alternatives consecutively; looking at the diagram, the eye instantaneously takes in all the possibilities of the total, organized pattern, the Gestalt. This twofold, paradoxical nature of *April March* is the nature of Borges' own work: a labyrinth with a plan, not always as schematically mapped as *April March*, but always provided with the necessary thread for finding one's way.

There are, then, two kinds of labyrinths, depending on the view taken, to be found in De Quincey and Borges. One is the labyrinth we see from the inside and cannot grasp: that is life itself, imaged in the palace of the Immortals for Borges and the city of London for De Quincey. The other is the labyrinth whose structure is open to our view so that we experience it as labyrinthine and yet are not prisoners of its deceptions. It is the labyrinth of art. In the preceding paragraphs I quoted some expressions of this latter type from both Borges and De Quincey; but now I would like to go a step further and suggest that the oeuvre of each is labyrinthine with this exception: De Quincey's works are labyrinths without discernible plans; they are like the universe Borges describes when he writes that reality is perhaps ordered, "but in accord with divine laws—I translate: with inhuman laws—that we shall never completely perceive" (*F*, 33). De Quincey captures that picture, reflects it perfectly, but Borges creates a work that "may be a labyrinth, but it is a labyrinth woven by men, a labyrinth destined to be deciphered by men" (*F*, 3). The two kinds of labyrinths are compared in "The Immortal":

> *I had crossed a labyrinth, but the bright City of the Immortals terrified and repulsed me. . . . In the palace, which I explored imperfectly, the architecture lacked a purpose. It abounded in corridors without exits, high unreachable win-*

dows, ornate doors that opened into a cell or a shaft, incredible, inverted stairways with steps and balustrades leading down. (A, 14-15)

There is no clarity here. We view the labyrinth from a partial point of view ("I explored imperfectly") and what we get is monstrous complexity. But in the subterranean labyrinths that the narrator crossed in order to reach the structure described above, the point of view is different:

There were nine doors in that cellar; eight led to a labyrinth that deceptively opened into the same room; the ninth (through another labyrinth) led to a second circular room, identical to the first. I do not know the total number of rooms; my misfortune and anxiety multiplied them. (A, 13)

Confusion reigns here too ("I do not know the total"), but we get a picture of the labyrinths leading somewhere, eventually giving out on to other passages that take the narrator above ground. The fact that he chooses to *summarize* these lower labyrinths and to *describe* the one above ground is a key to the difference. He comprehends the lower labyrinths and can present them as entities, while the upper labyrinth is vaster than his imagination, so he can only mention some details. The upper labyrinth corresponds to the universe as Borges imagines it: it is his subject matter; the lower labyrinth corresponds to the fiction Borges writes about that universe: it is his form. That is, Borges sees the universe as a labyrinth, but can not affirm it, as Pope does: "A mighty maze! but not without a plan"[27] He is willing to imagine, along with Pope, that "All Nature is but art,"[28] but Borges lacks the point of view from which to prove that assertion, the point of view that Faust, another wanderer in the labyrinth, seeks in wanting to follow the sun:

> *Oh, that no wings lift me above the ground*
> *To strive and strive in his pursuit!*

In the eternal evening light
The quiet world would lie below
With every valley tranquil, on fire every height,
The silver stream to golden rivers flow.
Nor could the mountain with its savage guise
And all its gorges check my godlike ways;
Already ocean with its glistening bays
Spreads out before astonished eyes.[29]

Turning from that impossibility, as Faust himself does, Borges accepts the full weight of his despairing certainty (as Faust also does): if nature is art, that art is "unknown to thee."[30] Borges' view thus parallels one expressed in Addison's *Cato*, but does not rest on the same assumption of a grand order:

The ways of Heaven are dark and intricate,
Puzzled in mazes, and perplex'd with errors:
Our understanding traces 'em in vain,
Lost and bewilder'd in the fruitless search;
Nor sees with how much are the windings run,
Nor where the regular confusion ends.[31]

De Quincey's prose is labyrinthine. The reader finds himself "lost in a labyrinth of clauses" (X, 161) that mirror De Quincey's presentment of "labyrinthine truth" (X, 225). And that, of course, has been the great tragedy of most of De Quincey's work: condemned by classical, formal standards to the category of the less great because he could seldom elevate himself to an overview of his subjects and found himself wandering in his prose with the mortifying awareness that he was constructing "endless and labyrinthine sentences" (X, 158) that finally make up a "maze of diction" (X, 15). (There are few passages more pathetic than those in which De Quincey recognizes the snare he is weaving for himself and stops short with a postleptic awareness that has been the reader's for some time: "But I am insensibly wandering beyond the limits assigned me" [XIV, 129].) The endless process of De Quincey's style prevents him from stopping long enough or penetrating far enough to build the last wall or to rest at the center. The twisting prose and expanding digression are his symbol: I repeat, De Quincey *is* his style. Nevertheless there are passages in De Quincey that come close to realizing the end of presenting a lucid labyrinth. I am thinking, for instance, of the description in "Klosterheim," where the whole forest is seen as a labyrinth composed of many smaller ones of underbrush, light, and sound—a fitting emblem of De Quincey's writing.

Upon explaining the circumstances of the robbery, however, the officer caused his men to light a number of torches and advance into the wood. But the ground was so impracticable in most places, from tangled roots and gnarled stumps of trees, that it was with difficulty they could keep their footing. They were also embarrassed by the crossing shadows from the innumerable boughs above them; and a situation of greater perplexity for effective pursuit it was scarcely possible to imagine. Everywhere they saw alleys, arched high overhead, and resembling the aisles of a cathedral, as much in form as in the perfect darkness which reigned in both at this solemn hour of midnight, stretching away apparently without end, but more and more obscure, until impenetrable blackness terminated the long vista. Now and then a dusky figure was seen to cross at some distance; but these were probably deer; and, when loudly challenged by the yagers, no sound replied but the vast echoes of the forest. Between these interminable alleys, which radiated as from a centre at this point, there were generally thickets interposed. Sometimes the wood was more open, and clear of all undergrowth—shrubs, thorns, or brambles—for a considerable distance, so that a single file of horsemen might have penetrated for perhaps half a mile; but belts of thicket continually checked their progress, and obliged them to seek their way back to some one of the long vistas which traversed the woods between the frontiers of Suabia and Bavaria. (XII, 25)

De Quincey knew the heights, but he dwelt for the most part in the lower mazes, and, even more despairingly, in the catacombs; for, once in the labyrinth, he found that as he retraced and crossed his own steps repeatedly the awareness of repetition overburdened him with a sinking sense of reiteration, a sense reflected in his repetitive vocabulary:

I seemed every night to descend—not metaphorically, but literally to descend—into chasms and sunless abysses, depths below depths, from which it seemed hopeless that I could ever re-ascend. Nor did I, by waking, feel that I had re-ascended. (III, 35)

It is true that at the end of his works De Quincey often introduces a sudden rising movement, as J. Hillis Miller says:

Many of De Quincey's works have just this pattern of a descent deeper and deeper into hopeless darkness, followed at the last moment by a sudden ascent into light. This movement is the basic pattern of his narrative art, appearing in "Klosterhiem," his longest story, in "The Daughter of Lebanon," in the "Dream Fugue" attached to "The Vision of Sudden Death," in his essay on Joan of Arc, and in "Revolt of the Tartars."[32]

But in each case the ascent is an inexplicable, miraculous event harshly fulfilling the requirements of form by putting an end to the thing. On the other hand, in Borges the extensive labyrinth leads up to a revelation that it itself embodies. Even in "Feeling in Death" Borges wanders in a maze before reaching the corner from which his vision expands through the immediate to the eternal:

The afternoon preceding that evening, I was in Barracas: a locality I customarily did not visit and whose distance from the ones I later visited immediately gave a strange flavor to that day. My evening there had no special aim; since it was pleasant, after dinner I went out to walk and to remember. I did not want to predetermine the direction of that walk; I strove for a maximum number of probabilities in order not to wear out my anticipation with the obligatory prevision of any one of them. I realized to the poorest possible extent what is called walking at random; I accepted the most obscure invitations of chance without any other conscious prejudice than merely casting a side glance at the wide avenues and streets. Nevertheless a kind of customary gravitation took me far away toward some neighborhoods whose name I want always to remember because they inspire my reverence. (*OI*, 26)

It is the final vision, the overview, however, that matters here as elsewhere in Borges. Thus in "The Approach" the concluding myth is the largest, most basic statement of the preceding material; in "Death and the Compass" the last lines place the murder of Lönnrot in an infinitely repeating series; in "Examination of the Work of Herbert Quain," the critical approach ("Examination") permits an intelligible, bird's-eye view of Quain's labyrinth ("the Work"). Always in Borges there is, from the start or more usually at the finish, a view from above which is the clarifying device of his plot or argument. If we can allow, for a moment, a distinction between form and content, we can say that the overview is the shape he gives to his matter. With the grandiose example of De Quincey before him, Borges discovered a way for using the labyrinth to express chance and establish order. What is even more amazing is that Borges' mastery develops from De Quincey, who, though he seldom managed to make it work for him, had the key ready at hand.

(3) In the last of the three passages I want to consider, De Quincey writes about the books he read as a boy and names one that figures prominently in Borges as it does in so much Spanish literature—*The Arabian Nights*. (Once again we have evidence of the two writers frequenting the same literature. This time, however, De Quincey's report of

what he read was to affect Borges profoundly, for here De
Quincey introduces a labyrinthine situation but follows it
with a possible solution.) De Quincey tells of despising the
story of Aladdin except for one section "which fixed and
fascinated my gaze, in a degree that I never afterwards for-
got, and did not at that time comprehend" (I, 128). The section concerns a magician's search for a child who will be able
to obtain the magic lamp because he is an innocent whose
horoscope and constitution predict his special life:

*Where shall such a child be found? Where shall he be
sought? The magician knows: he applies his ear to the earth;
he listens to the innumerable sounds of footsteps that at that
moment of his experiment are tormenting the surface of the
globe; and amongst them all, at a distance of six thousand
miles, playing in the streets of Baghdad, he distinguishes the
peculiar steps of the child Aladdin. Through this mighty labyrinth of sounds, which Archimedes, aided by his* arenarius,
*could not sum or disentangle, one solitary infant's feet are
distinctly recognized on the banks of the Tigris, distant by
four hundred and forty days' march of an army or a cara-
van.* (I, 128-29)

The magician's power, as De Quincey concludes, is a twofold vatic gift:

*First, he has the power to disarm Babel itself of its confu-
sion. Secondly, after having laid aside as useless many bil-
lions of earthly sounds, and after having fastened his mur-
derous attention upon one insulated tread, he has the power,
still more unsearchable, of reading in that hasty movement
an alphabet of new and infinite symbols; for, in order that
the sound of the child's feet should be significant and intelligible, that sound must open into a gamut of infinite compass. The pulses of the heart, the motions of the will, the
phantoms of the brain, must repeat themselves in secret hieroglyphics uttered by the flying footsteps. Even the articu-*

late or brutal sounds of the globe must be all so many lan-
guages and ciphers that somewhere have their correspond-
ing keys—have their own grammar and syntax; and thus the
least things in the universe must be secret mirrors to the
greatest. Palmistry has something of the same dark sublim-
ity. (I, 129)

Here is a typical, nonarchitectural De Quincey labyrinth with
the usual space-time function (the boy is six thousand miles
away; his future is implicit in his horoscope); but the magician embodies a new element. Without the immense, ideal
overview, he is still able to cut through all that is extraneous and penetrate to his object, which he discovers by means
of "secret hieroglyphics." Keeping in mind the analogy between De Quincey's imagining existence as labyrinthine and
his construction of a mimetic style, we see that the magician
possesses the skill that De Quincey's own essays so demonstrably lack. To lay aside all that is useless, to avoid distraction and the wayward corridors of digression, was beyond
De Quincey—it went against his nature and his vision. In his
great projects unable to proceed by a direct route from starting point to conclusion, he still acknowledged that ability in
others and in small ways caught the mysterious hieroglyphics that were there to be read. In his essay on Lamb for example, he indicates that the answer to the puzzle of Lamb's
character is to be found in the detection of a secret alphabet:

The syllables lurk up and down the writings of Lamb which
decipher his eccentric nature. His character lies there dis-
persed in anagram; and to any attentive reader the regath-
ering and restoration of the total word from its scattered
parts is inevitable without an effort. (V, 219)

And he returns to the notion of natural hieroglyphics bearing the clue to meaning frequently, as in the following:

The forehead [Sir Walter Scott's] was not remarkably lofty—
and, by the way, some artists, in their ardour for realizing

their phrenological preconceptions, not suffering nature to surrender quietly and by slow degrees her real alphabet of signs and hieroglyphic characters, but forcing her language prematurely into conformity with their own crude speculations, have given to Sir Walter Scott a pile of a forehead (II, 25)

The prevailing character of any natural object, no matter how little attractive it may be for beauty is always interesting for itself, as the character and hieroglyphic symbol of the purposes pursued by Nature in the determination of its form, style of motion, texture of superficies, relation of parts, &c. (I, 361)

So frequent is De Quincey's use of this image that Lane Cooper remarks:

The word hieroglyphics, *so common with our author, doubtless pleased his ear, and it calls up also vague visual sensations to the reader; but it is not for the senses chiefly. With De Quincey it is rather on the order of a negative idea. . . . Matters seemingly without significance, apparently disjointed circumstances, are by a sudden effort of his mind thrown into relation, and forced, in their very paucity and slenderness of indication, to render up an unmistakable story.*[33]

In other words *hieroglyphics* for De Quincey (as for Sir Thomas Browne, who also uses the word frequently) is the reading of the secret mirrors that in the least things reveal the greatest; it is a doctrine of correspondence that he believed he commanded in conversation: "a logical instinct for feeling in a moment the secret analogies or parallelisms that connected things else apparently remote" (III, 332). But in his writing, this feeling always gives way to the perception of lesser connections and greater differences, leaving him, after having cut through tangles of thought and history by swift analogical insight, to dissipate that insight by meandering distinctions: sameness always gives way in De Quincey to difference, unity to digression, clarity to obfuscation.

For our consideration of Borges, it is significant that a magician reads the hieroglyphics and peers into the secret mirrors of the universe, since Borges himself employs "magic" correlation. The process Cooper describes as standing behind De Quincey's notion of hieroglyphics is, in fact, the process of Borges' essays and fictions: "Matters seemingly without significance, apparently disjointed circumstances, are by a sudden effort of his mind thrown into relation, and forced, in their very paucity and slenderness of indication, to render up an unmistakable story." Borges is the magician whose stories correlate the minutest details with the greatest actions, whose essays lay aside all useless words—his art is essential and constricted—to focus on the two, three, or more passages, that, when extracted from the mass of all writing, suddenly reveal a connection where none appeared before. Borges is the magician who puts his ear to one text, Kafka's or his own, and hears the isolated, distant sounds of similar thoughts, a skill inherent in the procedure of his prose. Unlike De Quincey, who emphasizes "the philosophy of transition and connection, or the art by which one step in an evolution of thought is made to arise out of another" (II, 65) as the capital secret of prose composition, Borges is ruthlessly paratactic, both in grammar and thought. The procedure began in Ultraism when he advocated the "deletion of intervening sentences, the transitions,"[34] continued in his early writings where he patterned himself on the abrupt editing he found in von Sternberg's films, and developed into the exaggerated manner evident in "The Intruder." In the course of making transitions, De Quincey's writing opens new subjects and wanders into new paths; theoretically each of his works is illimitable transition. Borges, on the other hand, by focusing on "magic" correlations and "secret mirrors" relates things abruptly, precluding diffuseness. Staccato allusion, as at the beginning of "Note on (toward) Bernard Shaw" (*OI*, 217), often substitutes in Borges for what is transition and digression in De Quincey, so that we have in the style itself a direct cutting through barriers in Borges, an indirect route in De Quincey. Finally, Borges is the magician for whom there is a hidden language in all things— in the stripes of a tiger's coat, as in "The Writing of God," in the scar on a man's face, as in "The Shape of the Sword," or in the works of a man's mind, as in the epilogue to *El Hacedor*:

A man proposes to himself the task of sketching the world. Through the years he populates a space with images of provinces, kingdoms, bays, ships, islands, fish, rooms, instruments, stars, horses and people. A little before his death, he discovers that this patient labyrinth of lines traces the image of his face. (*H*, 103)

Borges' justification (his justification, in the role of gramaticus, of his own work) of such hieroglyphic techniques is to be found in "A Vindication of the Kabbala," where he explains: "I do not want to vindicate the doctrine, but the hermeneutic or cryptographic procedures which lead to it" (*D*, 55). These procedures, when applied to literature, lead to the conception of a text where "the collaboration of chance is calculable at zero" (*D*, 59) so that every detail, every magic detail, prognosticates and refers. Borges' writing reasons the universe Kabbalistically; his own fiction is cryptographic and requires a literary Kabbalism for its proper understanding. De Quincey is mentioned in that vindication, and when asked what first interested him in the Kabbala, Borges replied: "I think it was through De Quincey, through his idea that the whole world was a set of symbols or that everything meant something else."[35]

The notion Borges refers to is treated at length in De Quincey's essay "Modern Superstitions," where he writes of omens and magic predictions; but a more typical example of De Quincey's alertness to Kabbalistic possibilities—more typical because it is coupled with his refusal to make use of them—and one that fits Borges' application of the doctrine to fiction as well occurs in "Homer and the Homeridae":

It startles us to find lurking in any man's name a prophecy of his after career; as, for instance, to find a Latin legend— "And his glory shall be from the Nile" (Est honor a Nilo) *concealing itself in the name* Horatio Nelson. *But* there *the prophecy lies hidden, and cannot be extracted without a painful corkscrew process of anagram. Whereas, in* Demosthenes, *the handwriting is plain to every child: it seems witchcraft—and a man is himself alarmed at his own predestinating name.* (VI, 33)

Although he breaks down *Demosthenes* into *demos* (the people) and *sthenos* (strength) and shows that *Homer* can be prophetically deciphered as "blind man" and "metaphorical joiner" or "cabinet maker," De Quincey argues against such interpretations, insisting that "prophetic" names are back formations based on the person's achievements. In fiction, however, Borges is free to employ this traditional device of prophetic onomancy and he does so by calling Homer *Cartaphilus* and in inventing other names like *Funes, Red Scharlach, Stephen Albert, Dahlmann,* which are secret mirrors of the characters' destiny. Such secret mirrors force an awareness on the reader that is beyond that of the characters themselves. While they are lost, we work our way through the labyrinth, perceiving an order usually hidden from them until the last, revelatory moment. A quotation from "Examination of the Work of Herbert Quain" epitomizes this dimension of Borges' fiction: "The reader of that singular book is more perspicacious than the detective" (*F*, 79). This dimension is entirely lacking, naturally, in De Quincey's autobiographical writing, where the plane of the action is the plane of narration, and no clues are forthcoming.

The principle of secret mirrors is a form of repetition, but whereas repetition through the Eternal Return confers meaning and significance as well as the fundamentally phantasmal nature of life in Borges, it produces a horror in De Quincey that is unabated. In Borges, of course, the horror is there too, because repetitions deny our individual selves and the solidity of material reality, but Borges' work employs the same theory and system to guarantee esthetic form as to devastate the characters that the form encloses. The reader is satisfied (formally) by the very repeating details which disintegrate the people in the stories. De Quincey, unfortunately, almost always found himself in the same position as Borges' characters, unable to shift from personal dilemma to esthetic or metaphysical solution. (In part, this is the result of De Quincey's relying mostly on the close-up of autobiographical expression; Borges, by contrast, chooses the longer perspective of fiction or literary history.) In De Quincey there is nothing that resembles the relationship of Lönnrot and Scharlach; De Quincey is always the victim. For him, the repetitions are always a chaos, where, in the words of Goethe's dedication to *Faust*, "Grief is renewed, laments retrace the maze/Of Life's strange labyrinthian career."[36] Looking at one of the passages that perhaps stirred Borges' imagination and certainly matches one of his favorite situations, we can see how De Quincey fails to come away with Borges' kind of constructed, imagined order:

There are cases occasionally occurring in the English drama and the Spanish where a play is exhibited within a play. To go no further, every person remembers the remarkable instance of this in Hamlet. *Sometimes the same thing takes place in painting. We see a chamber, suppose, exhibited by the artist, on the walls of which (as a customary piece of furniture) hangs a picture. And, as this picture again might represent a room furnished with pictures, in the mere logical possibility of the cast we might imagine this descent into a life below a life going on ad infinitum.* (X, 3)

The introvolution, as De Quincey calls it, offers no satisfaction to him, even though the play within the play is obviously a mirror, although not very secret, of *Hamlet* itself. And it is precisely on this point that Borges and De Quincey differ. They both posit the repetition and intuit the possible order, but where Borges forces essence to triumph over particularity and declares an identity of events or items, De Quincey's mind forces him to abandon the possibility. On the one hand he can say, "I must yet believe that the 'soul of the world' has in some instances sent forth mysterious types of the cardinal events in the great historic drama of our planet" (X, 28), which is the very germ of Borges' stories like "Theme of the Traitor and Hero"; but then, in another place he is obliged to say:

As with external objects, so with human actions: amidst their infinite approximations and affinities, they are separated by circumstances of never-ending diversity. History may furnish her striking correspondences; biography her splendid parallels; Rome may in certain cases appear but the mirror of Athens, England of Rome; and yet, after all, no character can be cited, no great transaction, no revolution of "high-viced cities," no catastrophe of nations, which, in the midst of its resemblances to distant correspondences in other ages, does not include features of abundant distinction, and individualizing characteristics so many and so important as to yield its own peculiar matter for philosophical meditation and its own separate moral. Rare is the case in history, or (to speak with suitable boldness) there is none, which does not involve circumstances capable, to a learned eye, without any external aid from chronology, of referring it to its own age. The doctrine of Leibnitz, on the grounds of individuality in the objects of sense, may, in fact, be profitably extended to all the great political actions of mankind. Many pass, in a popular sense, for pure transcripts or duplicates of similar cases in past times; but, accurately speaking, none are such truly and substantially. Neither are the differences by which they

are severally marked and featured interesting only to the curiosity or to the spirit of minute research. All public acts, in the degree in which they are great and comprehensive, are steeped in living feeling and saturated with the spirit of their own age; and the features of their individuality,—that is, the circumstances which chiefly distinguish them from their nearest parallels in other times, and chiefly prevent them from lapsing into blank repetitions of the same identical case—are generally the very cardinal points, the organs, and the depositories which lodge whatever best expresses the temper and tendencies of the age to which they belong. So far are these special points of distinction from being slight or trivial that in them par excellence *is gathered and concentrated whatever a political philosopher would be best pleased to insulate and to converge within his field of view.*
(V, 357-58)

The necessity to discriminate leads De Quincey away from the mythic and leaves him, finally, with no system for linking events and characters comparable to that of Borges; it leaves him with the feeling of disgust and ultimately without a structure:

It always struck me as disgusting that, in going round the sun, we must be passing continually over old roads, and yet have no means of establishing an acquaintance with them: they might as well be new for every trip. Those chambers of ether, through which we are tearing along night and day (for our *train stops at no stations), doubtless, if we could put some mark upon them, must be old fellows perfectly liable to recognition. And yet, for want of such a mark though all our lives flying past them and through them, we can never challenge them as old acquaintances. The same thing happens in the desert: one monotonous iteration of sand, sand, sand, unless where some miserable fountain stagnates, forbids all approach to familiarity: nothing is circumstantiated or differenced: travel it for three generations, and you are no nearer to identification of its parts; so that it amounts to traveling through an abstract idea. There is no Aristotelian* αυαγωριοσ, *no recognition.* (X, 31)

Contrast that passage with the following in "The Library of Babel":

The library is unlimited and periodic. *If an eternal traveller should cross it in any direction, he would confirm at the end of centuries that the same volumes recur in the same disorder (which, repeated, would be an order: the Order). My solitude rejoices in this elegant hope.* (F, 95)

The universe, which, as Borges' narrator says in the first line of the story, "others call the Library" (*F*, 85), is orderly disorder and Borges' story is the expression an "elegant hope." But De Quincey is unable to make that one supposition ("if an eternal traveller") that underlies Borges' fiction and is repeated there in many forms, most notably in "The Immortal." And because he cannot do that, the Eternal Return is useless to De Quincey. For him, everything is new under the sun because he cannot recognize it as old:

More truly and more philosophically, it may be said that there is nothing old under the sun, no absolute repetition. It is the well-known doctrine of Leibnitz, that amongst the familiar objects of our daily experience there is no perfect identity. In finite change, illimitable novelty, inexhaustible difference, these are the foundations upon which nature builds and ratifies her purpose of individuality,—*so indispensable, amongst a thousand other great uses, to the very elements of social distinctions and social rights.* (VII,357)

De Quincey sees the repetitions serially ("sand, sand, sand") and cannot recognize the identity of terms; that is, cannot telescope them chronologically as Borges does so that they may become one, the series a single point. Borges confounds the grim confounder esthetically and metaphysically by inventing and elaborating a system, so we remember the victory rather than the artificiality of his "elegant hope." De Quincey fails to find a way or to invent a unifying principle and what we remember are the depths and confusions of his failure. The universal library for him is a horror:

In my youthful days, I never entered a great library . . . but my predominant feeling was one of pain and disturbance of mind. . . . Here, said I, are one hundred thousand books, the worst of them capable of giving me some pleasure and instruction; and before I can have had time to extract the honey from one-twentieth of this hive, in all likelihood, I shall be summoned away. This thought, I am sure, must have often occurred to yourself; and you may judge how much it was aggravated when I found that, subtracting all merely professional books . . . from the universal library of Europe, there would still remain a total of not less than twelve hundred thousand books over and above what the presses of Europe are still disemboguing into the ocean of literature. . . . Consequently, three hundred and sixty-five per anum . . . one thousand every triennium; that is, ten thousand for thirty years—will be as much as a man who lives for that only can accomplish. From the age of twenty to eighty, therefore—if a man were so unhappy as to live to eighty—the utmost he could hope to travel through would be twenty thousand volumes. . . . All this arithmetical statement you must not conceive to relate to any fanciful case of misery. No; I protest to you that I speak of as real a case of suffering as ever can have existed. (X, 38-39)

De Quincey's arithmetic of despair is not unknown in the Library of Babel, but Borges' elegant, superhuman hope is unknown to De Quincey. In the same universal library, the pale rejoicing of theoretical intelligence confronts the dark despondency of speculative emotion.

The substance of De Quincey's vision, both as it derives from his reading and from his dream world, is essentially the same substance we encounter in Borges. They dream the same subjects in the same library. The form put upon that substance is what distinguishes the two writers. Borges finds in De Quincey (takes from him? shares with him? confirms in him?) a mind so close to his own, both in conceiving the world and expressing that conception, that as he told me of Nietzsche, who would not praise Emerson because it would be too much like praising himself, Borges never tells how much of himself there is in De Quincey. But turning to De Quincey on the basis of the spare hints Borges does give, we find there a newly defined sense of De Quincey's imagination. Borges adopts the universal image of the labyrinth; and in doing so awakens us to the less systematically presented but no less moving and forceful evocation of that image in De Quincey. He trains our eye to see in De Quincey another shadow of the great artificer, ever constant, ever changing. Once that awareness is ours, there is no longer any reason to see De Quincey as the tangential figure he has seemed for so long. Instead there is every reason to view him as the other side of Borges' coin. De Quincey's vision is synaptic, and his is the art of expression; Borges' view is synoptic, and his is the art of formulation. The one is classic, slender, realized, the other romantic, boundless, reaching: "The obverse and the reverse of this coin are, for God, the same" (*A*, 52).

Notes

1. Quoted by Enid Starkie in *Baudelaire* (New York, 1958), 28.
2. The writings of Simon Ginzburg and Christian D. Ginsburg are also referred to. See Scholem's bibliography.
3. Not appropriate to my argument at this point, but pleasing to consider is the possibility that a third name in the story, that of the detective Lonnröt, while certainly chosen because of the *rot-red* significance, may also owe something to that of the famous detective Poirot, whose name, we are told, "conveys an odd sense of unreality." Remember that Poirot's friend and Watson-like aide "lives and flourishes—but on the other side of the world. He is now in the Argentine." (See

Agatha Christie, *"The Murder of Roger Ackroyd "* [London, 1977], 19,21.)

4. "Nominalist and Realist," *Essays*, 439. Borges quotes the passage in an abbreviated translation in *"La flor de Coleridge"* (*OI*, 19) and again in his preface to the translation of *Representative Men* (Buenos Aires, 1949), xiii.

5. *"La flor de Coleridge,"* *La Nación* (September 23, 1945), see *OI*, 9-23.

6. T. S. Eliot, "Tradition and Individual Talent," *Selected Essays* (New York, 1950) 6-7.

7. Op. Cit., 9.

8. Op. Cit., 11.

9. With José E. Clemente (Buenos Aires).

10. *The Collected Writings of Thomas De Quincey*, ed. David Masson (Edinburgh, 1889-1890), VI, 28-29. All further references to De Quincey, unless otherwise noted, are to this edition and will be included parenthetically in the text.

11. *The Dream* (New York, 1924), 317.

12. *The First Men in the Moon, Novels of Science*, 69.

13. Op. Cit., 165.

14. *The Mine and the Mint* (Carbondale, IL, 1965), 154.

15. *SUR* 92 (May,1942): 60.

16. See VI, 338, 358, 359 for examples.

17. *Complete Essays*, 446.

18. *The Works of Sir Thomas Browne*, ed. Charles Sayle (Edinburgh, 1912), III, 7.

19. I am wrong—and right—as I learned after writing this. When Borges was in New York in 1968, I asked him if he ever revealed the answer to the riddle, "Yes, sometimes." Would he tell me? And I knew at once my error: he turned and looked at his wife for a moment and then said, "Not now; tomorrow. I'd like to keep you guessing for one more day." The following day at a reception I reminded him of his promise. He leaned over and whispered into my ear so that no one else could hear: "Well, the act or what Whitman says 'the divine husband knows from the work of fatherhood.'—when I first heard about this act, when I was a boy, I was shocked, shocked to think that my mother, my father had performed it. It is an amazing discovery, no? But then too it is an act of immortality, a rite of immortality, isn't it?"

   Borges' sense of decorum further explains the form of the story while his childhood shock helps explain the appearance of dirt in the rite itself. For the source of his Whitmanesque euphemism, see "From Pent-Up Aching Rivers" in the "Children of Adam" section of *Leaves of Grass, Complete Poetry*, 70.

20. *The Mine and the Mint*, 10.

21. For a detailed account of the hoax and the sources of my information see De Quincey's note to "Walladmor, a Pseudo-Waverly Novel"

(XIV, 132-45) and *The Mine and the Mint*, 92-97.

22. *The Mine and Mint*, 64.

23. For an analysis of this phenomenon in Emerson, see Richard Poirier's chapter "Is There an I for an Eye?" in *A World Elsewhere* (New York, 1966) 50-92.

24. *The Short Stories of H. G. Wells* (London, 1960), 625.

25. *Complete Essays,* 261-62.

26. Op. Cit.

27. Alexander Pope, "Essay on Man," *Poetical Works* (Boston, 1852), 231.

28. Op. Cit., 239.

29. Johann Wolfgang von Goethe, *Faust*, trans. Walter Kaufmann (New York, 1962), 141, 143.

30. Pope, *Works*, 239.

31. Joseph Addison, *The Miscellaneous Works*, ed. A. C. Guthkelch (London, 1914), II, 356.

32. "Thomas De Quincey," *The Disappearance of God* (New York, 1965), 76. Through negligence I did not read Mr. Miller's analysis of De Quincey until I had worked out my own interpretation; and reading De Quincey with Borges in mind, I came to focus on many of the same passages that Mr. Miller had. Since my intention is obviously different from his, however, and his conclusions are agreeably antagonistic to my own, I have forsworn agreeing or disagreeing with him at every point.

33. *The Prose Poetry of Thomas De Quincey* (Leipzig, 1902), 61-62.

34. "Ultraísmo," *Nosotros*: 468.

35. "Interview," *Paris Review* (Winter-Spring, 1967): 161.

36. Goethe, *Faust*, 65.

SUMMATION: "THE IMMORTAL"

The universal literary figure, the relationship to De Quincey, and the symbol of the labyrinth all come together in Borges' story "The Immortal," which is the perfection of his allusive method in a work that is more than ever a literature of literature. Beyond that, "The Immortal" is Borges' statement of themes that have preoccupied many twentieth-century writers, in a form comparable to that of Conrad, Joyce, Eliot, but still personal, authentic. "The Immortal" is the culmination of Borges' art.

The Universal Literary Figure

The epigraph to "The Immortal" establishes the familiar theme in Borges' work and introduces the singleness of authorial mind that is the story's subject:

Salomon saith, There is no new thing upon the earth. So that as Plato had an imagination, that all knowledge was but remembrance; so Salomon giveth his sentence, that all novelty is but oblivion.
Francis Bacon: Essays LVIII (A, 7)

Four authors—Plato, Solomon, Bacon, and Borges himself—are here made to collaborate in expressing the Eternal Return in an intellectual or mental sense. This apparent plurality of minds and demonstrable unity of statement in an allusive tissue is at once the theme and the technique of the story, which uses the literary figure to reformulate definitively the principles of personality and time found throughout Borges. It is the same theme he treats in "Everything and Nothing," but that sketch is commentary and a summary; "The Immortal" is a presentation and a demonstration.

In "Everything and Nothing" Borges writes of Shakespeare: "No one was so many men as that man, who, like the Egyptian Proteus, could exhaust all the appearances of being" (*H*, 44). The pun on "no one" divulges the removed, all-knowing approach Borges takes in order to distill the essence of his subject. The distillation, however, is a little lifeless, droning; and the monotone is relieved only by the octave shift in the last sentences, when God speaks. "Everything and Nothing," like so much in *El Hacedor*, is a summation of previous work, but sapped of almost all energy, subdued by nostalgia. More varied, more complex is "The Immortal," which treats the same subject but from the inside, so that the reader's understanding develops gradually and dramatically, along with that of the character. Furthermore, at the end of "Everything and Nothing," all is solved, resolved, while at the conclusion of "The Immortal" the sense of mystery, and complex mystery at that, still lingers. The one is a rapid disclosure, the other an intricate unfolding; and the intricacy comes not from the treatment alone but from the conception, because in "The Immortal" Borges takes the possibilities of both *everything* and *nothing* more seriously. The story shows that Homer's work is nothing—nothing extraordinary, that is—and that Homer is literally everything, *everyone* in the story.

The paradoxical everythingness and nothingness of Homer is indicated elsewhere by the expressly generic title of "El Hacedor," "The Maker," which Borges bestows upon him; but in "The Immortal" the two exhaustive attributes are simultaneous modes of his work and personality. The story itself is a little *Odyssey*, and that, of course, is tribute to the universal, mythic proportions of Homer's work, which nourishes subsequent writings; but the story in no way proposes the greatness or superiority of the Homeric epic, instead showing its mere inevitability in the scheme of things:

Homer composed the Odyssey. *Given an infinite period of time, with infinite circumstances and changes, the impossible thing is not to compose the* Odyssey, *at least once. No one is anyone; a single immortal is all men.* (A, 20-21)

The *Odyssey* belongs not to Homer but to History; it is nothing more or less than the story of the world. But it belongs to Language as well, for as Borges argues in "Versions of Homer," it is impossible "to know what belongs to the poet and what pertains to the idiom" (*D*, 107), and, therefore, the only certainty about Homer's style, his literary personality, "is the impossibility of separating what pertains to the writer from what pertains to the idiom" (*D*, 108). Logically, then, not Homer but everyone has written (and continues to write) the *Odyssey*; in the end, as Cartaphilus writes, "*only words remain*" (*A*, 26). The most exact indication of the universal composition of Homer is the phrase "Pope's *Iliad*" on the first page of "The Immortal" (*A*, 7), an indication supported by a reference to "Pope's *Odyssey*" that Emerson makes in the course of arguing that all literature has been written by one person.[1] The logic is clear: if "a single man is all men," then a single author is all authors, all men ("The genius is all," says Emerson[2]), and all men are immortal because Homer is immortal. We are all Homer. Thus, this story, which gives what we have always lacked and so often desired—a biography of Homer—takes away far more than it gives:

Like Cornelius Agrippa, I am god, I am hero, I am philosopher, I am demon and I am world, which is a wearisome way of saying that I am not. (*A*, 21)

Exhaustive amplitude is a trait of the cipher.

As so often in Borges, the confirmation of being obliterates, but notice the peculiar absence of definite and indefinite articles in that quoted series and also notice the constant present tense. The added complexity in "The Immortal," one characteristically indicated by a suppression, is that character is not only multiple and sequential as presented in "Theme of the Traitor and Hero," "The Circular Ruins," and even in Part V of "The Immortal"; character is single and simultaneous as well: the apparent multiplicity of Types or Ideas exists in the present tense. Homer is all men *now*. That bloody horseman who dies at Rufus' feet in Part I is the same

Rufus who undertakes an identical journey and dies in similar circumstances at the end of Part I; the Rufus speaking to Argos is Homer, who has forgotten that he is Homer, speaking to Homer, who has nearly forgotten the *Odyssey* he composed 1,000 years ago. The Princess of Lucinge reads Homer; Pope and his employees write Homer; Joseph Cartaphilus sells Homer; Nahum Cordovero comments on Homer. All are aspects of Homer in a literary, mental sense.

This simultaneous multiplicity is revealed by personal pronouns in "The Immortal." The story begins, unusually for Borges, not with "I" but with "we" (*ofrecemos*), shifts to Homer's first–person (*que yo recuerde*), moves naturally between the first person plural (*partimos*) and first person singular (*devisé*) in the course of narration, and then in Part IV shifts subtly to another "we," one that includes the Immortals:

Neither was his own destiny interesting. His body was a submissive domestic animal and each month the alms of a few hours sleep, a little water, and a scrap of meat were enough for him. Let nobody wish to reduce us to ascetics. There is no more complex pleasure than thought and we gave ourselves over to it. (A, 21)

Finally the story ends with the first person (*a mi entender*). The confusion or explanation and contraction is partially clarified by Homer's statement: "The story I have narrated seems unreal because in it are mixed the incidents of two different men" (*hombres distintos, A*, 24). But "different," "distinct" are themselves ambiguous and apply more to the grammar than to the psychology or history of the character. An analogous situation in Emerson is more illuminating.

The same kind of shifts in person have been noted by Richard Poirier in Emerson's "Nature," and they show us, says Poirier, "the speaker's capacity to relinquish his particular identity and assume an ever more inclusively general one."[3] In Borges, the grammatical shift reenacts the myth of the Simurg, which begins with discrete "I"s and culminates in a "we." In fact, that myth, found at the end of "The Approach," with its difficult journey, its pilgrims falling by the wayside, its passage through Vertigo and Annihilation, its final revelation that all are one (the Immortal Simurg) informs Borges' later, as well as his earlier, story. The events in "The Immortal" are thus to be read in two ways: first, as apparent particulars, of person, place, thing, and time; and second, as the manifestation of a single character, who writes the entire fiction (including preface, narrative, and postscript), but who is absent from the story as himself, except in so far as he is all and everywhere. Without giving his readers the benefit of an explanatory note, Borges has employed the same device Strindberg said he used in *Dream Play*:

In this dream play . . . the Author has sought to reproduce the disconnected but apparently logical form of a dream. Anything can happen; everything is possible and probable. Time and space do not exist; on a slight groundwork of reality, imagination spins and weaves new patterns made up of memories, experiences, unfettered fancies, absurdities and improvisations.

The characters are split, double and multiply; they evaporate, crystallise, scatter and converge. But a single consciousness holds sway over them all—that of the dreamer. For him there are no secrets, no incongruities, no scruples and no law. He neither condemns nor acquits, but only relates, and since on the whole, there is more pain than pleasure in the dream, a tone of melancholy, and of compassion for all living things, runs through the swaying narrative.[4]

In what it says about characterization as well as narrative procedure, Strindberg's note is the best description of the story. There is one immortal who is all the rest: the story's title is pointedly singular; Homer is the universal author.

Men are immortal, then, like the rest of the universe: "To be immortal matters very little; except for man, all crea-

tures are immortal since they do not know about death . . ."
(*A*, 20). As Sir Thomas Browne writes in "Religio Medici":

*For as though there were a Metempsuchosis, and the soul
of one man passed into another, Opinions do find, after certain Revolutions, men and minds like those that first begat
them. To see our selves again, we need not look for Plato's
year: every man is not only himself; there hath been many
Diogenes, and as many Timons, though but few of that name:
men are liv'd over again, the world is now as it was in Ages
past; there was none then, but there hath been some one
since that parallels him, and is, as it were, his revived self.*"[5]

Emerson recognized that immortality and also stressed our
suppression of it: "We hide this universality if we can, but
it appears at all points."[6] Man has repressed his immortality
or he is moved to forget it, a wish Emerson also understood:

*But it is not the intention of Nature that we should live by
general views. We fetch fire and water, run about all day
among the shops and markets, and get our clothes and shoes
made and mended, and are the victims of these details; and
once in a fortnight we arrive perhaps at a rational moment.
If we were not thus infatuated, if we saw the real from hour
to hour, we should not be here to write and to read, but
should have been burned or frozen long ago. She would
never get anything done, if she suffered Admirable Crichtons
and universal geniuses.*[7]

Our principal antidotes to universality and immortality are
death and forgetting. Because they confirm our mortality and
our individual identity, death and forgetting make the universe bearable, real for us. On this point of forgetting I have
already noted Borges' story "Funes the Memorious," and I
would also want to point to De Quincey, who, like Borges,
feels assured "that there is no such thing as ultimate *forgetting*" (III, 437) but who nevertheless describes forgetting as
a gift and an art:

that art which the great Athenian Themistocles noticed as
amongst the desiderata *of human life—that gift which, if in*
some rare cases it belongs only to the regal prerogatives of
the grave, fortunately in many thousands of other cases is
accorded by the treachery of the human brain. Heavens!
what a curse it were, if every chaos, which is stamped upon
the mind by fairs such as that London fair of St. Bartholomew
in years long past, or by the records of battles and skirmishes
through the monotonous pages of history, or by the cata-
logues of libraries stretching over a dozen measured miles,
could not be erased, but arrayed itself in endless files inca-
pable of obliteration, as often as the eyes of our human
memory happened to throw back their gaze in that direction!
Heaven be praised, I have forgotten everything. (I, 387)

Man lives by dying, that is, by forgetting; only God or an Immortal lives by remembering all. Thus, "The Immortal" proceeds by a series of deaths or equivalent lapses of memory
that give to the story its seemingly disjunctive form, the "disconnected but apparently logical form of a dream," as
Strindberg puts it. On the other hand, these deaths and
forgettings, as we shall see, are shams and illusions, and the
inner reality, captured by the procedure of the story and described in the career of Homer, is one of eternal life and all-
encompassing memory.

Death makes men "precious and pathetic" (*A*, 22);
remove it or the knowledge of it and they are no longer precious or pathetic. Hence the curious description of "The
Immortal" in the epilogue to *El Aleph* as an "outline of an
ethic for immortals" (*A*, 171). The story proposes a system
of values, indeed a way of living or reading (which are much
the same thing in Borges), an ethic of supreme equality in
life (notice the phrase "the republic of immortal men" in Part
IV), of sublime impersonality in literature. All claims to
originality or invention—of experience or writing—as well
as all accusations of plagiarism and influence are destroyed:
"There is no new thing upon the earth." Books, like men, are

no longer to be valued as either precious or pathetic: there is all eternity in which to write the Homeric epics, and it was inevitable that they should be written; there is all eternity to complete the on-going work described in "The Dream of Coleridge," and a sentiment of loss about the missing lines of "Kubla Khan" is simply misguided and misplaced in time. Freed from the values death imposes, literature can at last be seen for what it is: "In the beginning of literature was myth, and also in the end" (*H*, 38). The ascendency of myth, of a literary collective consciousness in "The Immortal" may be guessed when we realize, in contrast to other stories about literary figures like Pierre Menard or Herbert Quain, how little there is about writing or planning of a book in "The Immortal"; how little, even, of criticism, for this is a story whose intention is to question the basis of most criticism and appreciation of literature, which develop from a notion of limits to man's life, from limits, that, the story argues, do not exist. It is the responsibility of literature, then, to deny mortality, to deny oblivion by ignoring the sleep of death and the sleep of forgetting and by emphasizing in their place the eternal dream of life and memory. Literature must be timeless memory: to be true, to be archetypically real, literature based on such a belief must deny its own novelty, and the position of the author must be that of grand remembrancer. Ironically, then, Cordovero's attack in the postscript on the integrity of Homer's text is our assurance of its universal validity. The more it is nothing in itself, the more the story is everything.

"The Immortal" thus realizes a great victory over time and space and personality, but it is finally despondent and futilitarian. As "New Refutation of Time" ended with "*And yet, and yet . . .*" (*OI*, 256), "The Immortal" leaves us with a feeling of loss rather than of gain. The implicit morality and political ethic of the story are at first noble but then dispiriting: the "perfection of tolerance" (*A*, 20) that the Immortals have achieved leads inevitably to a perfection of disdain and inactivity. And while we can accept the eternity of literature, the necessity for seeing people as eternal shades instead of flitting realities is too much for us. We want to believe that we are, which is to say, that we shall die. Therefore the story leaves us with the fundamental antinomy of Borges' work: the achievement of metaphysical vision antagonistic to our very selves. Even Homer cannot bear the strain of his discovery and lapses into forgetfulness and apparent death: "Again I am mortal, I repeated, again I am like all men. That night I slept until dawn" (*A*, 23). Of course he is not mortal; all the signs contradict it: "I repeated" and the twice-repeated "again" call upon the Eternal Return, and the ellipsis with which the succeeding paragraph begins as well as the sleep into which Homer falls signal a new beginning based on forgetting. "The Immortal," Borges' incarnation of the universal writer, ends by dissipating that same literary figure. And so Borges joins that great train of writers who confer immortality only to deride it and lament it, that train which includes Petronius, Swift, De Quincey, Tennyson, and Eliot.

De Quinceyan Imagery

De Quincey is called upon to supply the scene-meaning at the very center of "The Immortal," and as we might guess, it is a picture of disorder and meaningless reiteration. But so that we shall not miss the point, the postscript refers us directly to De Quincey's *Writings* (III, 439), where we read a recollection of some Piranesi etchings Coleridge once described:

Many years ago, when I was looking over Piranesi's "Antiquities of Rome," Coleridge, then standing by, described to me a set of plates from that artist, called his "Dreams," and which record the scenery of his own visions during the delirium of a fever. Some of these (I describe only from memory of Coleridge's account) represented vast Gothic halls; on the floor of which stood mighty engines and machinery, wheels, cables, catapults, &c., expressive of enormous power put forth, or resistance overcome. Creeping

215

along the sides of the walls, you perceived a staircase; and upon this, groping his way upwards, was Piranesi himself. Follow the stairs a little farther, and you perceive them reaching an abrupt termination, without any balustrade, and allowing no step onwards to him who should reach the extremity, except into the depths below. Whatever is to become of poor Piranesi, at least you suppose that his labours must now in some way terminate. But raise your eyes, and behold a second flight of stairs still higher, on which again Piranesi is perceived, by this time standing on the very brink of the abyss. Once again elevate your eye, and a still more aerial flight of stairs is descried; and there, again, is the delirious Piranesi, busy on his aspiring labours: and so on, until the unfinished stairs and the hopeless Piranesi both are lost in the upper gloom of the hall. With the same power of endless growth and self–reproduction did my architecture proceed in dreams.

This passage is definitive of what J. Hillis Miller calls "the Piranesi effect" in De Quincey,[8] an effect we have all experienced, apparently, but with less frightening overtones, in discovering a disquieting infinity on the label of a box of salt or can of cocoa. Borges' picture of the City of the Immortals is closely patterned on this passage, from the general impression of purposeless repetition to the details of the staircases that "died without reaching anywhere" (*A*, 15), and even to the conditional quality imposed because the scene is only recalled, and recalled from another's description, not actually witnessed. On this point, the reference is furtively expressive since no such Piranesi etching exists, and we do not even know who invented—De Quincey or Coleridge— the one described by De Quincey. The postscript thus accuses the narrative of being false for plagiarizing De Quincey, who in turn is equally false.[9] More significantly, De Quincey's image specifies the abomination at the core of life's labyrinth for Borges: at the center, or "cell" as De Quincey calls it (VII,

203), there is no resting place, not even a destructive monster, but instead another labyrinth without plan or end. In effect, there is no center, but only the Piranesi effect of labyrinth within labyrinth, and "What we all dread most," Father Brown says, "is a maze with no centre."[10] Both De Quincey and Borges collaborate in describing such a maze. The labyrinth of the Immortals should lead to death, to a termination, to eternal rest; instead it turns upon itself and centrifugally flings the searchers out into newer and newer existences. De Quincey's visual Piranesi effect is here made to serve the office of a horrifying, distempered "Vision of Er."

The City of the Immortals is the symbolic center of Borges' universe, and from it emanates all the anxiety undermining that world. As in "The Approach," Borges usually withholds the final vision and concentrates on the way to the center, leaving the character on the very doorsill of revelation, but in "The Immortal" we are conducted to this center and enter into the absolute mythic reality that Mircea Eliade tells us is associated with such places:

The center, then, is pre-eminently the zone of the sacred, the zone of absolute reality. . . . The road leading to the center is a "difficult road" . . . , and this is verified at every level of reality: difficult convolutions of a temple (as at Borobudur); pilgrimage to sacred places (Mecca, Hardwar, Jerusalem); danger-ridden voyages of the heroic expeditions in search of the Golden Fleece, the Golden Apples, the Herb of Life; wandering in labyrinths; difficulties of the seeker for the road to the self, to the "center" of his being, and so on. The road is arduous, fraught with perils, because it is, in fact, a rite of the passage from the profane to the sacred, from the ephemeral and illusory to reality and eternity, from death to life, from man to divinity.[11]

The Library of Babel is one representation of this reality, and the City of the Immortals is a more terrifying one still. Of its sacred nature there can be no doubt: we are told that the gods have built it, and the Immortals do live there; but, instead of giving rise "to a life that is real, enduring and effective,"[12] this perverse heaven gives rise to an existence that is nightmarish, eternal, and futile, for "*the gods who built it were mad*" (*A*, 14). This city

is so horrible that its mere existence and perpetuation, even in the center of a hidden desert, contaminates the past and the future and in some way compromises the heavenly bodies. While it lasts, no one in the world can be valiant or happy. (*A*, 16)

This description goes beyond De Quincey's personal nightmares, and the word "horrible" can serve as our introduction to this loathsome realm, the Conradian heart of darkness. The odyssey of "The Immortal" is a Conradian journey to the center of the world, another journey to the center of Africa, where Rufus encounters the same reality as Mr. Kurtz: "The horror! The horror!"[13] Once there, there is nothing for either Homer/Rufus or Marlow to do but to turn around and rethread the windings of their approach. The mythic structure of "The Immortal" is thus supported by the mythological universe of Conrad, where to seek is to wander in a labyrinth—of adventure for the characters, of Marlow's style for the reader—and to find is to discover the abyss. Marlow says of Kurtz: "True, he had made that last stride, he had stepped over the edge, while I had been permitted to draw back my hesitating foot."[14] Conrad is actually worked into "The Immortal" by having Homer ship on the *Patna*, Jim's boat in *Lord Jim*, and the importance of Conrad to Eliot as well as to Borges serves to unite the three in their depiction of a world where, if all is not exactly desert, as in "The Immortal" and *The Waste Land*, everything wears "a vast and dismal aspect of disorder,"[15] a world where there is no meaning and no utterance beyond the cry for death.[16]

    The meeting of De Quincey, Chesterton, Conrad, and Borges in a common image is striking because they illuminate each other's thought. Chesterton, for example,

serves to remind us that the labyrinth was originally a bury-
ing place. Looking at "a vast black bulk of the cyclopean
building" in "The Point of a Pin," Father Brown says:

It reminds one of Coppée's poem about the Pharaoh and the
Pyramid. The house is supposed to be a hundred houses; and
yet the whole mountain of buildings is only one man's tomb.[17]

And Flambeau describes another labyrinth that also connects
that structure with the grave:

"Died," repeated Flambeau, "and that's about as much as
we can say. You must understand that towards the end of his
life he began to have those tricks of the nerves not uncom-
mon with tyrants. He multiplied the ordinary daily and
nightly guard around his castle till there seemed to be more
sentry-boxes than houses in the town, and doubtful charac-
ters were shot without mercy. He lived almost entirely in a
little room that was in the very centre of the enormous laby-
rinth of all the other rooms, and even in this he erected an-
other sort of central cabin or cupboard, lined with steel, like
a safe or battleship. Some say that under the floor of this
again was a secret hole in the earth, no more than large
enough to hold him, so that, in his anxiety to avoid the grave
he was willing to go into a place pretty much like it."[18]

In fact, we should have guessed, on the basis of "The Cult
of the Phoenix," that the City of Immortals would be a vast
graveyard, a universal mausoleum; but if we did not guess,
Borges puts the information in our way:

On finally disentangling myself from that nightmare, I found
myself manacled and thrown into an oblong niche, no big-
ger than an ordinary sepulcher, shallowly excavated in the
sharp slope of a mountain. . . . About a hundred irregular
niches, like mine, furrowed the mountain and the valley. (A,
10-11)

The nightmare is one labyrinth ("disentangling myself": "desen*red*arme") and the city is another.[19] Between them lies the grave and rebirth. We might even have known from the beginning that the labyrinth, in its oldest, Egyptian form (the form invoked by the setting of "The Immortal") is precisely a symbol of life through death, as C. N. Deedes tells:

Above all, the Labyrinth was the centre of activities concerned with those greatest of mysteries, Life and Death. There men tried by every means known to them to overcome death and to renew life. The Labyrinth protected and concealed the dead king-god in order that his life in the afterworld might be preserved. . . . The Labyrinth, as tomb and temple, fostered the development of all art and literature, activities which in those days possessed a religious and life-giving significance.[20]

It is the peculiar virtue of Borges' story, however, to have seen the potential horror in such a resurrection symbol and to have put De Quincey's famous passage so dramatically to work. Nevertheless, we might remind ourselves that Borges did not have to rely on De Quincey's Gothic nightmare, except as the singularly fine example it is. He could have drawn, and in some ultimate way does, on Chesterton's equally fantastic architecture:

Immediately beneath and about them the lines of the Gothic building plunged outwards into the void with a sickening swiftness akin to suicide. There is that element of Titan energy in the architecture of the Middle Ages that, from whatever aspect it be seen, it always seems to be rushing away, like the strong back of some maddened horse. This church was hewn out of ancient and silent stone, bearded with old fungoids and stained with the nests of birds. And yet, when they saw it from below, it sprang like a fountain at the stars; and when they saw it, as now, from above, it poured like a cataract into a voiceless pit. For these two men on the tower

*were left alone with the most terrible aspect of the Gothic:
the monstrous foreshortening and disproportion, the dizzy
perspectives, the glimpses of great things small and small
things great; a topsy-turvydom of stone in the mid-air. Details of stone, enormous by their proximity, were relieved
against a pattern of fields and farms, pygmy in their distance.
A carved bird or beast at a corner seemed like some vast
walking or flying dragon wasting the pastures and villages
below. The whole atmosphere was dizzy and dangerous, as
if men were upheld in air amid the gyrating wings of colossal genii; and the whole of that old church, as tall and rich
as a cathedral, seemed to sit upon the sunlit country like a
cloudburst.*[21]

"Dizzy and dangerous" (Chesterton is always more jovial
and buoyant than Borges, even when detailing the hideous):
the phrase applies to Piranesi climbing the fantastic staircase
in De Quincey's memory, and it applies to the City of the
Immortals as well. That it comes from Chesterton may serve
to remind us that Borges' allusions, by putting us into a universal vein of imagery, direct us to vaster land than the legend on the sign indicates.

What the reference in Borges' postscript does not tell
us is that much background information for "The Immortal"
can be found in another of De Quincey's essays, "Homer and
the Homeridae," and that while this essay, in relation to
Borges' story, fits into the category I call congenerous, it
does present another image that is perhaps even more basic
to this story than the labyrinth itself.

In "The Immortal" we read of the multitudinous survival of Homer down to our present time when he is discovered to be, in a typical Borges' pun, an "antiquarian," whose
form is understandably exhausted: "He was . . . a worn-out
and earthen man, with grey eyes and grey beard and singularly vague features" (*A*, 7). This is a comedown from the
colorful existence he had even as a Roman whose name was
brightly, perhaps doubly tinted: Marcus Flaminius Rufus.

(*Rufus* is Latin for red, and while *Flaminius* may evoke "flame" or "red" for us, it comes from the Latin *flamen*, meaning priest, in which case it may call to mind the gray priest in "The Circular Ruins," so notably associated with fire.) The waning of primordial fires into ash is a recurring pattern in Borges, who, adopting the everpresent of the Eternal Return, nevertheless describes life as if it were gradually burning out in each repetition, getting paler as it moves from the crimson life-blood of myth—"The Red Adam of Paradise" (*OP*, 69)—to the paler rose color of the historical past—the wall in "Feeling in Death" (*OI*, 246) belonging to the 1890s—to the pale grayness of the contemporaneous. The pattern is pinpointed by one of the metaphysical schools of Tlön:

Another school declares that all time has already transpired and that our life is scarcely the memory or twilight reflection, now undoubtedly falsified and mutilated, of an irrecoverable process. (*F*, 23)

The diminishing intensity of life veins Borges' work with melancholy and explains the backward urge of his mind, first to the time of childhood and then to the mythic past. De Quincey felt such an urge too, and in a sense both writers are "escapists"; but, in particular, De Quincey's application of the aging, diminishing quality of the world to Homer, as he expressed it in "Homer and the Homeridae" seems to have caught Borges' fancy.

In that essay Borges could have read of a Homer who is "the general patriarch of Occidental Literature" (VI, 7); of a Homer who could not write, like the Argos who composed the Odyssey but cannot make intelligible signs in the sand; of a Homer born in Smyrna like "the antiquarian Joseph of Smyrna (*A*, 7); of a Homer who "at the islands of Ios, of Chios, and of Crete . . . had a standing invitation" (VI, 35), like that same Cartaphilus who is buried at Ios, one of the traditionally ascribed burial places of Homer; of a Homer who never existed and whose poems were composed by many different men; and even of a Homer who was himself one and yet many like the Homer in Part V of Borges' story:

Others, like our Jacob Bryant, have fancied that he was not merely coeval with those heroes, but actually was one of those heroes—viz. Ulysses; and that the "Odyssey," therefore, rehearses the personal adventures, the voyages, the calamities of Homer himself. It is our old friend the poet, but with a new face; he is now a soldier, a sailor, a king, and, in case of necessity, a very fair boxer. (VI, 18)

Such correspondences, and the others like them, are curious, and it is quite possible that Borges first encountered them in De Quincey; but what is really striking in the De Quincey essay is a metaphysical equation of the survival of Homer's text to the survival of his body, and a consequent description of Homer as a monstrous ancient.

Homer, they say, is an old—old—very old man, whose trembling limbs have borne him to your door; and, therefore—what? Why, he ought to look very old indeed. Well, good man, he does look very old indeed. He ought, they say, to be covered with lichens and ivy. Well, he is covered with lichens and ivy. And sure I am that few people will undertake to know how a man looks when he is five hundred years old by comparison with himself at four hundred. Suffice it here to say, for the benefit of the unlearned, that not one of our own earliest writers, hardly Thomas of Ercildoune, has more of the peculiar antique words in his vocabulary than Homer. (VI, 76)

Here, as throughout De Quincey's essay, Homer is his poems, so that archaic words in an already ancient text become lichens on the old man's body—an astonishing image, one that would please Borges and perhaps lead him to join it with another of De Quincey's favorite figures, appropriate to this picture of Homer but not actually invoked in "Homer and the Homeridae."

The figure of Swift's Struldbrugg comes to De Quincey's mind whenever he wants to image the decrepit survival of the ancient world into the modern. Of course he does not think of Homer as decrepit (even though his imagination leads him to picture Homer that way), so that Struldbruggs are not found in "Homer and the Homeridae"; but the following passage shows De Quincey's typical use of the image:

The Romans were essentially the leaders in civilisation, according to the possibilities then existing; for their earliest usages and social forms involved a high civilisation, whilst promising a higher: whereas all Moslem nations have described a petty arch of national civility—soon reaching its apex, and rapidly barbarising backwards. This fatal gravitation towards decay and decomposition in Mahometan institutions, which at this day exhibit to the gaze of mankind one uniform spectacle of Mahometan ruins,—all the great Moslem nations being already in the Struldbrug* state, and held erect only by the colossal support of Christian powers,—could not . . . have been healed by the Arabian prophet.*

*To any reader who happens to be illiterate, or not extensively informed, it may be proper to explain that Struldbrugs *were a creation of Dean Swift. They were people in an imaginary world, who were afraid of dying, and who had the privilege of lingering on through centuries when they ought to have been dead and buried, but suffering all the evils of utter superannuation and decay; having a bare glimmering of semi-consciousness, but otherwise in the condition of mere vegetables.* (VII, 275)

Those Mahometan institutions now in ruins cast good light on the horrendous city of the Immortals in Borges' story, and

Homer in that story certainly qualifies as a Struldbrugg. The allusion, as De Quincey's charming condescension makes clear, is to Swift, and to the only part of Swift that has any meaningful connection with Borges—the Third Book of *Gulliver's Travels*. But just as quickly, it calls to mind Petronius' Sibyl, invoked by Eliot in the epigraph to *The Waste Land* and Tennyson's "Tithonus," to name only two versions of the myth that probably has its widest currency in English through Coleridge's "Ancient Mariner." As the "Everlasting Jew" the myth is noted by De Quincey:

"The Everlasting Jew":—*The German name for what we English call the Wandering Jew. The German imagination has been most struck by the duration of the man's life, and his unhappy sanctity from death: the English by the unrestingness of the man's life, his incapacity of repose.* (VII, 27)

Borges' story is another version of this myth, one that significantly differs from De Quincey's interpretation of Homer but could, nonetheless, have been suggested by it:

When you describe Homer, or when you hear him described, as a lively picturesque old boy (by the way, why does everybody speak of Homer as old?), full of life, and animation, and movement, then you say (or you hear say) what is true, and not much more than what is true. (X, 308)

De Quincey insists on Homer's liveliness, but he gives no images to that liveliness; Petronius, Swift, Tennyson, Eliot, and Borges all envision a weary immortal with a single desire: to die.

What Borges has done is apply the myth of the Everlasting Jew to literature, making the eternal figure the author himself. In doing so, Borges writes another entry in an old controversy and establishes himself with those who believe that *we* are the ancients. He mentions this argument in his preface to Ray Bradbury's *Martian Chronicles*: "The Renaissance had already observed, through the words of Giordano Bruno and Bacon, that we, not the Men of Genesis and Homer, are the true ancients."[22] Bradbury looks to the future of 2004, and we feel, Borges notes, "the gravitation, the vast and vague accumulation of the past."[23] Borges looks to the past, of course, but we feel the same thing. What distinguishes Borges in the Quarrel of the Ancients and Moderns is that he sees no final superiority on either side— all the fight has been taken out of the Battle of the Books. The human mind for him, as for De Quincey, is a palimpsest, "A membrane or roll cleansed of its manuscript by reiterated successions" (XIII, 341). Patches of writing from various ages and in various languages show through, but he sees the writing getting ever weaker, ever vaguer as initial rubrics are gradually faded by consecutive forgettings and rewritings. Ancient or Modern, all is a reflection of an archetype, and therefore less than real.

Allusion

The truest thing about "The Approach" was myth, and one of the most nearly real things in "The Immortal" is a made-up book. "Real," that is, in that it tells a kind of truth about the story and provides a thread for the labyrinth Borges has carefully built, so that reader, unlike character, will not be left with meaningless confusions at the core. This thread is given in the postscript, which is a manifest rationale for the story, but one that is integral and dramatic, for unlike the notes to *The Waste Land*, in "The Immortal" there is no change of authorial voice from introductory section to postscript that frame the narrative. What Eliot tells us in his notes is demonstrably, authoritatively factual; what the narrator of "The Immortal" tells us is pure fiction, that is, invention based on fact. In this respect, Borges has gone a step beyond either Joyce or Eliot in his relation to both text and reader, following a tendency that has been exploited by Nabokov, as I indicated earlier, in *Pale Fire*. The device arises from one of the oldest conventions of fiction and is common to the novel from the time of Cervantes, but the reflecting diptych of critical fiction and fictional criticism in a peculiarly compact, intellectual, literary format is characteristically Borgesian. Before him, no one astounded or pleased in quite that way.

The thread, or solution to the story's form and meaning, is put into a summary of an imaginary book entitled *A Coat of Many Colours*. As a whole, the story follows the usual pattern of *presentation* (introduction, parts I, II, III), *discussion* (parts IV, V), and *solution* (postscript); and the postscript itself conforms to the fundamental procedure of *proposition* (summary of *A Coat of Many Colours*) and *rejection* (concluding paragraph) that we have seen at the end of "New Refutation of Time" and the beginning of "The Approach," the same pattern described in an item from the bibliography of Pierre Menard's works:

> *(e) a technical article on the possibility of enriching chess by eliminating one of the rook's pawns. Menard proposes, recommends, discusses, and concludes by rejecting such an innovation. (F, 48)*

This pattern indicates the degree to which Borges' work and his system are hypothetical projections or constructions of the intellect; they are "pure" in this respect, not valid philosophical schemes, not "true" for Borges in the sense that Schopenhauer's metaphysic, say, was true for Schopenhauer but, rather, lucid improbabilities. The pattern is also a measure of the degree to which Borges' work is intellectual *play*, resting frequently on a jest. Few words in his vocabulary are more repeated than "game" or "play" (*juego*), and there is no better word to describe the effect his work has on readers. Certainly there is a strong element of play in his summary of the nonexistent critical study, *A Coat of Many Colours*, a summary that is nothing more or less than a meaningful joke.

A *Coat of Many Colours*, like a Borges' essay, classifies "The Immortal" and places it in a literary tradition. The class is that of the cento, and the tradition includes the centos of classical antiquity as well as works by Ben Jonson, Alexander Ross, George Moore, and T. S. Eliot, each of whom created works comprized of *retazos* (*A*, 26) or remnants of other works. Both the title, *A Coat of Many Colours*, and the author's name, Nahum Cordovero, however, disclose an artifice within artifice that is the hallmark of Borges. *A Coat of Many Colours* is an appropriate name for the book because it recalls the biblical Joseph's famous garment and thus invokes *Joseph* Cartaphilus, but also because *cento* is Latin for rag cushion or patchwork quilt, an etymological definition that gives new meaning to the word *retazo*. The book's title is equally appropriate to the story; in fact, the briefly imagined book stands in exact relationship to the produced story as a picture within a picture: the one is the compressed, analytic reflection of the other, almost to the point of a one-to-one correspondence. For if Homer, that imaginary author, wrote "The Immortal," compiled the postscript in fact, then a no less imaginary author, Nahum Cordovero, wrote the study; but once again, as with the title, we must read hieroglyphically. *Nahum*, the first name of this writer who provides a key to our perplexities about the text, means "comforter" or "source of comfort" in Hebrew,[24] while *Cordovero* is similarly, Kabbalistically prophetic: Moses Cordovero is the name of a famous Kabbalist writer whom Scholem calls the greatest theoretician of Jewish mysticism.[25] The word *cordovero* itself can be broken down into *string* (the Latin *chorda*, meaning catgut, derives from the Greek *khorde*, meaning yarn) and *true*: Nahum Cordovero is literally a latter-day Ariadne! The typically Borgesian twist in this word game is that the utterly false and fantastic source provides accurate information, pointing to the inner structure and outer reality of the story, for Cordovero concludes that "the whole document is apocryphal" (*A*, 26). The apocryphal naming the apocryphal: that is the Piranesi effect, that is the true Borges. Also Borgesian is the sense of humor. There is only grim humor and wryness in *The Waste Land*, and there is no deep laughter in "The Immortal"; but Borges is seldom without sly wit—*El Hacedor* is a notable exception. We saw the beginnings of that wit in feebler form in *Universal History of Infamy*; now we see it as subordinated effect and still another way in which Borges' writing may properly be described as *juego* or "game."

The main body of the postscript is a list, another of Borges' connective series, ranging from classical antiquity to the times of Bernard Shaw. The books alluded to fall into two fundamental, overlapping categories: the paradigmatic of form and the paradigmatic of content. No artless referential allusions here: each item is expressive; in sum they are substantive. The first group needs little explanation: it establishes the precedent for creating literature from literature, and it is made up of works based on other works, like Alexander Ross' *Virgilius Evangelizans*, a poem in Virgilian Latin dealing with the life of Christ, and George Moore's *The Brook Kerith*, a turgid historical novel about Christ in deliberately anachronistic biblical language. In both cases, what Borges is getting at, clearly, is a tendency of literature to recapture old subjects in old language based on previous writing. It is a tendency we have marked in Borges' own writing, and it is one the narrator of "The Immortal" calls to our attention in the introduction: "The original is written in English and abounds in Latinisms" (*A*, 7). Borges' verb ("*redactado*" not the more usual "*escrito*") in this sentence is especially important, implying as it does that the manuscript is not so much written as rewritten, a fact substantiated by the Latinisms. But what matters is that each of the writers specifically referred to has a direct bearing on the theme of the Immortal as Borges develops it.

Christ is literally the everlasting Jew, and therefore Ross's poem celebrates the Immortal in still another guise, while Moore's novel, like Lawrence's *The Man Who Died*, shows that the Crucifixion was not fatal to Jesus, who merely

229

underwent the imitative death of coma and revived to live another life in his own lifetime. (An appropriate subtitle for Moore's nearly forgotten novel could be taken from his completely forgotten play *The Making of an Immortal*, which deals with a writer.) Jonson, too, in his poem on Shakespeare contributes to the theme. The postscript cites "Ben Jonson, who defined his contemporaries with remnants from Seneca" (*A*, 26), and Borges obviously has in mind, as a corollary to Homer's universal immortality, the everything and nothingness of Jonson's contemporary, Shakespeare. Otherwise, Shakespeare, so appropriate to Borges' theme, would be conspicuously absent from "The Immortal." Turning to the text of Jonson's poem memorializing Shakespeare, we see that a particular passage even further reinforces the theme and technique of Borges' story:

> And though thou hadst small Latine, *and lesse* Greeke,
>   *From thence to honour thee, I would not seeke*
> *For names; but call forth thund'ring* Aeschilus,
>   Euripides, *and* Sophocles *to us,*
> Paccuvius, Accius, *him of* Cordova *dead*
>   *To life againe . . .*[26]

The method of involving other authors is Borges', and the resurrection of Seneca, "him of *Cordova* dead," is a reenactment of "The Immortal." The procedure hinges on "contemporaries"—literature can make contemporaries of Virgil and Alexander Ross; it can raise from the dead, as in the case of Jonson and Seneca. The Immortal is Author; his immortality is Literature.

The last precedent cited by Cordovero is the most important: *The Waste Land* provides not only an analogous form but parallel content as well. In a word, both *The Waste Land* and "The Immortal" are centos that come to pretty much the same conclusion:

> *"These fragments I have shored against my ruins . . ."*[27]

When the end approaches, wrote Cartaphilus, images of what is remembered no longer remain: only words remain. Words, mutilated and displaced words, words of others, were the poor dole left him by the hours and the centuries. (A, 26)

The Tithonus-like weariness of Borges' Homer is reflected in Eliot's Tiresias, who, like De Quincey's Homer, is ancient in other than a personal sense. Moreover, both works are world visions, moving between the ancient and modern, the East and the West, presenting the world as a desert ruin; both employ the device of the narrator who is all the characters and whose memory is their medium of existence; both are self-consciously mythic and rely on the quest or search for their central action and employ the metaphor of thirst as the fundamental yearning, a thirst both for the River of Life and the River of Death; both are ostentatiously learned and employ literary allusion as matter and method. If there is a striking difference, it is the characterizing one that Eliot's poem is social, religious, irrationalistic, and concerned with the kinds of love, while Borges' story is abstracted from society, fantastic, intellectual, cogent, and unconcerned with human relations. Both works are modified monologues, though it is worthwhile noting that sometimes in Eliot's we lose sight of the central figure (as in parts of "The Game of Chess"), while in Borges' story the central figure is an almost constant focus. (In Borges there is a general tendency to limit narrative to one figure, and to one figure who is not in vital, emotional contact with others, to whom other people figure largely as ideas or stimuli to action. This is a condition of Borges' lonely world, and it is a severe limitation upon the possibilities of his fiction; but, on the other hand, it is the condition that enables him to operate in an atmosphere almost purely speculative and imaginary. Then too, there is often a suggestion, never developed, sometimes censured, of political and moral implications in Borges. I have noted one example in "The Immortal," and I do not think it would be hard to derive a fairly cogent, if not satisfactory, ethic from his writings. But such an effort, so essential to an understanding of parts of Eliot, is foreign to Borges' writing, which presents morality, like murder, as one of the fine arts.) But how can two men who have such a similar vision, and a similar imagery, who rely on the same schemes, as of the Eternal Return (embodied in Eliot in the Tarot cards and the chess game, which symbols are among Borges' favorites), how can two such men create such formally different works? The answer lies, again, in the vantage point. Eliot, at least in *The Waste Land*, is on the order of De Quincey, and Borges works more in the vein of Joyce, whose writings also function on the principle of the Eternal Return. I am speaking, of course, of esthetic dispositions that tend toward the open, aspiring, inevitably inconclusive and those that tend toward the closed, formulated, finished work. Specifically, Eliot's view in *The Waste Land*, as we can gather from the related "Gerontion," is from within the labyrinth:

> . . . *Think now*
> *History has many cunning passages, contrived corridors*
> *And issues . . .*[28]

and he shows a character who, like De Quincey, "can connect/ Nothing with nothing,"[29] even though he does exist in a work that, like De Quincey's, is busy making parallels. Borges, in contrast, leads his character to the moment of awareness: "Everything became clear to me that day" (*A*, 19). Joyce, Eliot, Borges are all labyrinthine; all employ the image and symbol of the labyrinth; but Joyce and Borges, by their use of magic correlation, which is an ordering expression of the Eternal Return, create labyrinths that are complete and decipherable; all three aim at mystification, but Eliot chooses that mystification as a final intention. One advantage that emerges from such a comparison is the possibility of uniting our views of Borges, Joyce, Eliot (and Yeats too, of whom Borges writes: "Like so many others, he conceived a cyclical doctrine of history"[30]) in the study of a common theme—the Eternal Return. Such a comparison is beyond the scope of my present interest, but it indicates once again the synthesizing quality of Borges' work, and, by association, implies its value.

The second group of allusions in the postscript has less to do with the technique of the cento and more with the substance of the story. In each instance something has been borrowed from the acknowledged source and interpolated into "The Immortal," but these are not cases of literal theft or simple annexation. Pliny is a good example. On the surface, it would seem that the allusion to *Natural History* is referential, an allusion to informative writing that is the source of the passage in question. In fact "source" seems to be the right word here, for Borges does take a description from Pliny and filter it into his own text. In Part I of "The Immortal," where Cordovero finds an interpolation from Pliny, we read:

We left from Arisnoë and entered the scorched desert. We crossed the land of the troglodytes, who devour snakes and lack all verbal communication; that of the garamantes, who keep their females in common and nourish themselves on lions; that of the augyls, who worship only Tartarus. We wearied other deserts, where the sand is black, where the traveler must usurp the hours of night because the fervor of day is intolerable. From far off I caught sight of the mountain that gave its name to the Ocean: on its slopes grows spurge, which neutralizes poisons; on its summit live the satyrs, a nation of cruel, savage men, given to lust. That those barbarous regions, where the earth is mother of monsters, could shelter in their bosom a famous city, seemed inconceivable to all of us. We continued our journey since it would have been a dishonor to retreat. A few rash men slept with their faces exposed to the moon; fever burned them; in the depraved water of the cisterns others drank madness and death. (A, 9-10)

And in the section of Pliny to which Cordovero precisely directs us we do find the framework for the description in Borges:

In the middle of the desert some place the Atlas tribe and next to them the half-animal Goat-Pans and the Blemmyae and Gamphasantes and Satyrs and Strapfoots.

The Atlas tribe have fallen below the level of human civilization, if we can believe what is said; for they do not address one another by any names, and when they behold the rising and setting sun, they utter awful curses against it as the cause of disaster to themselves and their fields, and when they are asleep they do not have dreams like the rest of mankind. The Cave-dwellers hollow out caverns, which are their dwellings; they live on the flesh of snakes, and they have no voice, but only make squeaking noises, being entirely devoid of intercourse by speech. The Garamates do not practice marriage but live with their women promiscuously. The Augilae only worship the powers of the lower world. The Gamphasantes go naked, do not engage in battle, and hold no intercourse with any foreigner. The Blemmyae are reported to have no heads, their mouth and eyes being attached to their chests. The Satyrs have nothing of ordinary humanity about them except human shape. The form of the Goat-Pans is that which is commonly shown in pictures of them. The Strapfoots are people with feet like leather thongs, whose nature it is to crawl instead of walking. The Pharusi, originally a Persian people, are said to have accompanied Hercules on his journey to the Ladies of the West. Nothing more occurs to us to record about Africa.[31]

The borrowing, however, is neither exact nor artless. Of course Borges has condensed Pliny, but then he has also blended his sources, creating a pastiche of pastiches, as in the fragment about men being fevered, burned to death by the moon, which is not found in that part of Pliny and which may have come to Borges through De Quincey:

In p. 50 of the "Annotations" upon Glanvill's Lux Orientalis
*the author . . . having occasion to quote from the Psalms
"The sun shall not burn thee by day, neither the moon by
night" in order to illustrate that class of cases where an
ellipsisis to be suggested by the sense rather than directly
indicated, says "The word* burn *cannot be repeated, but some
other more suitable verb is to be supplied." A gentleman,
however, who has lately returned from Upper Egypt, &c.,
assures me that the moon* does *produce an effect on the skin
which may as accurately be expressed by the word "burn"
as any solar effect.* (X, 454-55)

Most meaningful in the excerpt from Pliny is that the description of these monstrous peoples is fitted into a geographical
sequence that suggests a journey and that Homer himself is
cited as an authority for the information:

*Eastward of all of these there are vast uninhabited regions
spreading as far as the Garamantes and Augilae and the
Cave-dweller—the most reliable opinion being that of those
who place two Ethiopias beyond the African desert, and especially Homer, who tells us that the Ethiopians are divided
into two sections, the eastward and the westward.*[32]

The clear implication is that Homer has made the trip, knows
the land firsthand, an implication that reinforces Borges'
identification of Homer as Rufus, the man who makes the trip
to the City of the Immortals. The relationship between
Borges and Pliny is active: if Borges borrows from Pliny, he
enriches the Pliny text by eliciting a new meaning.

The other sources are used similarly. The actual reference is not exhaustive, and if we take the trouble to con-
sult the passage in question, we find something new in the
story and often in the source as well. Skipping over the De
Quincey passage, which I have already discussed, we can
compare "A letter from Descartes to the ambassador Pierre
Chanut" (A, 26) with Borges' version:

If I had been only as wise as they say savages persuade themselves monkeys are, I should never have been known by anyone as a maker of books: for it is said that they imagine that the monkeys would be able to speak if they wished, but that they refrain from doing it so that they will not be forced to work.[33]

I recalled that it is famous among the Ethiopians that the monkeys deliberately do not speak so that they will not be forced to work, and I attributed Argus' silence to suspicion or fear. (A, 17)

This is the direct correspondence, but more interesting is the motto Descartes takes from Seneca's *Thyestes* at the end of the same letter:

And so I think the best thing I can do from now on is to abstain from writing books; and having taken for my motto:

> *Death lies heavy upon that man who,*
> *unusually well known to others, dies*
> *unknown to himself.*[34]

In Descartes' allusion to antiquity, and to the same figure Jonson employs and Cordovero mentions, Borges shows the centrifugal force of literature; and by noting the sense of Seneca's lines we are directed to the pathos of the conversation between Rufus and Homer, who has become a dog-like creature and forgotten his own nature. There is a worse death: to be famous to all, and to die unknown to oneself. Notice, however, that neither the allusion in the postscript nor the passage about the monkeys in the narrative directly evokes this motto. The evocative quality of this allusion is only remotely present, almost silent, as is customary in Borges. Nevertheless, if the motto serves for Descartes, it likewise can serve for Borges' story, for each of us, having forgotten that we are Homer, dies famous throughout the world but unrecognized by ourselves.

As with the first group of allusions I considered from the postscript, the last in the second group is the most important: Cordovero directs us to *Back to Methuselah*, Act V,[35] but once again, while he points in the right direction, his scope is not nearly broad enough. The parallels between the Shaw play and Borges' story are close and pervasive, even though the attitude taken toward immortality in each differs. Shaw's theme, as described by Borges, is optimistic, corrective, while the one we have seen in Borges is dejected and dispiriting:

In Man and Superman *he declares that heaven and hell are not places but conditions of the human spirit; in* Back to Methuselah *that man ought to resolve to live 300 years so as not to die at 80 in full immaturity with a golf club in his hand, and that the physical universe began by Spirit and shall return to Spirit.*[36]

Here then is another ethic for immortals and one that brings the world back to its originating spirit as well, but Borges' story is far from the joking argument for creative evolution that Shaw's play is. Nevertheless Borges found much to his use and liking in Shaw's "cerebral capers" (69).

Shaw's play, as his preface states, shows that "human life is continuous and immortal" (23), and it uses the mythic image of the Wandering Jew (112) as well as the literary unity Borges hypothesizes: "An ancient writer whose name has come down to us in several forms, such as Shakespeare, Shelley, Sheridan, and Shoddy" (219), and it even voices the fundamental notion of art as dream when Eve tells Adam of certain of their sons

who borrow and never pay; but one gives them what they want, because they tell beautiful lies in beautiful words. They can remember their dreams. They can dream without sleeping. They have not will enough to create instead of dreaming; but the serpent said that every dream could be willed into creation by those strong enough to believe in it. (98)

237

In the last act, which is commended to our attention by Cordovero, the time is A.D. 31,920, yet the matter is the same as that of Borges' antiquity, and the point is made that tomorrow is "the day that never comes" (311). In this world beyond Bradbury, the most specific locus of comparison between the two texts is the Swiftian notion, complicated by the Emersonian doctrine of compensation, that the Immortals have grown completely indifferent because in the end all things balance out. In Borges we read:

Instructed by centuries of practice, the republic of immortal men had achieved the perfection of tolerance and almost of disdain. It knew that in an infinite term all things happen to every man. On account of his past or future virtues, every man deserves all goodness, but also deserves all treachery because of his past or future infamies. (A, 20)

This is the intolerable ethic Borges extracts with all the irony of the defeated victor, while in *Back to Methuselah* we find that Shaw's immortals, like Borges', are indifferent to discomfort and pleasure, for, as they recognize: "Everything happens to everybody sooner or later if there is time enough. And with us there is eternity" (271). But the passage we remember from Shaw's play as being most Borgesian of all is one in a completely different vein; one, nevertheless, where eras, texts, authors coalesce into one unified cultural senility:

There is a prehistoric saying that has come down to us from a famous woman teacher. She said: "Leave women; and study mathematics." It is the only remaining fragment of a lost scripture called The Confessions of St. Augustin, the English Opium Eater. *That primitive savage must have been a great woman, to say a thing that still lives after three hundred centuries.* (310)

Like the other allusions, the one to *Back to Methuselah* has its secret aspect too. In the third act, not the fifth, which Cordovero directs us to, we can find a solution for the apparent death of Homer, which is related in the introduction of "The Immortal": "In October the princess heard from a passenger on the *Zeus* that Cartaphilus had died at sea on returning to Smyrna and that they had buried him on the island of Ios" (A, 7).[37] Nowhere in the text does Borges offer an explanation for this apparent death, but if we turn to the third act of Shaw's play we find a character quoting a report that "points out that an extraordinary number of first-rate persons . . . have died by drowning during the last two centuries" (155) . The explanation for these drownings, which surely includes the death of Cartaphilus at sea, is given by a near-immortal archbishop who ran into bureaucratic problems trying to collect his pension at the age of ninety-seven because he looked so young. His solution was simple: pretend to die and start life all over again.

I did kill myself. It was quite easy. I left a suit of clothes by the seashore during the bathing season, with documents in the pocket to identify me. I then turned up in a strange place, pretending that I had lost my memory, and did not know my name or my age or anything about myself. Under treatment I recovered my health, but not my memory. I have had several careers since I began this routine of life and death. I have been an archbishop three times. When I persuaded the authorities to knock down all our towns and rebuild them from the foundations, or move them, I went into the artillery, and became a general. I have been a President. (172)

Even the question of Homer's burial is solved by this archbishop, who, in his architectural plans, may even remind us of Borges' Homer. When asked how he can have been President Dickenson, whose body was cremated and whose ashes lie in St. Paul's, the archbishop replies:

They almost always found the body. During the bathing season there are plenty of bodies. I have been cremated again and again. At first I used to attend my own funeral in disguise, because I had read about a man doing that in an old romance by an author named Bennett, from whom I remember borrowing five pounds in 1912. But I got tired of that. I would not cross the street now to read my last epitaph. (172)

Here then is the sham death practiced by the Immortals so as not to arouse suspicion, and here too is the necessary loss of memory to permit the renewal of life. This death-by-water motif is further suggested by Homer's explanation that "on the fourth of October, 1921, the *Patna*, which was carrying me to Bombay, had to cast anchor in a port on the Eritrean coast" (*A*, 23). The *Patna*, "a local steamer as old as the hills," carrying "eight hundred pilgrims (more or less),"[38] is Jim's boat in Conrad's *Lord Jim*, and we read there a Captain Brierly, who commits suicide by jumping overboard. Jim, on the other hand, also jumps ship in the crucial moment of his life, and Conrad has him explain: "It was as if I jumped into a well—into an everlasting deep hole. . . ."[39] In light of Borges we read this passage somewhat differently and are not surprised to find another character urging the following plan for Jim, "Let him creep twenty feet underground and stay there" (157), and still another remarking, "Bury him in some sort" (157). Of course this is what in effect happens and Jim, "the youngest human being now in existence" (157), revives to lead a new life.

This last allusion to Conrad demands our recognition that "The Immortal" is immensely more allusive than Borges admits. The *Lord Jim* allusion really tells us nothing about "The Immortal," but it invokes the same theme from other writings and thus establishes the mirror relationship in literature that the Immortals recognize in life:

Among the Immortals . . . each act (and each thought) is the echo of others that preceded it in the past, without apparent principle, or the faithful omen of others that will repeat it, to the point of vertigo, in the future. There is no thing that

is not lost, as it were, amidst indefatigable mirrors. Nothing
can occur only once, nothing is preciously precarious.
(A, 22)

Allusion is thus the device that reflects one work in another;
and despite the lack of apparent principle in repetition that
the Immortals describe, allusion repeats meaningfully, ordering the chaos that is at once literature and life. Thus we have
in the story major themes alluded to, as in the case of "the
nightingale of the Caesars" (*A*, 17), which invokes Keats'

> *The voice I hear this passing night was heard*
> *In ancient days by emperor and clown* [40]

And we have minor works, like the reference to a novel by
Ellis Cornelia Knight, which Borges probably read of in De
Quincey's review of another book (V, 151). The novel's title
tells us about all we need to know of it: *Marcus Flaminius*;
or *a view of the military, political and social life of the Ro-*
mans: in a series of letters from a patrician to his friend; in
the year DCC.LXII. from the foundation of Rome to year
DCC.LXIX. There are no significant parallels in the novel to
Borges' story, except perhaps for one lamenting letter that
in part reads: "death flies from the cavern of despair and only
delights to overthrow the pompous fabrics of hope: your
friend still lives; his youth and the strength of his constitution have once more snatched him from the arms of freedom."[41] This last-minute reference, gathered magpie fashion
by Borges in the course of his reading, establishes a pole, and
an end, to the range of allusion I have been noting in "The
Immortal." From the basic outline of Eliot's *The Waste Land*,
which supplies the form of Borges' story, and the specific
material of Shaw's *Back to Methuselah*, which supplies
much of the content, to Miss Knight's *Marcus Flaminius*,
which supplies at least a single item, we have the entire rank
of allusion. One could spend more time filling in the degrees
and undoubtedly Borges will give rise to his own academic
industry, just as Eliot and Joyce have; but, more important,

what concerns all readers of Borges and not just the detectives is the purpose and meaning of these allusions.

Borges has taken care to see that all readers will know the allusive nature of "The Immortal," even if they do not grasp the extent of that allusiveness. Hence all readers are aware of the substantive as well as the secret quality in this work. Like *Ulysses*, like *The Waste Land*, "The Immortal" uses allusion not only as a means to an end but as an end itself. Each of the allusions contributes to our awareness of literature as universal memory, which, in not seeming to lose sight of anything guarantees the survival of all, is, in a word, immortality. To break down the story into its constituent allusions is an inevitable desire of the inquiring mind, but to do so takes one no closer to the monistic meaning of the narrative that has as its purpose the fictional embodiment of the philosophy Borges reads in Emerson: "a faith which eliminates circumstances, and which declares that every man is all men and that there is no one who is not the universe."[42] On the other hand, to be at least aware of these borrowings is to be in touch with the secret meaning of the story, is to read it Kabbalistically, hieroglyphically, to solve its puzzle with the clues given.

In the use of allusion Borges never pushed further than "The Immortal." Nor did he ever write another story that so completely embodies his metaphysical and literary theories; for, in this one narrative, he actually creates a character of extraordinary implication and presents him a situation where we perceive a phase of his emergence and disintegration. The character, the only character, I think, in all of Borges, is the literary Over-Soul. Emerson, in his notes to an essay on the Over-Soul, had jotted down the following observations:

> *There is one soul.*
> *It is related to the world.*
> *Art is its action thereon.*
> *Science finds its methods.*
> *Literature is its record.*[43]

Borges takes the first of these jottings as his premise and the last as his method. Emerson said he liked to read "for the lustres, as if one should use a fine picture in a chromatic experiment, for its rich colours" (439). Borges seems to read that way in preparation for his stories, and in reading him we do the same, noting the allusions—some of them—for the originals they are, and in this way we discover, with Emerson, that "it is a greater joy to see the author's author, than himself" (439).

The author's author is first of all Borges, because of the involutions of his fictional worlds; but then the author's author is the figure Borges' essays define with tireless precision, whose spirit moves in and above Borges' work to bring it into line with all other works. It is toward an intimation of this spirit that all his works move, asking the same fantastic question we ask when, in different terms, we consider literary history and tradition:

> *The player is also prisoner*
> *(the phrase is Omar's) of another table*
> *of black nights and white days.*
>
> *God moves the player, and he the piece.*
> *What god behind God begins the plot of*
> *dust and time and dream and agony?* (*H*, 60)

Borges began by introducing his own imaginary passages into already existing books, then progressed to the fabrication of imaginary books with bits of real ones worked in, and finally created a single character who not only is responsible for this story, but for all literature, the author of authors: the Immortal. That creation represents a mastery by order and reason of infinite chaos; that it is, ironically, a destruction of everything personal and real only epitomizes the character of his achievement and the dilemma of our irrational existence.

Borges' is the hand that points: his essence is a direction away from his own substance. To see beyond his work—really, to see through it to other writings—is the greatest necessity, and achievement, of his labor. He stands midway between the cataphysical characters of his stories and the metaphysical spirit of literature, reflecting primary light onto tertiary beings. He does this with intricate allusion, and if we are tempted to undervalue his genius because he seems to borrow all that is his, let us remember what De Quincey wrote of Coleridge, with generosity and accuracy, a statement that applies to each of these three—Coleridge, De Quincey, Borges—in different ways, but that, in that minor variation of a perpetual gesture, constitutes their literary identity. De Quincey writes: "If he took—he gave. Constantly he fancied other men's thoughts his own; but such were the confusions of his memory that continually, and with even greater liberality, he ascribed his own thoughts to others" (II, 228).

Notes

1. *Complete Essays*, 439.
2. Op. Cit., 437.
3. *A World Elsewhere*, 67.
4. "Author's Note," *Six Plays of Strindberg*, trans. Elizabeth Sprigge (New York, 1955), 193.
5. *Religio Medici and Other Writings* (New York, 1951), 7-8.
6. *Complete Essays*, 447.
7. Op. Cit., 442.
8. *The Disappearance of God*, 67.
9. The etchings De Quincey (and Coleridge?) apparently had in mind are the *Carceri d'invenzione*, which Borges labels an influence on *Vathek* and describes as "etchings, praised by Beckford, which represent mighty palaces that are also inextricable labyrinths" (*OI*, 191).

     See Miller (*The Disappearance of God*, 69n.), who gives a brief explanation and directs the reader to other pertinent sources.
10. *Father Brown Stories*, 235.
11. *Cosmos and History*, 17-18. It is relevant that the throne at Borobudur was an empty one—the void was king. Jean Grenier emphasizes this

significant void in *Conversations on the Good Uses of Freedom*, trans. Alexander Coleman (Cambridge, Mass., 1967).

12. Op. Cit.

13. Joseph Conrad, *The Heart of Darkness and the Secret Sharer* (New York, 1950), 131.

14. Op. Cit., 134.

15. Joseph Conrad, *Lord Jim* (Cambridge, 1958), 225.

16. In his *Introducción a la literatura inglesa* (Buenos Aires, 1965), which he wrote in collaboration with María Ester Vázquez, Borges calls Conrad "one of the great novelists and story tellers of English literature"(55), and describes the theme of Lord Jim—"the obsession with honor and the shame of having been a coward"(55)—in such a way as to suggest a relationship between that novel and his story "The Shape of the Sword."

17. *Father Brown Stories*, 690.

18. Op. Cit., 306.

19. "Disentangle" is "*desen*red*arme*" and "red" means "net." Does this hieroglyphic breaking down of "*desen*red*arme*" gives us another reason for Borges' predilection for the color *red*? A bilingual pun, certainly is not beyond him.

20. *The Labyrinth*, ed. S. H. Hooke (New York, 1935), 42.

21. *Father Brown Stories*, 129.

22. *Martian Chronicles* (Buenos Aires, 1955), 8.

23. Op. Cit.

24. Eric Partridge, *Name This Child* (London, 1959), 93.

25. *Major Trends in Jewish Mysticism*, 252.

26. "To the memory of my beloved the Author Mr. William Shakespeare: and what he has left us," *The Oxford Book of Seventeenth Century Verse* (Oxford, 1934), 177.

27. T. S. Eliot, *The Complete Poems and Plays*, 50.

28. Op. Cit., 22.

29. Op.Cit., 46.

30. *Introducción a la literatura inglesa*, 62.

31. *Pliny, Natural History*, trans. W. H. Rackam and W. H. S. Jones, V (London, 1938-1963), viii, 44-45. Note that "Troglodytae" is given as "Cave-dwellers" in this translation whereas Borges uses the more Latinate, and thus more significant, "trogloditas," the equivalent of our "troglodytes."

32. Op. Cit., viii, 43.

33. *Correspondence*, VII (Paris, 1960), 199-200.

34. Op. Cit., viii, 43.

35. George Bernard Shaw, *Back to Methuselah* (Baltimore, 1961). All subsequent references are included parenthetically in the text.

36. *Introducción a la literatura inglesa*, 54.

37. In the Spanish, of course, "at sea" reads "*en el mar*," literally "*on* the sea" or "*in* the sea."

38. *Lord Jim*, 12-13.
39. Op. Cit., 32.
40. "Ode to a Nightingale," *The Poetical Works of Keats*, 208.
41. *Marcus Flaminius* (London, 1808), 24.
42. "Estudio preliminar to *Representative Men*," xiii.
43. *Complete Essays*, xxi.

INTERVIEW

I went to Buenos Aires in July 1966 with a grant, an encouraging note from the *Paris Review*, and no Spanish to speak. The day before I left, there was a military coup d'etat; on the day itself a fellow passenger collapsed on the gangway to the helicopter in the 106–degee heat. Both omens impressed others lightly: when I questioned the stewardess, she smilingly told me that the man had died; in Argentina a dignified lady at dinner told me not to worry about the *coup*: "Are the telephones still working? Well, there," she purred, "you see! It was a Courréges coup, only a matter of new boots."

Of course I had written Borges earlier about interviewing him, and his mother had responded in English: call as soon as you arrive, at 1:30 on any day. I called after two days, from a pay phone in a bar, and when her rasped voice responded, naturally enough, in Spanish, I dwindled to incomprehension and hung up. For a couple of days I wandered, wondering how I could ever make good on the grant, the magazine offer. In the Paner book shop on Calle Callao, the owner, Ernesto Bungue, spotted me as a moping American. He smiled, first at my plight, kindly, then into the telephone, whimsically: "Hello, Georgie? There's an American here who wants to interview you. Can he come by the library?"

So, when you read Borges recalling tall, shy young men who had asked him questions in New York, you'll realize that he was not only recalling but also acknowledging his present questioner, as he did a bit later, jabbing at my untimid necktie. In later years, he sometimes ignored the person of the interviewer, chiefly propping his monologue with them; but he interested himself in our interview, and the edited transcription retains some of that playful interest.

When I first went to the National Library, of which he was then the director, Borges entered the anteroom a few minutes later, to chuckles from fellow workers. (Other times when he came in, always wearing a beret and a dark grey flannel suit hanging loosely from his shoulders and sagging over his shoes, people stopped talking for a moment, pausing, perhaps out of respect, perhaps out of empathetic hesitation for a man who is not entirely blind.) It seems that he had asked one of them to deliver a package; and, when whoever it was got to the address, she discovered an empty lot—and one more instance of the Borges many readers ignore while hefting his profound melancholy and the metaphysic of which he declared himself an apostate before he swore out its articles. "Always there are jokes, little practical jokes," his secretary Susana Quinteros, told me. Later she gave me a copy of Adolfo Bioy Casares's novel *The Invention of Morel* with an inscription in Spanish that reads: "So that you may get to know other Argentinian authors besides Borges." (Everywhere I found the same curious disbelief about my interest in Borges, and it usually culminated in a statement to the effect that Borges wasn't Argentine at all, he was European. Of course this was long before the last days when he used to sit in a store window on Saturdays to sign copies of his *Complete Works*.)

Each day, Quinteros told me, Borges arrived at the library where it was now his custom to dictate letters and poems that she typed out and read back to him. Following his revisions, she would make two or three, sometimes four copies of each poem before Borges was satisfied. Some afternoons she read to him, and he would carefully correct her English pronunciation. Occasionally, when he wanted to think, she said, he would leave his office and slowly circle the library's rotunda, high above the readers at tables below. For me, this image of his removed presence characterized both his comportment and the respect with which he was treated at the library.

Now, told of my presence, Borges asked Quinteros to show me into his office, where I waited for five or seven minutes. I wondered if he was giving me time to look around. Anyway, I did. The room, recalling an older Buenos Aires, was not really an office, but a large, ornate, high-ceilinged chamber in the freshly renovated library. On the walls—but far too high to be easily read, as if hung with diffidence—were various academic certificates and literary citations as well as several Piranesi etchings, recalling the nightmarish Piranesi ruin in "The Immortal." Over the fireplace hung a large portrait, which Quinteros later explained to me in a fitting, if unintentional echo of a basic Borgesian theme: "*No importa.* It's a reproduction of another painting."

At diagonally opposite corners of the room stood two large, revolving bookcases that held the books Borges most frequently consulted, all arranged in a certain order and never varied so that he could find them by position and size. The dictionaries, for instance, were collected together, among them an old, sturdily rebacked, well-worn copy of Webster's *Encyclopedic Dictionary of the English Language* and an equally well-worn Anglo-Saxon dictionary. Among the other volumes, ranging from books in German and English on theology and philosophy, literature and history, were the complete *Pelican Guide to English Literature*, the *Modern Library Francis Bacon*, Holander's *The Poetic Eddas*, *The Poems of Catullus*, Forsyth's *Geometry of Four Dimensions,* several volumes of Harrap's *English Classics*, Parkman's *The Conspiracy of Pontiac*, and the Chambers edition of *Beowulf.* Recently, Ms. Quinteros said, Borges had been reading The *American Heritage Picture History of the Civil War*, and just the night before he had taken to his home, where his mother, in her nineties, read aloud to him, Washington Irving's *Life of Mahomet.*

I had scarcely time to jot down these titles, when Borges entered through the scarcely opened door as if he were trying to sneak in unobserved—a feat through that massive doorway. Standing far from me in that formal chamber, he held a small book to his face, not an inch away from his eyes, and slowly read a number of lines, his whole head grazing the rows. The book pocketed, he withdrew the watch he kept in his outside breast pocket, depending from a chain hooked through the eyelet of his lapel. (He read the watch too, though at a greater distance, in an epitomizing gesture.) Finally, he approached: "Well now, we have to work." As he crossed the room, I had my first full-face look at him.

Borges' walk was tentative, and he carried a cane that he used like a divining rod. He was short, with combed-back grey hair that looked slightly unnatural in the way it rose from the back of his large head. His features were vague, softened by age, partially erased by the paleness of his skin. His voice, too, was unemphatic, almost a drone, seeming, possibly because of the unfocused expression of his eyes, to come from another person behind the face, and his gestures and expressions were lethargic—typified by the involuntary droop of one eyelid.

As I saw later, when he laughed—and he laughed often—his features wrinkled into what actually resembled a wry questioned mark; and he was apt to make a sweeping or clearing gesture with his arm and to thump his hand on the table. Most of his statements took the form of rhetorical questions, but in asking a question he wanted answered, Borges displayed now a looming curiosity, now a shy, almost pathetic incredulity. When he chose, as in telling a joke, he adopted a crisp, dramatic tone, and his quotation of a line from Oscar Wilde would have done justice to an Edwardian actor. His accent and diction defied easy classification: a cosmopolitan diction emerging from a Spanish background, educated by correct English speech and influenced by American movies. (Certainly no Englishman ever pronounced *piano* as *pie-ano*, and no American says *a-née-a-hilates*.) His words slurred softly into one another, allowing suffixes to dwindle so that *couldn't* and *could* were virtually indistinguishable. Slangy and informal when he wanted to be, more typically he was formal and bookish in his speech, relying, quite naturally, on phrases like *that is to say* and *wherein*. (When he used *hooligans*, it was as if believed those he was describing would have chosen precisely the same word.) He almost always linked his sentences with a narrative *and then* or a logical *consequently*. Most of all, Borges was shy. Retiring, even self-obliterating, he avoided personal statements as much as possible and obliquely answered questions about himself by talking about other writers, using their words and even their books as emblems of his own thought.

I have tried to preserve the colloquial quality of his English speech—an illuminating contrast to his writings and a revelation of his intimacy with a language that has figured so importantly in the development of his writing. For those who wonder, and they should: I sent Borges a copy of the transcribed, edited interview along with a few queries. He answered those queries promptly through his secretary and expressed his satisfaction with the faithfulness to his words, a satisfaction he repeated when this interview was published.

You don't object to my recording our conversation?

No, no. You fix the gadgets. They are a hindrance, but I will try to talk as if they're not here. Now, where are you from?

From New York.

Ah, New York. I was there and I liked it very much. I said to myself: "Well, I have made this, this is my work."

You mean the walls of the high buildings, the maze of the streets?

Yes. I rambled about the streets—Fifth Avenue—and got lost, but the people were always kind. I remember answering many questions about my work from tall, shy young men. In Texas they had told me to be afraid of New York, but I liked it. Well, are you ready?

Yes, the machine is already working.

Now, before we start, what kind of questions are they?

Mostly about your own work and about English writers you have expressed an interest in.

Ah, that's right. Because if you ask me questions about the younger contemporary writers, I'm afraid I know very little about them. For about the last seven years I've been doing my best to know something of Old English and Old Norse. Consequently, that's a long way off in time and space from the Argentine, from Argentine writers, no? But if I have to speak to you about the *Finnsburg Fragment* or the elegies or the *Battle of Brunanburg* . . .

Would you like to talk about those?

No, not especially.

What made you decide to study Anglo-Saxon and Old Norse?

I began by being very interested in metaphor. And then in some book or other—I think in Andrew Lang's *History of English Literature*—I read about the kennings, metaphors of Old English, and in a far more complex fashion of Old Norse poetry. Then I went in for the study of Old English. Nowadays, or rather today, after several years of study, I'm no longer interested in the metaphors, because I think that they were rather a weariness of the flesh to the poets themselves—at least to the Old English poets.

To repeat them, you mean?

To repeat them, to use them over and over again, and to keep on speaking of the *hronrad, waelrad,* or "road of the whale" instead of "the sea"—that kind of thing—and "the sea-wood," "the stallion of the sea" instead of "the ship." So I decided finally to stop using them—the metaphors, that is; but, in the meanwhile, I had begun studying the language and I fell in love with it. Now I have formed a group—we're about six or seven students—and we study every day. We've been going through the highlights of *Beowulf*, the *Finnsburg Fragment*, and *The Dream of the Rood*. Also, we've gotten into King Alfred's prose. Now we've begun learning Old Norse, which is rather akin to Old English. I mean the vocabularies are not really very different: Old English is a kind of halfway house between the Low German and the Scandinavian.

Epic literature has always interested you very much, hasn't it?

Always, yes. For example, there are many people who go to the cinema and cry. That has always happened; it has happened to me also. But I have never cried over sob stuff, or the pathetic episodes. But, for example, when I saw the first gangster films of Sternberg, I remember that when there was anything epic about them—I mean Chicago gangsters dying bravely—well, I felt that my eyes were full of tears. I have felt epic poetry far more than lyric or elegy. I always felt that. Now, that may be, perhaps, because I come from military stock. My grandfather, Colonel Borges, fought in the border warfare with the Indians, and he died in a revolution. My great grandfather, Colonel Suárez, led a Peruvian calvary charge in one of the last great battles against the Spaniards. Another great uncle of mine led the vanguard of San Martín's army—that kind of thing. And I had, well, one of my great-great-grandmothers was a sister of Rosas*—and I'm not especially proud of that relationship, because I think of Rosas as being a kind of Perón in his day; but, still, all those things link me with Argentine history and also with the idea of a man's having to be brave, no?

But the characters you pick as your epic heroes—the gangster, for example—are not usually thought of as epic, are they? Yet you seem to find the epic there.

---

*Juan Manuel de Rosas (1793-1877) was an Argentine military dictator.

I think there is a kind of—perhaps—low epic in him, no?

Do you mean that since the old kind of epic is apparently no longer possible for us, we must look to this kind of character for our heroes?

I think that as to epic poetry or as to epic literature, rather— if we except such writers as T. E. Lawrence in his *Seven Pillars of Wisdom* or some poets like Kipling, for example, in "Harp Song of the Dane Women" or even in the stories—I think nowadays, while literary men seem to have neglected their epic duties, the epic has been saved for us, strangely enough, by the Westerns.

I have heard that you have seen the film West Side Story *many times.*

Many times, yes. Of course, *West Side Story* is not a Western.

No, but for you it has the same epic qualities?

I think it has, yes. During the century, as I say, the epic tradition has been saved for the world by, of all places, Hollywood. When I went to Paris, I felt I wanted to shock people, and when they asked me—they knew that I was interested in the films, or that I had been, because my eyesight is very dim now—and they asked me, "What kind of film do you like?" And I said, "Candidly, what I most enjoy are the Westerns." They were all Frenchmen; they fully agreed with me. They said, "Of course we see such films as *Hiroshima, mon amour* or *L'Anée dernière à Marienbad* out of a sense of duty; but, when we want to amuse ourselves, when we want to enjoy ourselves, when we want, well, to get a real kick, then we see American films."

Then it is the content, the "literary" content of the film, rather than any of the technical aspects of the movies that interests you?

I know very little about the technical part of movies.

If I may change the subject to your own fiction, I would like to ask about your having said that you were very timid about beginning to write stories.

Yes, I was very timid, because when I was young I thought of myself as a poet. So, I thought: "If I write a story everybody will know I'm an outsider, that I am intruding in forbidden ground." Then I had an accident. You feel the scar. If you touch my head, here, you will see. Feel all those mountains, bumps? Then I spent a fortnight in a hospital. I had nightmares and sleeplessness—insomnia. After that they told me that I had been in danger, well, of dying, that it was really a wonderful thing that the operation had been successfull. I began to fear for my mental integrity; I said, "Maybe I can't write anymore." Then my life would have been practically over, because literature is very important to me. Not because I think my own stuff particularly good, but because I know that I can't get along without writing. If I don't write, I feel, well, a kind of remorse, no? Then I thought I would try my hand at writing an article or a poem. But I thought: "I have written hundreds of articles and poems. If I can't do it, then I'll know at once that I am done for, that everything is over with me." So I thought I'd try my hand at something I hadn't done: if I couldn't do it, there would be nothing strange about it, because why should I write short stories?—It would prepare me for the final overwhelming blow: knowing that I was at the end of my tether. I wrote a story called, let me see, I think, *"Hombre de la esquina rosada,"* and everyone enjoyed it very much.* It was a great relief to me. If it hadn't been for that particular knock

---

*This is, perhaps, a slip of memory: the story was "Pierre Menard, autor del Quijote," published in *SUR* 56 (May 1959).

on the head I got, perhaps I would never have written short stories.

And perhaps you would never have been translated?

And no one would have thought of translating me. So it was a blessing in disguise. Those stories, somehow or other, made their way: they got translated into French, I won the Formentor Prize, and then I seemed to be translated into many tongues. The first translator was Ibarra. He was a close friend of mine, and he translated the stories into French. I think he greatly improved upon them, no?

Nestor Ibarra, not Roger Caillois, was the first translator?

He and Roger Caillois. At a ripe old age, I began to find that many people were interested in my work all over the world. It seems strange: many of my writings have been done into English, Swedish, into French, into Italian, into German, into Portuguese, into some of the Slav languages, into Danish. And always this comes as a great surprise to me, because I remember I published a book—that must have been way back in 1932, I think—and at the end of the year I found out that no less than thirty-seven copies had been sold!

Was that the Universal History of Infamy?

No, no. *History of Eternity.* At first I wanted to find every single one of the buyers to apologize because of the book and also to thank them for what they had done. There is an explanation for that. If you think of thirty-seven people—those people are real; I mean, everyone of them has a face of his own, a family, he lives in his own particular street. Why, if you sell, say two thousand copies, it is the same thing as if you had sold nothing at all, because two thousand is too vast—I mean, for the imagination to grasp. While thirty-seven people—perhaps thirty-seven are too many, perhaps seventeen would have been better or even seven—but still, thirty-seven are still within the scope of one's imagination.

Speaking of numbers, I notice in your stories that certain numbers occur repeatedly.

Oh, yes. I'm awfully superstitious. I'm ashamed about it. I tell myself that, after all, superstition is, I suppose, a slight form of madness, no?

Or of religion?

Well, religion, but . . . I suppose that if one attained one hundred and fifty years of age, one would be quite mad, no? Because all those small symptoms would have been growing. Still, I see my mother, who is ninety, and she has far fewer superstitions than I have. Now, when I was reading, for the tenth time, I suppose, Boswell's *Johnson*, I found that he was full of superstition and, at the same time, that he had a great fear of madness. In the prayers he composed, one of the things he asked God was that he should not be a madman, so he must have been worried about it.

Would you say that it is the same reason—superstition—that causes you to use the same colors—red, yellow, green—again and again?

But do I use green?

Not as often as the others, but, you see, I did a rather trivial thing: I counted the colors in . . .

No, no. That is called *estilística*; here it is studied. No, I think you'll find yellow.

But red too, often moving, fading into rose.

Really. Well, I never knew that.

*It's as if the world today were a cinder of yesteryear's fire—
that's a metaphor you use. You speak of "Red Adam," for
example.*

Well, the word *Adam*, I think, in the Hebrew means "red
earth." Besides, it sounds well, no? *Rojo Adan.*

*Yes, it does, but that's not something you intend to show: the
degeneration of the world by the metaphorical use of color?*

I don't intend to show anything! *(Laughter)* I have no intentions.

Just to describe?

I describe. I write. Now, as for the color yellow, there is a
physical explanation of that. When I began to lose my sight,
the last color I saw or the last color, rather, that stood out—
because of course now I know that your coat is not the same
color as this table or of the woodwork behind you—the last
color to stand out was yellow, because it is the most vivid
of colors. That why you have the Yellow Cab Company in
the United States. At first they thought of making the cars
scarlet. Then somebody found out that at night or when there
was a fog that yellow stood out in a more vivid way than
scarlet. So, you have yellow cabs because anybody can pick
them out. Now, when I began to lose my eyesight, when the
world began to fade away from me, there was a time among
my friends . . . well, they made, they poked fun at me, because I was always wearing yellow neckties. Then they
thought I really liked yellow although it really was too glaring. I said, "Yes, to you, but not to me, because it is the only
color I can see, practically!" I live in a grey world, rather like
the silver-screen world. But yellow stands out. That might
account for it. I remember a joke of Oscar Wilde's: a friend
of his had a tie with yellow, red, and so on in it, and Wilde
said, "Oh, my dear fellow, only a deaf man could wear a tie
like that!"

He might have been talking about the yellow necktie I have on now.

Ah, well . . . I remember telling that story to a lady who missed the whole point. She said, "Of course, it must be because being deaf he couldn't hear what people were saying about his necktie." That might have amused Oscar Wilde, no?

I'd like to have heard his reply to that.

Yes, of course. I never heard of such a case of something being so perfectly misunderstood. The perfection of stupidity. Of course, Wilde's remark is a witty translation of an idea: in Spanish as well as in English you speak of a "loud" color. A "loud color" is a common phrase, but then the things that are said in literature are always the same. What is important is the way they are said. Looking for metaphors, for example: when I was a young man I was always hunting for new metaphors. Then I found out that really good metaphors are always the same. I mean, you compare time to a road, death to sleeping, life to dreaming–and those are the great metaphors in literature because they correspond to something essential. If you invent metaphors, they are apt to be surprising during the fraction of a second, but they strike no deep emotion whatever. If you think of life as a dream, that is a thought, a thought that is real or at least that most men are bound to have, no? "What oft was thought but ne'er so well expressed." I think that's better than the idea of shocking people, than finding connections between things that have never been connected before, because there is no real connection, so the whole thing is a kind of juggling.

Juggling just words?

Just words. I wouldn't even call them real metaphors because in a real metaphor both terms are really linked together. I have found one exception—a strange, new, and beautiful metaphor from Old Norse poetry. In Old Norse poetry a battle is spoken of as the "play of swords" or the "encounter of spears." But in Old Norse, and I think also in Celtic poetry, a battle is called a "web of men." That is strange, no? Because in a web of men you have a pattern, a weaving of men, *un tejido.* I suppose in medieval battle you got a kind of web because of having the swords and spears on opposite sides and so on. So there you have, I think, a new metaphor; and, of course, with a nightmare touch about it, no? The idea of a web made of living men, of living things, and still being a web, still being a pattern. It is a strange idea, no?

It corresponds, in a general way, to the metaphor George Eliot uses in Middlemarch, *that society is a web, and one cannot disentangle a strand without touching all the others.*

(With great interest) Who said that?

George Eliot, in Middlemarch.

Ah, *Middlemarch!* Yes, of course! You mean the whole universe is linked together, everything linked. Well, that's one of the reasons the Stoic philosophers had for believing in omens. There's a paper, a very interesting paper, as all of his are, by De Quincey on modern superstition, and there he gives the Stoic theory. The idea is that since the whole universe is one living thing, then there is a kinship between things that seem far off. For example, if thirteen people dine together, one of them is bound to die within the year. Not merely because of Jesus Christ and the Last Supper, but also because all things are bound together. He said—I wonder how that sentence runs—that everything in the world is a secret glass or secret mirror of the universe.

You have often spoken of people who have influenced you, like De Quincey . . .

De Quincey greatly, yes, and Schopenhauer in German. Yes, in fact, during the First World War, I was led by Carlyle— Carlyle, I rather dislike him: I think he invented Nazism and so on: one of the fathers or forefathers of such things—well, I was led by Carlyle to a study of German, and I tried my hand at Kant's *Critique of Pure Reason.* Of course, I got bogged down as most people do—as most Germans do. Then I said, "Well, I'll try their poetry, because poetry has to be shorter because of the verse." I got hold of a copy of Heine's *Lyrishces Intermezzo* and an English-German dictionary, and, at the end of two or three months, I found I could get on fairly well without the aid of a dictionary. I remember the first English novel I read through was a Scottish novel called *The House with the Green Shutters.*

Who wrote that?

A man called Douglass. Then that was plagiarized by the man who wrote *Hatter's Castle*—Cronin—there was the same plot, practically. The book was written in the Scots dialect—I mean people, instead of saying *money*, speak of *baubees* or instead of *children*, *bairns*—that's an Old English and Norse word also—and they say *nicht* for *night*: that's Old English.

And how old were you when you read that?

I must have been about—there were many things I didn't understand—I must have been about ten or eleven. Before that, of course, I had read the *Jungle Books*, and I had read Stevenson's *Treasure Island*, a very fine book. But the first real novel was that novel. When I read that, I wanted to be Scotch, and then I asked my grandmother, and she was very indignant about it. She said, "Thank goodness that you're not!" Of course, maybe she was wrong. She came from

Northumberland; they must have had some Scottish blood in them. Perhaps even Danish blood way back.

With this long interest in English and your great love of it . . .

Look here, I'm talking to an American: there's a book I *must* speak about—nothing unexpected about it: that book is *Huckleberry Finn*. I thoroughly dislike *Tom Sawyer*. I think that *Tom Sawyer* spoils the last chapter of *Huckleberry Finn*. All those silly jokes. They are all pointless jokes; but I suppose Mark Twain thought it was his duty to be funny, even when he wasn't in the mood. The jokes had to be worked in somehow. According to what George Moore said, the English always thought: "Better a bad joke than no joke."

I think that Mark Twain was one of the really great writers, but I think he was rather unaware of the fact. But, perhaps in order to write a really great book, you must be rather unaware of the fact. You can slave away at it and change every adjective to some other adjective, but perhaps you can write better if you leave the mistakes. I remember what Bernard Shaw said, that as to style, a writer has as much style as his conviction will give him and not more. Shaw thought that the idea of a game of style was quite nonsensical, quite meaningless. He thought of Bunyan, for example, as a great writer because he was convinced of what he was saying. If a writer disbelieves what he is writing, then he can hardly expect his readers to believe it. In this country, though, there is a tendency to regard any kind of writing—especially the writing of poetry—as a game of style. I have known many poets here who have written well—very fine stuff, with delicate moods and so on—but if you talk with them, the only thing they tell you is smutty stories or speak of politics in the way that everybody does, so that, really, their writing turns out to be a kind of sideshow. They had learned writing in the way that a man might learn to play chess or play bridge. They were not really poets or writers at all. It was a trick they had learned, and they had learned it thoroughly. They had the whole thing at their finger ends. But most of them—except for four or five, I should say—seemed to think of life as having nothing poetic or mysterious about it. They take things for granted. They know that when they have to write, then, well, they have to suddenly become rather sad or ironic.

To put on their writer's hat?

Yes, put on the writer's hat and get into a right mood, and then write. Afterward, they fall back on current politics.

(Borges' secretary, Susana Quinteros enters) Excuse me. Señor Campbell is waiting.

Ah, please ask him to wait a moment. Well, there's a Mr. Campbell waiting. The Campbells are coming.

When you wrote your stories, did you revise a great deal?

At first I did. Then I found out that when a man reaches a certain age he has found his real tone. Nowadays, I try to go over what I've written after a fortnight or so, and of course there are many slips and repetitions to be avoided, certain favorite tricks that should not be overworked. But I think that what I write nowadays is always on a certain level and that I can't better it very much, nor can I spoil it very much either. Consequently I let it go, forget all about it, and think about what I'm doing at the time. The last things I have been writing are *milongas*, popular songs.

Yes, I saw a volume of them, a beautiful book.

Yes, *Para seis cuerdas*, meaning, of course, the guitar. The guitar was a popular instrument when I was a boy. Then you would find people strumming the guitar, not too skillfully,

at nearly every street corner of every town. Some of the best
tangos were composed by people who couldn't write them
or read them. But, of course, they had music in their souls,
as Shakespeare might have said. So they dictated them to
somebody: they were played on the piano, and they got written down and they were published for the literate people. I
remember I met one of them—Ernesto Poncia. He wrote
"Don Juan," one of the best tangos before the tangos were
spoiled by the Italians in La Boca and so on; I mean, when
the tangos came from the *criolla*. He once said to me: "I have
been in jail many times, Señor Borges, but always for man-
slaughter!" What he meant to say was that he wasn't a thief
or a pimp.

In your Antología Personal . . .

Look here, I want to say that book is full of misprints. My
eyesight is very dim, and the proofreading had to be done by
somebody else.

I see, but those are only minor errors, aren't they?

Yes, I know, but they creep in, and they worry the writer,
not the reader. The reader accepts anything, no? Even the
starkest nonsense.

What was your principle of selection in that book?

My principle of selection was simply that I felt the stuff was
better than what I had left out. Of course, if I had been cleverer, I would have insisted on leaving out those stories, and
then, after my death, someone would have found out that
what had been left out was really good. That would have
been a cleverer thing to do, no? I mean, to publish all the
weak stuff, then to let somebody find out that I had left out
the real things.

You like jokes very much, don't you?

Yes, I do, yes.

But the people who write books about your books, your fiction in particular . . .

No, no—they write far too seriously.

They seldom seem to recognize that some of them are very funny.

They are meant to be fun. Now a book will come out called *Crónicas de H. Bustos Domecq*, written with Adolpho Bioy Casares. That book will be about architects, poets, novelists, sculptors, and so on. All the characters are imaginary, and they are all very up-to-date, very modern. They take themselves very seriously; so does the writer. But they are not actually parodies of anybody. We are simply going as far as a certain thing can be done. For example, many writers from here tell me: "We would like to have your message." You see, we have no message at all. When I write, I write because a thing has to be done. I don't think a writer should meddle too much with his own work. He should let the work write itself, no?

You have said that a writer should never be judged by his ideas.

No, I don't think ideas are important.

Well then, what should he be judged by?

He should be judged by the enjoyment he gives and by the emotions one gets. As to ideas, after all, it is not very important whether a writer has some political opinion or other, because a work will come through despite them as in the case of Kipling's *Kim*. Suppose you consider the idea of the empire of the English—well, in *Kim* I think the characters one really is fond of are not the English but many of the Indians, the Mussulmans. I think they're nicer people. And that's because he thought them—NO! NO! not because he thought them nicer—because he *felt* them nicer.

What about metaphysical ideas then?

Ah, well, metaphysical ideas, yes. They can be worked into parables and so on.

Readers very often call your stories parables. Do you like that description?

No, no. They're not meant to be parables. I mean, if they are parables ... (*long pause*) ... that is, if they are parables, they have *happened* to be parables, but my intention has never been to write parables.

Not like Kafka's parables then?

In the case of Kafka, we know very little. We only know that he was very dissatisfied with his own work. Of course, when he told his friend, Max Brod, that he wanted his manuscripts to be burned, as Virgil did, I suppose he knew that his friend wouldn't do that. If a man wants to destroy his own work, he throws it into a fire, and there it goes. When he tells a close friend of his: "I want all the manuscripts to be destroyed," he knows that the friend will never do that, and the friend knows that he knows and he knows that the other knows that he knows and so on and so forth.

It's all very Jamesian.

Yes, of course. I think that the whole world of Kafka is to

be found in a far more complex way in the stories of Henry James. I think that they both thought of the world as being at the same time complex and meaningless.

Meaningless?

Don't you think so?

No, I don't really think so. In the case of James . . .

But in the case of James, yes. In the case of James, yes. I don't think he thought the world had any moral purpose. I think he disbelieved in God. In fact, I think there's a letter written to his brother, the psychologist William James, wherein he says that the world is a diamond museum, let's say a collection of oddities, no? I suppose he meant that. Now in the case of Kafka, I think Kafka was looking for something.

For some meaning?

For some meaning, yes. And not finding it, perhaps. But I think that they both lived in a kind of maze no?

I would agree to that. A book like The Sacred Fount, *for example.*

Yes, *The Sacred Fount* and many short stories. For example, "The Abasement of the Northmores," where the whole story is a beautiful revenge, but a revenge that the reader never knows will happen or not. The woman is very sure that her husband's work, which nobody seems to have read or care about, is far better than the work of his famous friend. But maybe the whole thing is untrue. Maybe she was just led by her love for him. One doesn't know whether those letters, when they are published, will really come to anything. Of course, James was trying to write two or three stories at one time. That's the reason why he never gave any explanation. The explanation would have made the story poorer. He said: *"The Turn of the Screw* was just a pot-boiler, don't worry about it." But I don't think that was the truth. For instance, he said, "Well, if I give explanations, then the story will be poorer, because the alternative explanations will be left out." I think he did that on purpose.

I agree. People shouldn't know.

People shouldn't know, and, perhaps he didn't know himself!

Do you like having the same effect on your readers?

Oh, yes. Of course I do. But I think the stories of Henry James are far above his novels. What's important in the stories of Henry James are the situations created, not the characters. *The Sacred Fount* would be far better if you could tell one character from the other, but you have to wade through some three hundred pages in order to find out who Lady So-and-so's lover was; and then, at the end, you may guess that it was So-and-so and not What's-his-name. You can't tell them apart; they all speak in the same way; there are no real characters. Only the American seems to stand out. If you think of Dickens, well, while the characters don't seem to stand out, they are far more important than the plot.

Would you say that your own stories have their point of origin in a situation, not in a character?

In a situation, right. Except for the idea of bravery, of which I'm very fond—bravery, perhaps, because I'm not very brave myself.

Is that why there are so many knives and swords and guns in your stories?

Yes, that may be. Oh, but there are two causes there: first, seeing the swords at home, because of my grandfather and my great-grandfather and so on. Seeing all those swords. Then I was bred in Palermo, it all was a slum then, and people always thought of themselves—I don't say that it was true, but that they always thought of themselves—as being better than the people who lived on a different side of the town, as being better fighters and that kind of thing. Of course, that may have been rubbish. I don't think they were especially brave. To call a man, or to think of him, as a coward, that was the last thing; that's the kind of thing he couldn't stand. I have even known of a case of a man coming from the southern side of the town in order to pick a quarrel with somebody who was famous as a knifer on the north side and getting killed for his pains. They had no real reason to quarrel: they had never seen each other before; there was no question of money or women or anything of the kind. I suppose it was the same thing in the West, in the States. Here the thing wasn't done with guns but with knives.

Using the knife takes the deed back to an older form of behavior?

An older form, yes. Also, it is a more personal idea of courage, because you can be a good marksman and not especially brave; but if you're going to fight your man at close quarters, and you have knives . . . I remember I once saw a man challenging another to fight, and the other caved in; but he caved in, I think, because of a trick. One was an old hand, he was seventy, and the other was a young and vigorous man: he must have been between twenty-five and thirty. Then the old man, he begged your pardon, he came back with two daggers, and one was a span longer than the other. He said: "Here, choose your weapon." So he gave the other the chance of choosing the longer weapon and having an advantage over him, but that also meant that he felt so sure of himself that he could afford that handicap. The other apologized and caved in, of course. I remember that a brave man, when I was a young man in the slums, he was always supposed to carry a short dagger, and it was worn here, like this (*pointing to his armpit*), so it could be taken out a moment's notice, and the slum word for the knife—or one of the slum words— well, was *el hierro*, "the iron," but of course that means nothing special. But one of the names, and that's been quite lost—it's a pity—was *el vaivén*, the "come and go." In the words "come and go" (*making a sawing motion*), you see the flash of the knife, the sudden flash.

It's like a gangster's holster?

Exactly, yes, like a holster—on the left side. Then it could be taken out a moment's notice, and you scored *el vaivén*. It was spelled as one word, and everyone knew it meant knife. *El hierro* is rather poor as a name, because to call it "the iron" or "the steel" means nothing, while *el vaivén* does.

(*Susana Quinteros enters again*) *Señor Campbell is still waiting.*

Yes, yes, we know. The Campbells are coming.

Two writers I wanted to ask you about are Joyce and Eliot. You were one of the first readers of Joyce, and you even translated part of Ulysses *into Spanish, didn't you?*

Yes, I'm afraid I undertook a very faulty translation of the last page of *Ulysses*. Now, as to Eliot, at first I thought of him as being a finer critic than a poet; now I think that sometimes he is a very fine poet, but as a critic I find that he's too apt to be always drawing fine distinctions. If you take a great critic, let's say Emerson or Coleridge, you feel that he has read a writer and that his criticism comes from his personal experience of him, while in the case of Eliot, you always think—at least I always feel—that he's agreeing with some professor or slightly disagreeing with another. Consequently, he's not creative. He's an intelligent man who's drawing fine distinctions, and I suppose he's right; but, at the same time, after reading, to take a stock example, Coleridge on Shakespeare, especially on the character of Hamlet, a new Hamlet has been created for you, or the same after reading Emerson on Montaigne or whoever it may be. In Eliot there are no such acts of creation. You feel that he has read many books on the subject—he's agreeing or disagreeing—sometimes making slightly nasty remarks, no?

Yes, that he takes back later.

Yes, yes, that he takes back later. Of course, he took those remarks back later because at first he was what might be called nowadays "an angry young man." In the end, I suppose he thought of himself as being an English classic, and then he found that he had to be polite to his fellow classics, so that, afterwards, he took back most of the things he had said about Milton or even against Shakespeare. After all, he felt that in some ideal way they were all sharing the same academy.

Did Eliot's work, his poetry, have any effect on your own writing?

No, I don't think so.

I have been struck by certain resemblances between The Waste Land *and your story "The Immortal."*

Well, there may be something there, but in that case I'm quite unaware of it, because he's not one of the poets I love. I should rank Yeats far above him. In fact, if you don't mind my saying so, I think that Frost is a finer poet than Eliot. I mean a finer poet. But I suppose Eliot was a far more intelligent man; however, intelligence has little to do with poetry. Poetry springs from something deeper. It's beyond intelligence; it may not even be linked with wisdom. It's a thing of its own; it has a nature of its own. Undefinable. I remember—of course, I was a young man—I was even angry when Eliot spoke in a slighting way of Sandburg. I remember he said that classicism is good—I'm not quoting his words but the drift of them—because it enabled us to deal with such writers as Mr. Carl Sandburg. When one calls a poet "mister," (*laughing*) it's a word of haughty feelings: it means a Mr. So-and-so who has found his way into poetry and has no right to be there, who is really an outsider. In Spanish, it's still worse, because sometimes when we speak of a poet, we say "El Doctor So-and-so." Then that annihilates him, that blots him out.

You like Sandburg then?

Yes, I do. Of course, I think Whitman is far more important than Sandburg; but when you read Whitman, you think of him as literary, perhaps a not too learned man of letters, who is doing his best to write in the vernacular and who is using slang as much as he can. In Sandburg the slang seems to come naturally. Now, of course there are two Sandburgs: there is the *rough*, but there is also a very delicate Sandburg, especially when he deals with landscapes. Sometimes when he is describing the fog, for example, you are reminded of a Chinese painting. While in other poems of Sandburg you think, rather, of, well, gangsters, hoodlums—that kind of people. But I suppose he could be both, and I think he was equally sincere: when he was doing his best to be the poet of Chicago and when he wrote in quite a different mood. Another thing that I find strange in Sandburg is that Whitman—but, of course, Whitman is Sandburg's father— Whitman is full of hope, while Sandburg writes as if he were writing in the two or three centuries to come. When he writes of the American expeditionary forces or when he writes about empire or the war or so on, he writes as if all those things were dead and gone by.

There is an element of fantasy in his work, then, which leads me to ask you about the fantastic. You use the word a great deal in your writing, and I remember that you call Green Mansions, *for example, a fantastic novel.*

Well, it is.

How would you define "fantastic" then?

I wonder if you *can* define it. I think it's rather an intention in a writer. I remember a very deep remark of Joseph Conrad—he is one of my favorite authors—I think it is in the foreword to something like *The Dark Line*, but it's not that . . .

The Shadow Line?

The Shadow Line. In that foreword he said that some people have thought that the story was a fantastic story because of the captain's ghost stopping the ship. He wrote—and that struck me because I write fantastic stories myself—that to deliberately write a fantastic story was not to feel that the whole universe is fantastic and mysterious, nor that it meant a lack of sensibility for a person to sit down and write something deliberately fantastic. Conrad thought that when one wrote, even in a fantastic way, about the world, one was writing a fantastic story, because the world itself is fantastic and unfathomable and mysterious.

You share this belief?

Yes. I found that he was right. I talked to Bioy Casares, who also writes fantastic stories—very, very fine stories—and he said: "I think Conrad is right." Really, nobody knows whether the world is realistic or fantastic, that is to say, whether the world is a natural process or whether it is a kind of dream, a dream that we may or may not share with others.

You have often collaborated with Bioy Casares, haven't you?

Yes, I have always collaborated with him. Every night I dine at his house, and then, after dinner, we sit down and write.

Would you describe your method of collaboration?

Well, it's rather queer. When we write together, when we collaborate, we call ourselves H. Bustos Domecq. Bustos was as great-great-grandfather of his. Now, the queer thing is that when we write, and we write mostly humorous stuff— even if the stories are tragic, they are told in a humorous way or they are told as if the teller hardly understood what comes of the writing, if we are successful, and sometimes we are— why not? after all, I'm speaking in the plural, no?—when our writing is successful, then what comes out is something quite different from Bioy Casares' stuff and my stuff: even the jokes are different. So we have created between us a kind of third person; we have somehow begotten a third person that is quite unlike us.

A fantastic author?

Yes, a fantastic author, with his likes, his dislikes, and a personal style that is meant to be ridiculous; but, still, it is a style of his own, quite different from the kind of style I write when I try to create a ridiculous character. I think that's the only way of collaborating. Generally speaking, we go over the plot together before we set pen to paper—rather, I should talk about typewriters, because he has a typewriter. Before we begin writing, we discuss the whole story. Then we go over the details; we change them, of course: we think of a beginning, and then we think the beginning might be the end or that it might be more striking if somebody said nothing at all or said something quite outside the mark. Once the story is written, if you ask us whether this adjective or this particular sentence came from Bioy or from me, we can't tell.

It comes from the third person.

Yes. I think that's the only way of collaborating, because I have tried collaborating with other people. Sometimes, it works out all right, but sometimes one feels that the collaborator is a kind of rival. Or, if not—as in the case of Peyrou— we began collaborating, but he is timid and a very courteous, a very polite kind of person; and, consequently, if he says anything and you make any objections, he feels hurt, and he takes it back. He says: "Oh, yes, of course, of course, yes, I was quite wrong. It was a blunder." Or, if you propose anything, he says: "Oh, that's wonderful!" Now, that kind of thing can't be done. In the case of me and Casares, we don't feel as if we are two rivals or even as if we were two men who play chess. There's no case of winning or losing. What we're thinking of is the story itself, the stuff itself.

I'm sorry, I'm not familiar with the second writer you named.

Peyrou. He began by imitating Chesterton and writing stories, detective stories, not unworthy and even worthy of Chesterton. But now he's struck a new line of novels whose aim is to show what this country was like during Perón's time. I don't care very much for that kind of writing. I understand that his novels are fine; but, I should say, from the historical, even the journalistic point of view. When he began writing stories after Chesterton—and then he wrote some very fine stories, one of them made me cry, but, of course, perhaps it made me cry because he spoke of the quarter I was bred in, Palermo, and of hoodlums of those days: a book called *La noche repetida*, with very, very fine stories about gangsters, hoodlums, hold-up men, that kind of thing. And

all that way back, let's say, well, at the beginning of the century. Now he has started this new kind of novel wherein he
wants to show what the country was like.

Local color, more or less?

Local color and local politics. Then his characters are very
interested, well, in graft, in loot, making money and so on.
As I am less interested in those subjects, maybe it's my fault,
not his, if I prefer his early stuff; but I always think of him
as a great writer, an important writer, and an old friend of
mine.

*You have said that your own work has moved from, in the
early times, expression, to, in the later times,* allusion.

Yes.

What do you mean by "allusion"?

Look, I mean to say this: when I began writing, I thought that
everything should be defined by the writer—for example, to
say "the moon" was strictly forbidden—that one had to find
an adjective, an epithet, for the moon. (Of course, I'm sim-
plifying things. I know it, because many times I have written "*la luna,*" but this is a kind of symbol of what I was doing.) Well, I thought everything had to be defined and that
no common turns of phrase should be used. I would never
have said "So-and-so came in and sat down," because that
was far too simple and far too easy. I thought I had to find
out some fancy way of saying it. Now I find out that those
things are generally annoyances to the reader. But I think the
whole root of the matter lies in the fact that when a writer is
young he feels somehow that what he is going to say is rather
silly or obvious or commonplace, and then he tries to hide
it under baroque ornament, under words taken from the sev-
enteenth-century writers; or, if not, and he sets out to be

modern, then he does the contrary: he's inventing words all the time or alluding to airplanes, railway trains, or the telegraph and telephone, because he's doing his best to be modern. Then, as time goes on, one feels that one's ideas, good or bad, should be plainly expressed, because, if you have an idea, you must try to get that idea or that feeling or that mood into the mind of the reader. If, at the same time, you are trying to be, let's say, Sir Thomas Browne or Ezra Pound, then it can't be done. So that I think a writer always begins by being too complicated: he's playing several games at the same time. He wants to convey a peculiar mood; at the same time, he must be a contemporary and, if not a contemporary, then he's a reactionary and a classic. As to the vocabulary, the first thing a young writer, at least in this country, sets out to do is to show his readers that he possesses a dictionary, that he knows all the synonyms, so we get, for example, in one line, "red," then we get "scarlet," then we get other words, more or less, for the same color: *purple*.

You've worked, then, toward a kind of classical prose?

Yes, I do my best now. Whenever I find an out-of-the-way word, that is to say, a word that may be used by the Spanish classics or a word used in the slums of Buenos Aires, I mean a word that is different form the others, then I strike it out, and I use a common word. I remember that Stevenson wrote that in a well-written page all the words should look the same way. If you write an uncouth word or an astonishing or an archaic word, then the rule is broken, and, what is far more important, the attention of the reader is distracted by the word. One should be able to read smoothly in it, even if you're writing metaphysics or philosophy or whatever.

Dr. Johnson said something similar to that.

Yes, he must have said it; in any case, he must have agreed with that. Look, his own English was rather cumbersome, and the first thing you feel is that he is writing in a cumbersome English—that there are far too many Latin words in it—but if you reread what is written, you find that behind those involutions of phrase there is always a meaning, generally an interesting and a new meaning.

A personal one?

Yes, a personal one. So, even though he wrote in a Latin style, I think he is the most English of writers. I think of him as—this is blasphemy, of course, but why not be blasphemous while we're about it?—I think that Johnson was a far more English writer than Shakespeare. Because, if there's one thing typical of Englishmen, it's their habit of understatement. Well, in the case of Shakespeare, there are no understatements. On the contrary, he is piling on the agonies, as I think the American said. I think Johnson, who wrote a Latin kind of English, and Wordsworth, who wrote more Saxon words—and there is a third writer whose name I can't recall, well, let's say Johnson, Wordsworth, and Kipling also—I think they're far more typically English than Shakespeare. I don't know why, but I always feel something Italian, something Jewish about Shakespeare, and perhaps Englishmen admire him because of that, because it's so unlike them.

And why the French dislike him, to the extent that they do: because he's so bombastic.

He was very bombastic. I remember I saw a film some days ago—not too good a film—called *Darling*. There some verses of Shakespeare are quoted. Now those verses are always better when they are quoted, because he is defining England, and he calls it, for example, "This other Eden, demi-paradise . . . This precious stone set in the silver sea" and so on, and, in the end, he says something like "this realm, this England." Now, when that quotation is made, the reader stops there, but in the text I think the verses go on, so that the whole point is lost. The real point would have been the idea of a man trying to define England, loving her very much and finding at the end that the only thing he can do is to say "England" outright—as if you said "America." But if he says "this realm, this land, this England" and then goes on "this demi-paradise" and so on, the whole point is lost, because "England" should always be the last word. Well, I suppose Shakespeare always wrote in a hurry, as the player said to Ben Jonson, and so be it. You've no time to feel that would have been the last word, the word "England" summing up and blotting out all the others, saying: "Well, I've been attempting something that is impossible." But he went on with it, with his metaphors and his bombast, because he was bombastic. Even in such a famous phrase as Hamlet's last words, I think: "The rest is silence." There is something phony about it; it's meant to impress. I don't think anybody would say anything like that.

In the context of the play, my favorite line in Hamlet *occurs just after Claudius' praying scene, when Hamlet enters his mother's chamber and says: "Now, Mother, what's the matter?"*

"What's the matter?" is the opposite of "The rest is silence." At least for me, "The rest is silence" has a hollow ring about it. One feels that Shakespeare is thinking: "Well, now Prince Hamlet of Denmark is dying: he must say something impressive," so he ekes out that phrase "The rest is silence." Now that may be impressive, but it is not true! He was working away at his job of poet and not thinking of the real character, of Hamlet the Dane.

When you are working, what kind of reader do you imagine you are writing for, if you do imagine one? Who would be your ideal audience?

Perhaps a few personal friends of mine. Not myself, because

279

I never reread what I've written. I'm far too afraid to feel ashamed of what I've done.

Do you expect the many people who read your work to catch the allusions and references?

No. Most of those allusions and references are merely put there as a kind of private joke.

A private joke?

A joke not to be shared with other people. I mean, if they share it, all the better; but, if they don't, I don't care a hang about it.

Then it's the opposite approach to allusion from that of, say, Eliot in The Waste Land?

I think that Eliot and Joyce wanted their readers to be rather mystified and so to be worrying out the sense of what they had done.

You seem to have read as much, if not more, nonfiction or factual material as fiction and poetry. Is that true? For example, you apparently like to read encyclopedias.

Ah, yes, I'm very fond of that. I remember a time when I used to come here to read. I was a very young man, and I was far too timid to ask for a book. Then, I was rather, I won't say poor, but I wasn't too wealthy in those days, so I used to come every night here and pick out a volume of the *Encyclopedia Britannica*, the old edition.

The eleventh?

The eleventh or twelfth, because those editions are far above the new ones. They were meant to be *read*. Now they are merely reference books. While in the eleventh or twelfth edition of the *Encyclopedia Britannica,* you had long articles by Macaulay, by Coleridge—no, not by Coleridge, by . . .

By De Quincey?

Yes, by De Quincey and so on, so that I used to take any volume from the shelves—there was no need to ask for them: they were reference books—and then I opened the book till I found an article that interested me; for example, about the Mormons or any particular writer. I sad down and read it because those articles were really monographs, really books or short books. The same goes for the German encyclopedia—Brockhaus or Meyers. When we got the new copy, I thought that was what they call the *Shorter Brockhaus*, but it wasn't. It was explained to me that because people live in small flats, there is no longer room for books in thirty volumes. Encyclopedias have suffered greatly; they have been packed in.

(Susana Quinteros, interrupting) I'm sorry. Está esperando el Señor Campbell.

Ah, please ask him to wait just a moment more. Those Campbells keep coming.

May I ask just a few more questions?

Yes, please, of course.

Some readers have found that your stories are cold, impersonal, rather like some of the newer French writers. Is that your intention?

No. *(Sadly)* If that has happened, it is out of mere clumsiness, because I have felt them very deeply. I have felt them so deeply that I have told them, well, using strange symbols, so that people might not find out that they were all more or less autobiographical. The stories were about myself, my personal experiences. I suppose it's the English diffidence, no?

Then a book like the little volume called Everness *would be a good book for someone to read about your work?*

I think it is. Besides the lady who wrote it is a close friend of mine. I found that word in Roget's *Thesarus*. Then I thought that word was invented by Bishop Wilkins, who invented an artificial language.

You've written about that.

Yes, I wrote about Wilkins, but he also invented a wonderful word that strangely enough has never been used by English poets—an awful word really, a terrible word. "Everness," of course, is a better word than "eternity," because eternity is rather worn now. "Ever-r-rness" is far better than German *Ewigheit*, the same word. But he also created a beautiful word, a word that's a poem in itself, full of hopelessness, sadness, and despair: the word "neverness." A beautiful word, no? He invented it, and I don't know why the poets left it lying about and never used it.

Have you used it?

No, no, never. I used "everness," but "neverness" is very beautiful. There is something hopeless about it, no? And there is no word with the same meaning in any other language or in English. You might say "impossibility," but that's very tame for "neverness": "Till world and fame to nothingness do sink"; but "nothingness," I think is weaker than "neverness." You have in Spanish *nadería*—many similar words—but nothing like "neverness." So if you're a poet, you should use that word. It's a pity for that word to be lost in the pages of a dictionary. I don't think it's ever been used. It may have been used by some theologian; it might have. I suppose Jonathan Edwards would have enjoyed that kind of word or Sir Thomas Browne perhaps, and Shakespeare, of course, because he was very fond of words.

You respond to English so well, you love it so much, how is it you have written so little in English?

Why? Why, I'm afraid. Fear. But next year, those lectures of mine that I shall deliver, I'll write them in English. I already wrote to Harvard.

You're coming to Harvard next year?

Yes. I'm going to deliver a course of lectures on poetry, and as I think that poetry is more or less untranslatable, and as I think English literature—that includes America—is by far the richest in the world, I will take most, if not all of my examples from English poetry. Of course, as I have my hobby, I'll try to work in some Old English verses, but that's English also! In fact, according to some of my students, it's far more English than Chaucer's English.

To get back to your own work for a moment: I have often wondered how you go about arranging works in those collections. Obviously the principle is not chronological. Is it similarity of theme?

No, not chronology; but sometimes I find out that I've written the same parable or story twice over or that two different stories carry the same meaning, and so I try to put them alongside each other. That's the only principle, because, for example, once it happened to me to write a poem, a not too good poem, and then to rewrite it many years afterwards. After the poem was written, some of my friends told me: "Well, that's the same poem you published some five years ago." And I said: "Well, so it is!" But I hadn't the faintest notion that it was. After all, I think that a poet has maybe five or six poems to write and not more than that. He's trying his hand at writing them from different angles and perhaps with different plots and in different ages and different characters, but the poems are essentially and innerly the same.

You have written many reviews and journal articles.

Well, I had to do it.

Did you choose the books you wanted to review?

Yes, I generally did.

So the choice does express your own tastes?

Oh yes, yes. For example, when somebody told me to write a review of a certain *History of Literature*, I found there were so many howlers and blunders, and as I greatly admire the author as a poet, I said: "No, I don't want to write about it, because if I write about it, I shall write against it." I don't like to attack people, especially now. When I was a young man, yes, I was very fond of it, but as time goes on, one finds that it is no good. When people write in favor or against any-body that hardly helps or hurts them. I think that a man can be helped, well, the man can be done or undone by his own writing, not by what other people say of him, so even if you brag a lot, and people say that you are a genius—well, you'll be found out.

Do you have any particular method for naming your characters?

I have two methods: one of them is to work in the names of my grandfathers, great-grandfathers, and so on. To give them a kind of, well, I won't say immortality, but that's one of the methods. The other is use names that somehow strike me. For example, in a story of mine, one of the characters who comes and goes is called Yarmolinsky, because the name struck me. It's a strange word, no? Then another character is called Red Scharlach, because *Scharlach* means scarlet in German, and he was a murderer. He was doubly red, no? Red Scharlach: Red Scarlet.

What about the princess with the beautiful name who occurs in two of your stories?

Faucigny Lucinge? Well, she's a great friend of mine. She's an Argentine lady. She married a French prince, and as the name is very beautiful—as most French titles are—especially if you cut out the Faucigny, as she does. She calls herself La Princesse de Lucinge. It's a beautiful word.

What about Tlön and Uqbar?

Oh, well, those are merely meant to be uncouth, so u-q-b-a-r.

Unpronounceable in a way?

Yes, more or less unpronounceable, and then *Tlön*: t-l is rather an uncommon combination, no? Then *ö*. The Latin *orbis tertius*: one can say it swimmingly, no? Perhaps in Tlön I may have been thinking of *traum*, the same word as the English "dream." But then it would have to be *Tröme*, but *Tröme* might remind the reader of a railway train. *T-l* was a queerer combination. I thought I had invented a word for imagined objects called *hrön*; yet, when I began learning Old English, I found that *hron* was one of the words for whale. There were two words, *wael* and *hron*, so the *hronrad* is the "whale-road," that is to say, "the sea" in Old English poetry.

Then the word you invented to describe an object perpetrated on reality by the imagination, that word had already been invented and was, in fact a hrön?

Yes, yes, it came to me. I would like to think that it came from my ancestors of ten centuries ago. That's a probable explanation, no?

Would you say that in your stories you have tried to hybridize the short story and the essay?

Yes, but I have done that on purpose. The first to point that out to me was Casares. He said that I had written short stories that were really sort of halfway houses between an essay and a story.

Was that partly to compensate for your timidity about writing narratives?

Yes, it may have been. Yes, because nowadays, or at least today, I began writing that series of stories about hoodlums of Buenos Aires. Those are straightforward stories. There is nothing of the essay about them or even of poetry. The story is told in a straightforward way, and those stories are in a sense sad, perhaps horrible. They are always understated. They are told by people who are also hoodlums, and you can hardly understand them. They may be tragedies, but the tragedy is not felt by them. They merely tell the story, and the reader is, I suppose, made to feel that the story goes deeper than the story itself. Nothing is said of the sentiments of the characters—I got that out of the Old Norse saga: the idea that one should know a character by his words and by his deeds but that one shouldn't get inside his skull and say what he was thinking.

So they are nonpsychological rather than impersonal?

Yes, but there is a hidden psychology behind the story, because if not the characters would be mere puppets.

What about the Kabbalah? When did you first get interested in that?

I think it was through De Quincey, through his idea that the whole world was a set of symbols or that everything meant something else. Then, when I lived in Geneva, I had two personal, two great friends—Maurice Abramowicz and Seymour Jichlinski. Their names tell you the stock they sprang from: they were Polish Jews. I greatly admired Switzerland and the nation itself, not merely the scenery and the towns; but the Swiss are very standoffish. One can hardly have a Swiss friend, because as they have to live on foreigners, I suppose they dislike them. That would be the same case with the Mexicans. They chiefly live on Americans, on American tourists, and I don't think anybody likes to be a hotel keeper, even though there's nothing dishonorable about it. But if you are a hotel keeper, if you have to entertain many people from other countries, well, you feel that they are different from you, and you may dislike them in the long run.

Have you tried to make your own stories Kabbalistic?

Yes, sometimes I have.

Using traditional Kabbalistic interpretations?

No. I read a book called *Major Trends in Jewish Mysticism.*

The one by Scholem?

Yes, by Scholem and another by Trachtenberg on Jewish superstitions. Then I have read all the books of the Kabbalah I have found and all the articles in the encyclopedias and so on, but I have no Hebrew whatever. I may have Jewish ancestors, but I can't tell. My mother's name is Acevedo; Acevedo may be a name for a Portuguese Jew, but, again, it may not. Now, if you're called Abraham, I think there is no doubt whatever about it, but as the Jews took Italian, Spanish, Portuguese names, it does not necessarily follow that if you have one of those names you come from Jewish stock. The word *acevedo,* of course, means a kind of tree; the word is not especially Jewish, though many Jews are called Acevedo. I can't tell. I wish I had some Jewish forefathers.

You once wrote that all men are either Platonists or Aristotelians.

I didn't say that. Coleridge said it.

But you quoted him.

Yes, I quoted him.

And which are you?

I think I'm Aristotelian, but I wish it were the other way. I think it's the English strain that makes me think of particular things and persons being real rather than the general ideas being real. But I'm afraid now that the Campbells are coming.

Before I go, would you mind signing my copy of Labyrinths?

I'll be glad to. Ah yes, I know this book. There's my picture, but do I really look like that? I don't like that picture. I'm not so gloomy, so beaten down?

Don't you think it looks pensive?

Perhaps, but so dark? So heavy? The brow . . . oh well.

Do you like this edition of your writings?

A good translation, no? Except that there are too many Latin words in it. For example, if I wrote, just say, *habitación oscura*—I wouldn't, of course, have written that, but *cuarto oscuro,* but just say that I did)—then the temptation is to translate *habitación* with "habitation," a word which sounds close to the original, but the word I want is "room." It is more definite, simpler, better. You know, English is beautiful language, but the older languages are even more beautiful: they had vowels. Vowels in modern English have lost their value, their color. My hope for English—for the English language—is America. Americans speak clearly. When I go to the movies now, I can't see much, but in the American movies, I understand every word. In the English movies, I can't understand as well. Do you ever find it so?

Sometimes, particularly in comedies. The English actors seem to speak too fast.

Exactly! Exactly. Too fast with too little emphasis. They blur the words, the sounds. A fast blur. No, America must save the language; and, do you know, I think the same is true for Spanish? I prefer South American speech. I always have. I suppose you in America don't read Ring Lardner or Bret Harte much any more?

They are read, but mostly in the secondary schools.

What about O. Henry?

Again, mostly in the schools.

And I suppose there mostly for the technique, the surprise ending. I don't like that trick, do you? Oh, it's all right in theory; in practice, that's something else. You can read them only once if there is just the surprise. You remember what Swift said: "the art of sinking." Now, in the detective story, that's different. The surprise is there too, but there are also the characters, the scene, or the landscape to satisfy us. But now I remember that the Campbells are coming, the Campbells are coming. They are supposed to be a ferocious tribe. Where are they?

BIBLIOGRAPHY

Works by Borges:
Clemente, José E. (ed.) *Obras Completas.* Buenos Aires, 1953-1967.
I. *Historia de la eternidad* (1953).
II.*Poemas 1928-1958* (1962).
III. *Historia universal de la infamia* (1954).
IV. *Evaristo Carriego* (1955).
V.*Ficciones* (1956).
VI. *Discusión* (1961).
VII. *El Aleph* (1966).
VIII. *Otras inquisiciones* (1960).
IX. *El hacedor* (1960).
X. *Obra poética* 1923-1964 (1967).
Borges, Jorge Luis, and Vázquez, María Esther. *Introducción a la literatura inglesa.* Buenos Aires, 1965.
Borges, Jorge Luis. *Inquisiciones.* Buenos Aires, 1925.
————. *El idioma de los argentinos.* Buenos Aires, 1928.
————, and Clemente, José E. *El lenguaje de Buenos Aires.* Buenos Aires, 1963.
————. *El tamaño de mi esperanza.* Buenos Aires, 1926.
————. "An Anthology of Contemporary Latin American Poetry," *Sur*, 102 (March 1943), 92-94.
————. "*Los laberintos policiales y Chesterton*," *Sur*, 10 (July 1935), 92-94.
————. "*Modos de G.K. Chesterton*," *Sur*, 22 (July 1936), 47-53.
————. "*Nota Preliminar*," *Sartor Resartus*, Buenos Aires, 1945.
————. Prologue to Ray Bradbury, *The Martian Chronicles*, Buenos Aires, 1955.
————. "*Ultraismo*," *Nosotros*, XV (December 1921), 467-71.

Works about Borges:
Adams, Robert Martin, "The Intricate Argentine," *Hudson Review*, XIX (Spring 1966), 139-46.
Alonso, Amado, "*Borges narrador*," *Sur*, 14 (November 1935), 105-15.
Anderson Imbert, Enrique, "*Nueva contribución al estudio de las fuentes de Borges*," *Filogía*, VIII (1962), 7-13.
Barrenechea, Ana María. *La expresión de la irrealidad en la obra de Jorge Luis Borges*, Mexico, D.F., 1957.
————. *Borges the Labyrinth Maker.* Edited and translated by Robert Lima. New York, 1965.
————, Speratti Piniero and, Emma Susana. *La literatura fantástica en argentina*, Mexico, D.F., 1957.
Bioy Casares, Adolfo. "*El jardín de los senderos que se bifurcan*," *Sur*, 92 (May, 1942), 60-65.
Briffault, Herma. "Labyrinths," *La Voz* (November, 1962), 15-16.

Capsas, Cleon. *The Poetry of Jorge Luis Borges, 1923-63*. Unpublished Ph.D. dissertation , University of Mexico, 1964.

Christ, Ronald. "Jorge Luis Borges, An Interview," *Paris Review*, 40 (Winter-Spring 1967), 116-64.

_____. "Borges' *Personal Anthology*," Commonweal, LXXXVI, 2 (September 29, 1967), 615-16.

De Man, Paul. "A Modern Master," *New York Review of Books*, III, 7 (November 19, 1964), 8-10.

Flores, Anges. "Magical Realism in Spanish American Fiction," *Hispania*, XXXVIII, 2 (May 1955), 187-92.

Irby, James E. *"Encuentro con Borges,"* appendix to *The Structure of the Stories of Jorge Luis Borges*. Unpublished Ph.D. dissertation, University of Michigan, 1962.

Jorge Luis Borges. L'Herne. Paris, 1964.

Rodríguez Monegal, Emir. *"Borges: teoría y práctica,"* *Número*, VI, 27 (December, 1955), 124-57.

Tamayo, Marcial, and Ruiz-Díaz, Adolfo. *Borges, enigma y clave*. Buenos Aires, 1955.

Vázquez, María Esther. *Everness*. Buenos Aires, 1965.

Yates, Donald Alfred. *The Argentine Detective Story*. Unpublished Ph.D. dissertation, University of Michigan, 1960.

Other Works Cited:

Addison, Joseph. *The Miscellaneous Works*, ed. A.C. Guthkelch. 2 vols. London, 1914.

Berkeley, George. "Three Dialogues Between Hylas and Philonous in Op position to Sceptics and Atheists," *The Harvard Classics*, XXXVII (New York, 1910), 201-302.

Browne, Sir Thomas. *Works*, ed. Charles Sayle. Edinburgh, 1912.

Chesterton, G.K. *The Father Brown Stories*. London, 1963.

Conrad, Joseph. *The Heart of Darkness* and *The Secret Sharer*. New York, 1950.

_____. *Lord Jim*. Cambridge, Mass., 1958.

Cooper, Lane. *The Prose Poetry of Thomas De Quincey*. Leipzig, 1902.

De Quincey, Thomas. *The Collected Writings*, ed. David Masson. 14 vols. Edinburgh, 1889-1990.

Descartes, René. *Correspondence*, ed. Charles Adam and Gerard Milhaud. 8 vols. Paris, 1960.

De Voto, Bernard. *Mark Twain's America*. Cambridge, Mass., 1951.

Eliade, Mircea. *Cosmos and History*. Translated by Willard R. Trask. New York and Evanston, 1959.

Eliot, T. S. *The Complete Poems and Plays*. New York, 1952.

_____. *Selected Essays*. New York, 1950.

Emerson, Ralph Waldo. *The Complete Essays and Other Writings*. New York, 1940.

Freeman-Mitford, A.B. Lord Redesdale. *Tales of Old Japan*. London, 1919.

French, Joseph Lewis. *The Book of the Rogue.* New York, 1926.

Von Goethe, Johann Wolfgang. *Faust.* Translated by Walter Kaufmann. New York, 1962.

Goldman, Albert. *The Mine and the Mint.* Carbondale and Edwardsville, Illinois,1965.

Gosse, Philip. *History of Piracy.* London, 1932.

Grenier, Jean. "Conversations on the Good Uses of Freedom." Translated by Alexander Coleman. Cambridge, Mass., 1967.

Haycraft, Howard (ed.). *The Art of the Mystery Story.* New York, 1947.

Hooke, S. H. *The Labyrinth.* New York, 1935.

Hulme, T. E. "Notes on Language and Style," *Criterion,* III, 12 (July 1925), 485-97.

Keats, John. *The Poetical Works.* Edited by H. W. Garrod. London, 1956.

Kenner, Hugh. *Paradox in Chesterton.* New York, 1947.

Knight, Ellis Cornelia. *Marcus Flaminius.* London, 1808.

Lévi-Strauss, Claude. *The Savage Mind.* Chicago, 1966.

Mallea, Eduardo. *Historia de una pasión argentina.* Buenos Aires,1940.

Matthiessen, F. O. *The Achievement of T. S. Eliot.* New York, 1959.

Miller, J. Hillis. *The Disappearance of God.* New York, 1965.

Moore, George. *The Brook Kerith.* New York, 1956.

————. *The Making of an Immortal.* New York, 1927.

Ortega y Gasset, José. "*Meditaciones de Quijote,*" *Obras Completas,* Madrid, 1957.

Parry, Edward Abbott. *Vagabonds All.* New York, 1926.

Pliny. *Natural History.* Translated by H. Rackam and W. H. S. Jones.10 vols. London, 1938-1963.

Pope, Alexander. *Poetical Works.* Boston, 1852.

Poirier, Richard. *A World Elsewhere.* New York, 1966.

Robbe-Grillet, Alain. *For a New Novel.* Translated by Richard Howard. New York, 1965.

Scholem, Gershom. *Major Trends in Jewish Mysticism.* New York, 1965.

Shaw, George Bernard. *Back to Methuselah.* Baltimore, 1961.

Some Imagist Poets. Boston and New York, 1915.

Sontag, Susan. *The Benefactor.* New York, 1963.

Starkie, Enid. *Baudelaire.* New York, 1958.

Stevenson, Robert Louis. *Treasure Island.* London, 1922.

Stoker, Bram. *Famous Impostors.* New York, 1910.

Strindberg, August. *Six Plays of Strindberg.* Translated by Elizabeth Sprigge. New York, 1955.

Trachtenberg, Joshua. *Jewish Mysticism and Superstition.* New York, 1939.

Wells, H. G. *The Dream.* New York, 1924.

————. *The First Men in the Moon, Novels of Science.* Edited by Donald A. Wollheim. New York, 1948.

————. *The Short Stories,* London, 1960.

Yung Lun Yüen. *History of the Pirates Who Infested the China Seas.* Translated by Karl F. Neumann. London, 1831.

INDEX

Index

Other Titles from
Lumen Books

Deconstructing the Kimbell:
An Essay on Meaning and Architecture
Michael Benedikt
ISBN: 0-930829-16-6

For an Architecture of Reality
Michael Benedikt
ISBN: 0-930829-05-0

The Architecture of Enric Miralles &
Carme Pinos
Peter Buchanan, Dennis Dollens,
Josep Maria Montaner, Lauren Kogod
ISBN: 0-930829-14-X

ANGST: Cartography
Moji Baratloo & Clif Balch
ISBN: 0-930829-10-7

Independent Projects:
Experimental Architecture, Design +
Research in New York
Anne Van Ingen & Dennis Dollens
ISBN: 0-930829-18-2

SITES Architecture 26
ISBN: 0-930829-37-9

Josep Maria Jujol:
Five Major Buildings 1913-1923
Dennis Dollens
ISBN: 0-930829-35-2

Written on a Body
Severo Sarduy
Translated by Carol Maier
ISBN: 0-930829-04-2

Borges in/and/on Film
Edgardo Cozarinsky
Translated by Gloria Waldman &
Ronald Christ
ISBN: 0-930829-08-5

Refractions
Octavio Armand
Translated by Carol Maier
ISBN: 0-930829-21-2

Space in Motion
Juan Goytisolo
Translated by Helen Lane
ISBN: 0-930829-03-4

Reverse Thunder, A Dramatic Poem
Diane Ackerman
ISBN: 0-930829-09-3

Sor Juana's Dream
Edited & Translated by Luis Harss
ISBN: 0-930829-07-7

Culture & Politics in Nicaragua:
Testimonies of Poets & Writers
Steven White
ISBN: 0-930829-02-6

Dialogue in the Void:
Beckett & Giacometti
Matti Megged
ISBN: 0-930829-01-8

The Animal That Never Was:
In Search of the Unicorn
Matti Megged
ISBN: 0-930829-20-4

Byron and the Spoiler's Art
Paul West
ISBN: 0-930829-13-1

Urban Voodoo
Edgardo Cozarinsky
ISBN: 0-930829-15-8

Under a Mantle of Stars
Manuel Puig
Translated by Ronald Christ
ISBN: 0-930829-00-X

SITES/Lumen Inc.
446 West 20 Street
New York, NY 10011
Phone/Fax 212-989-7944
Distributed by
Consortium
800-283-3572 (trade only)